Anonymus

Manresa

The spiritual exercises of St. Ignatius

Anonymus

Manresa
The spiritual exercises of St. Ignatius

ISBN/EAN: 9783741142291

Manufactured in Europe, USA, Canada, Australia, Japa

Cover: Foto ©Thomas Meinert / pixelio.de

Manufactured and distributed by brebook publishing software
(www.brebook.com)

Anonymus

Manresa

MANRESA:

OR THE

SPIRITUAL EXERCISES OF ST. IGNATIUS,

for General Use.

NEW EDITION.

LONDON: BURNS AND OATES.

1881

CONTENTS.

PART I.

FIRST WEEK.

FOURTH WEEK.

PART II.

PART III.

ABRIDGMENT OF THE FIRST PART OF THE EXERCISES.

PART IV.

Mysteries of the Life of our Saviour, distributed by St. Ignatius into fifty-one subjects of Meditation, with the passages from the Gospels indicated . . 331-354

PART V.

TABLES.

PREFACE.

THE name of "SPIRITUAL EXERCISES" indicates that the faithful who come to the school of St. Ignatius to make a retreat are called upon to use the faculties of their understanding and their heart. They come to act for themselves, not to see another act; in acting they come to exert themselves, not to give themselves up to barren contemplation; they come to exercise, not their body and its organs, but their soul and its chief powers—the understanding and the will.

The object of this undertaking, altogether interior and practical as it is, is clearly pointed out by the title even of the book.* Nothing vague, idle, or purely speculative, is to occupy man in the retreat. He comes to learn to conquer himself; to free himself from evil passions; to reform the disorder, great or little, of his past life, and to regulate it for the future by a plan conformable to the Divine will. Can man, during his short sojourn on earth,—become, too, by baptism a Christian the disciple and subject of Jesus Christ,—can he propose to himself an end more noble, more holy, more glorifying to his Creator?

To attain so high an end, many obstacles must be overcome, and many means made use of. Solitude; silence; cessation of ordinary business and study; all reading foreign to the Exercises; the setting aside of all

* "Spiritual Exercises; chosen with a view to lead Man to conquer himself, to disengage himself from the fatal influence of evil affections, and, with his heart thus set free, to trace out for himself the plan of a truly Christian life." "

preoccupation as to the future, and all thoughts (although pious) which are not in harmony with the work of each day; recollection of the senses; restraint of the eyes, and the obscurity which favours it; confession of sins, which puts an end to remorse and calms disquiet; finally, wise counsels, which prevent too much effervescence, exaltation, or fatigue,—which point out illusions, arouse languor, moderate indiscreet fervour;—such are the principal precautions taken to overcome the obstacles which might injure this work of reform.

The natural means employed, according to the degree of moral and physical strength of each one, are—examination of conscience; meditation; the study, or rather the contemplation, of Jesus Christ; reading of passages chosen from the holy Gospel and from the "Imitation of Jesus Christ;" penance; and recourse to the advice of a director.

Finally, by prayer, by mortification, by receiving the holy Sacraments of penance and the Eucharist, the assistance of God infinitely good is sought, in order to coöperate with the efforts of His faithful creature.

Thus, all obstacles being set aside, man employs all his resources in reforming himself, and God adds to His goodwill the succours of His grace and the coöperation of His infinite power.

The object of retreat is sublime. The means it employs are powerful; but are they equally certain, and are they chosen with wise discretion? Do they not excite in man, with danger to his head or his heart, sentiments more factitious than natural, constrained rather than spontaneous? St. Ignatius has foreseen this objection. "Let the nature, the length, the number of the exercises, be always suited," he says, "to the age, the capacity, the health, the good-will of the person in retreat; let no one be burdened; let each one do only what he can with profit, what he himself desires in the plenitude of his will, without ever going beyond his strength or the grace

of the moment, without ever passing the limits fixed for
him by a prudent director enlightened by experience."

Moreover, we have only to define the principal exercises we have named, to show evidently that they are all
as prudent and discreet as they are powerful and efficacious. These definitions will assist the reader in forming for himself a more exact idea of them, and one which
will become more readily practical.

1. *Examination.* When the attentive soul looks in
upon itself, in order to compare its thoughts, its words,
its actions, with the commandments of God and the
Church, to sigh over the opposition which it finds between its conduct and the Divine law, this exercise is
called " Examination," and is either general or particular,
according as it refers to all the faults committed, or to
only one kind,—*quotidien,* or that which is made every
day, or that which is preparatory to ordinary or extraordinary confession. St. Ignatius recommends this exercise above all others, as without doubt the most conducive to a knowledge and reform of ourselves, the most
favourable to reflection, and the least likely to lead to
exaltation and enthusiasm. He wishes this examination
to be made with exactness and frequently, but without
exaggeration or scruple.

The methods which St. Ignatius traces out for each
of these examinations are remarkable for their simplicity
and efficacy. The following is for the daily general examination : After you have recollected yourself, you will
thank God for the graces He has bestowed on you during
the day; you will then beg of Him light to know your
ingratitude, and grace to detest it. Then you will think
over the different hours or the different occupations of
the day, examining your thoughts, words, actions, or
omissions. After having seen the number of your faults,
you must repent of them by exciting yourself to sincere
sorrow ; and, finally, you will make a firm resolution to
avoid them for the future.

To arrive with certainty at amendment of life and the correction of our faults, the "Particular Examen" is still more useful. It goes direct to the predominant sin or vice of our character; in order to vanquish its enemies, it begins by isolating them, and attacks them one by one. The method of proceeding is this. Each morning you fix the exact point to be arrived at in this single combat. Every time during the day that you remark one of those faults which you wish to avoid above all others, you must offer to God some testimony of your repentance, and to yourself some means of recalling your fault, *e. g.* by placing your hand on your heart (in such a way that this sign cannot be remarked by others). After noon and at night you will seek in your conscience the number of your failures.† You must note the result of this inquiry, and compare your progress of the day with that of the day before, that of the week with the preceding week, being careful that your faults diminish each day. Thus you will bestow the same care in extirpating your faults and cultivating the opposite virtues, that the merchant does in calculating his receipts and expenses; the interest that a sick person takes in being informed of the progress of his cure or sickness; the constancy and vigilance of the general of an army, who is always well informed of the manœuvres and movements of the enemy.

Finally, with regard to an *examination preparatory to confession*, you may make use of a form. St. Ignatius gives a very abridged one, preferring to leave the director to add what is suitable to the capacity and disposition of each one, rather than to trace out himself a catalogue of sins, necessarily inapplicable to many. You may also, according to the method called "The first Manner of Praying," take the commandments of God and the Church, and the principal duties of your state, and on each one ask yourself the following questions: "What does this commandment or this duty prescribe? In what have I

* See p. 265.

been unfaithful?" Before going from one to the other,
make an act of contrition; and to offer some satisfaction
to God, and to obtain the grace of being more faithful
henceforward, recite a short prayer. By this means
your examination of conscience has the first of those
qualities it ought always to have—it has *sorrow*; it comprises, moreover, meditation and instruction. Hence
" The first Manner of Praying" should be taught to all,
and practised even when we are not preparing for confession.

2. *Meditation.* When the memory has recalled to the
soul the recollection of some dogmatical or moral truth,
when the understanding exerts itself to penetrate it, and
the will to submit to it, attach and devote itself to it, we
then say that we meditate. Meditation is also called the
" Exercise of the three Powers of the Soul."

The subject of the meditation should be considered
beforehand, and divided into two or three points which
fix the memory, and contain each one some circumstance
worthy of attention. From the commencement of the
exercise, the person in retreat must occupy his memory,
his imagination, his will, with the subject of the mystery
to be meditated on. This beginning is called the "prelude." The memory supplies the two or three points
prepared; the imagination forms a sort of picture of
them, if it can do so without constraint, and without
dwelling on it too long; the heart asks in a fervent
prayer that it may know and love. The whole is done
in the presence of Jesus Christ, who sees us, and in a
respectful attitude which renders to Him at once the
homage of our souls and of our bodies.

The soul, having thus seized the entire subject, has
only to be penetrated and nourished by it. Reflections,
colloquies, or conversations with God, affections, are the
necessary results of the remembrance, and the attentive
consideration of the objects. There the soul finds light,
emotion, a feeling of the Divine presence or of the Divine

will; there it rests without being anxious to proceed
farther. The body also is kept in the attitude which our
experience has shown to be most favourable to recollection.
This exercise, which lasts an hour, being finished, the
person in retreat must employ another quarter of an hour
in examining how he has conducted himself during the
hour he has conversed with the Lord, giving Him thanks
for any success, and sighing at His feet for whatever
negligences he has been guilty of.

This method, without comparing it with others, is
incontestably a simple, prudent, and practical one. There
is in it nothing subtle, embarrassing, or minute. The
flight of the soul is directed without being shackled;
the means which unite the soul to God are all employed
in it, but only in accordance with the end to be attained.
We find in it all that is useful, and nothing superfluous.

3. *Contemplation.* In this age, so little contemplative,
we must define exactly what is meant by contemplation.

We contemplate rather than meditate when, after the
memory has recalled the whole, or some detail, of the life
of our Lord Jesus Christ, the soul, in a state of profound
recollection, employs itself in seeing, hearing, considering
the different circumstances of the mystery, for the purpose of being instructed, edified, and moved by it. This
contemplation takes the name of "Application of the
Senses" when the soul nourishes itself at leisure, and
without the employment of the understanding, on all that
the mystery offers to it to see, to hear, to taste, to feel,
almost as if the fact present to the imagination passed
before the eyes, and affected all the bodily senses.

Thus, in meditation, it is the *understanding* which is
exerted on an abstract truth, of which it seeks to be convinced; in *contemplation*, it is the soul that applies itself
to the Incarnate Truth, which represents to itself the
practical teachings of the Man-God, which applies itself
to see, to hear, the Word made flesh—to "*contemplate*"
Him; such is the word which has been chosen to ex-

press these acts. Let us show, in a few words, that nothing is more conformable to the Divine will, to the practice of the Church and of the Saints, that nothing is more salutary to souls, than this contemplative view of Jesus Christ.

Why did the Son of God become man? To speak to our senses, to move us, to instruct us, by the great spectacles of the manger, of Thabor, and of Calvary; by this wonderful sight to fix our imaginations, to attach our hearts, while at the same time He redeems us by the bloody sacrifice of His death. "Blessed are the eyes that see what you see; blessed are the ears that hear what you hear," said the Saviour to His disciples; "for I say to you, that many prophets and kings have desired to see these things, and have not seen them" (Luke x. 23, 24). But if the just themselves, who lived before the Incarnation of the Word, were deprived of this powerful help, all those who are called to believe in the Gospel to the end of time ought to find their profit in it. Jesus Christ willed that the recital of His actions, the summary of His discourses, should be written by the inspiration of His Spirit, and promulgated through the entire world; He willed that all eyes should be turned towards Him as towards the true brazen serpent, the sight of which cures all the stings of the infernal serpent. The Good Shepherd knows His sheep, He wishes His sheep to know Him. Supreme High-Priest, He ordered His Apostles to preach His Gospel to every creature, promising life to those who believed in His words, and threatening with eternal death those who refused to believe in them.

Around the altar where He dwells, inaccessible to our senses, the Church, His spouse, never ceases to represent the mysteries of His life, death, and resurrection. The complete representation of all His mortal life, including the time that prepared His coming, the mission of the Holy Ghost, which consummated the work, and

the glorification of the Saints who havc been justified by
His merits, occupies the course of the year. The first
Sunday of Advent, the Church cries out, "Jesus Christ
our King is about to appear; come, let us adore Him."
At the great solemnities of Christmas, "Christ is born
for us; come, let us adore Him." At Easter, "The Lord
is risen indeed, alleluia."

All the offices and rites of the Church speak in the
same tone, tend to the same end. Our holy Mother, by her
songs, joyful or sorrowful, by the bright or the sad colour
of her ornaments, by the variety and beauty of her cere-
monies, by the decoration of her temples and altars, by
the use she makes in her cathedrals of painting, sculpture,
music, eloquence, poetry,—labours conformably to the in-
tentions of our heavenly Father in uniting us by all our
powers and faculties to the Word incarnate, crucified
and risen for us. She would, if possible, make all her
children, like the Apostles, hearers of His word and witnesses of His miracles; she wishes that each one of us
should be able to say with the beloved disciple, "That
which we have seen with our eyes, which we have heard,
and our hands have handled, this is what we believe and
preach unto you of the Word of Life" (1 John i. 1).

This idea of the Church has been fully understood
by the Saints. The Fathers, in their homilies, most frequently content themselves by quoting and explaining
some words of the Gospel; religious orders have taken
for statutes and rules the counsels or example of Jesus
Christ; true reformers sent by Heaven to revive in certain provinces, or among certain classes of the Church,
the true spirit which ought always to animate it, what
have they done? St. Francis, in recalling by his example
evangelical poverty and simplicity; St. Dominic, by
preaching the Rosary; St. Ignatius, by writing the Exercises; the Blessed Leonard of Port Maurice, by estab
lishing the "Way of the Cross;" Père de la Colombière,
by spreading every where the devotion of the Sacred

Heart,—aimed at nothing else than bringing those souls nearer to Jesus Christ who were losing sight of Him. And have not the greatest Saints in all ages been those who by constant contemplation have the best studied, and the most faithfully reproduced Jesus Christ in them-selves? Are not those predestined to heaven, says the Apostle, at the same time predestined to be conformable to the Divine model that the Father has given us in His Son? (Rom. viii. 29.)

It was doubtless these considerations, this design of God and His Church, that inspired St. Ignatius in the methods he has traced out for *contemplation, application of the senses, composition of place,* &c. We must beware of considering as curious or unnecessary the care which has been manifested by the Three Divine Persons in the circumstances of the Incarnation of the Word, and the Church in the structure and the details of her Liturgy.

But St. Ignatius does not wish his disciples to exer-cise themselves merely in contemplating Jesus Christ as the Teacher, the Model, the Saviour of all; he incessantly reminds them that they must study Him above all as *their* teacher, *their* model, *their* Saviour. He constantly incul-cates a truth too much forgotten among Christians, and yet one of the sweetest to the heart, and the most effica-cious for the reform of our lives, viz. that Jesus Christ said, did, and suffered for each one of us in particular what He said, did, and suffered for the whole human race.

Yes, the Man-God, in the immensity of His intelli-gence and His love, had present in His thoughts and in His heart each man, no less than the universal family of Adam; what He did for all He did for each one; and there is not any sinner on earth who may not say with as much truth as the Apostle, "Jesus Christ loved me, and gave Himself for me" (Gal. ii. 20). Yes, for me as if I was the only sinner among men; yes, for me, not less than for all. Would the sun light me more if I were the only one to receive his rays? So, if I had been the only sinner in the universe, the Divine Sun of justice would not have shed upon me less light or less warmth from His bosom. When I receive Jesus Christ at the holy table, with a multitude of other faithful, do I not receive Jesus Christ as entirely as if I were the only one in all the universe admitted to communion? So, in the manger; on the mountain, where He proclaimed the eight beatitudes; on the cross, where He consummated His sacrifice; on the altar, where He remains night and day,—Jesus Christ is my whole salvation and my life; each of His words is said for me; each of His actions and His sufferings is for me, and for my benefit. This principle, so productive of the fruit of salvation, is constantly recalled by St. Ignatius. He wishes this consideration to serve as a prelude to all the Exercises : " I will see from the beginning Jesus Christ with His eyes fixed on me. I will ask of Him the grace to understand with what intention, with what view, on what condition, He became man, poor, obedient, humble, for me ; what were His thoughts, His wishes, in dying for me, in rising again for me."

This solemn subject, which can be but touched upon in a preface, deserves profound study. We add yet another reflection. Before God, the intervals of time and place are nothing. His eternity is all time, and His immensity all place. For God nothing has been, all is ; nothing is out of Him, all is in Him. From this point of view, which is that of the Christian occupied in contemplating his Saviour, we have not to go back eighteen centuries to make the journey of the Holy Land, in order to find ourselves at Bethlehem or at Calvary. Bethlehem, Calvary, are before our eyes, and Jesus our Saviour is born there, dies there to-day, even this very moment. Thus it is for our instruction, for the redemption and salvation of our own souls, that the Man-God now comes into the world, now suffers, now dies. This is the foundation of contemplation; this is what should make it not only

easy and delightful, but above all efficacious and useful.
And this thought we have seen is that of God, of Jesus
Christ, of the Church. Since Jesus Christ is the Way,
the Truth, and the Life; since each one of His words is a
centre of light, each of His actions a precept or a counsel;
since to know Him is the end of a Christian, and, as the
Apostle says, " life eternal,"—we cannot place too much
value on all that brings us nearer to Him, and unites the
faithful soul to Him.

The means used by St. Ignatius to lead man to an
amendment of his life, which are, above all, examination
of conscience, meditation, and the contemplation of
Jesus Christ, being thus defined and appreciated, either
in themselves or in the method assigned to each one in
the book of Exercises, we must now consider the disposition of these means, or the progress and method of
the " Exercises" considered as a whole.

St. Ignatius supposes the Christian who presents him·
self at the entrance of the course to be of sound reason,
intelligent, animated by a courageous will, master of his
time and of his future, but yet a sinner; and of this sinner
he proposes to make a saint, and a great saint, for ever.
The enterprise is great, it is difficult; it is the grandest
work that apostolic zeal can propose to itself; it is the
work of Jesus Christ Himself. But how can man, whom
Jesus Christ has made His coöperator in the work of the
salvation of souls, unite to the Divine action the most
intelligent and efficacious means? Such is the prob-
lem that the author of the Exercises proposed to himself,
and the solution of which the Lord Himself revealed to
him, for there is in the method something more than a
mere masterpiece of human genius; the finger of God is
there.

In order to change, by the assistance of Divine grace,
a sinner into a saint, there is first the empire of evil to be
destroyed in the heart; then, the reign of good to be
established. This work once done, would not be durable

if not consolidated by foresight and avoidance of the obstacles which otherwise would react on this sudden revolution. Finally, it would not be complete if, begun by the imperfect but necessary sentiment of fear, it were not crowned by hope and love.

In another point of view, we may say that the sinner, to become a saint, must first have learned to sin no more; then to act and to suffer as a true disciple of Jesus Christ; and finally, that he must have, by love, an earnest of eternal rest and joy.

Hence the series of operations that St. Ignatius has distributed into four weeks, which comprise each an indefinite number of days, corresponding to what the ancients called the purgative, the illuminative, and the unitive ways.

The first week, which is principally addressed to the reason, is employed in destroying the reign of sin, or in reforming all that may be disorderly in the affections and the conduct.

Next, the faith of the Christian is called to the aid of the reason of man; and Jesus Christ presents Himself as the Saviour from sin, and as the model of the repentant sinner. Jesus Christ passed through the way of the commandments, or *common* life, then through the *perfect* life, or the way of counsels. Studied successively in these two states, He teaches us to act as a Christian, and as a perfect Christian. He becomes as it were the mould wherein the penitent takes the exterior and interior form of the true disciple of Jesus Christ; He is as it were the rule upon which henceforward his life will be ordered.

But the world, the flesh, and the devil will terribly persecute the neophyte, if he persist in his intention. St. Ignatius, therefore, during the third week, applies himself to forearm him on all sides against his enemies, visible and invisible.

Jesus Christ, on the eve of His death, has provided for him " a table," whence, according to the Psalmist, he

will draw strength against all his enemies (Ps. xxii. 27).
In His discourse after the Last Supper, the Son of God
fortifies him by the strongest encouragements and the
most sublime promises; then, suffering in soul and body,
from His agony in the Garden of Olives until His death
on the cross, He teaches him to undergo, without desist-
ing from his resolution, weariness, fear, sadness, humiliation, suffering, death. The work of the second week is
not only continued, it is, above all, corroborated, confirmed.

Finally, the true Christian is called from combat to
victory, from the tomb to resurrection, from earth to
heaven, from fear and hope to love. He exercises himself also, but in a sweeter manner,—in loving; it is Jesus Christ risen that he contemplates, and his apparitions
bring him each day an increase of peace. The hope of
eternal good rouses love in his heart; and this love, true,
efficacious, consummated by an entire abandonment of
himself into the hands of God, who has given Himself to
him, tends "to transform" him into the image of Jesus
Christ, the Divine object of his holy love.

The first week, intended for the purification of the
soul, begins by "the end of man," and ends by general
confession and receiving the Eucharist. The second is
occupied entirely in rendering the faithful like to Jesus;
it begins with the final end of the Christian, or the reign
of Christ, and concludes by the choice of a state of life,
or a plan of amendment in the state already chosen.
The third is employed in continuing and confirming the
work of the two first. Its special fruit should be resignation to sufferings, and the endeavour to find strength
against them in the Eucharist. The fourth week should
lead the Christian, regenerated and confirmed in grace,
to perfect love; it ends by the irrevocable donation of
ourselves to Jesus Christ.

When first entering into retreat, the sinner calls down
upon himself the grace that flows from the wounds of

Jesus Christ; he says incessantly, *Anima Christi, sanctifica me!* Become just, and strengthened in justice by this
Divine grace, he says to Him at the end of the last week,
" Since Thou hast given Thyself entirely to me, let me
now belong wholly to Thee: take me ; keep me !" *Suscipe, Domine, universam meam libertatem!* If he says at
first to Jesus Christ, as Jesus Christ Himself said to His
Father, "All Thine is mine ;" he adds at the end, "All that
is mine is Thine !" The gift is reciprocal, the exchange
perfect, the transformation is complete.

While the disciple thus advances by this way, which
leads from hell to heaven, St. Ignatius conducts him from
the more simple and easy to what appears at first the more
unusual and more arduous. First, he proposed to him
only considerations entirely rational, without prescribing
either time or method for making them, without even
giving them that name of meditation which alarms inex-
perience. Thus, he leads him to desire and willingly receive the methods of examination and meditation indicated above. The " Triple Sin," or the history of the
fallen angels, of Adam cast out of Paradise, of man
damned for his personal sin, shows, by the most natural
and the easiest application of all, how meditation is the exercise of the three powers of the soul, and what is the use
of the preludes and the colloquies. The subject of Hell,
which soon follows, and which ought to speak so strongly
to the imagination, serves as a model of the " Application
of the Senses." As soon as our Lord presents Himself,
it is by contemplation that we apply ourselves to studying Him as our model. What a first exercise had discovered to us, frequent repetitions should impress more
deeply on the soul. During the third and fourth weeks
certain views of faith, or considerations, as touching as
they are practical, are proposed for additional points of
contemplation.

In the work of each week the faithful is directed by
advice and rules which ought to actuate, direct, and, at

need, moderate his zeal. Among the multitude of lessons
that mystic theology might give him, and with which an
inexperienced person would not have failed to saturate
him, St. Ignatius, with a rare sobriety, a profound wisdom, an exquisite discernment, has chosen those most
suitable for his purpose. During the first week he in-
structs in examination of conscience, meditation, discernment of different spirits, which solicit to good or evil a
soul yet in sin or just emerging from it; he teaches the
necessity and the practice of penance; he teaches us to
know and to avoid scruples; he shows the advantages
and the facility of making a good general confession.

During the second week, he continues to enlighten
the steps of the person in retreat by rules for the discernment of spirits. He renders contemplation easy to him,
and directs him in the choice of a state, if he be in a position to choose one; and if his state is already fixed, he
teaches him to reform it, in the detail of his conduct, on
the model of Jesus Christ. If he has wealth to distribute, he recalls to him the rules of the Gospel.

The third week is best chosen to teach the disciple of
Jesus Christ, attentive in contemplating His sufferings,
the manner of conforming to his Divine model as to the
care to be given to the body, especially in his meals. For
the rest, the nearer the person in retreat draws to the
end, the more he acquires experience, and the less he requires to have this sort of rules multiplied for his instruction. St. Ignatius, though giving advice suitable to
the fourth week, and, in general, to paschal time, feast-
days, to the happy position of a soul that Jesus Christ
fills with His peace and inebriates with His joy,—does
not assign any special study for this time of happiness.

The different manners of praying, the meditations on
the life of our Saviour, the observations on scruples, on
alms, the rules of orthodox faith, of discernment of spirits,
are, as a body of reserve, placed near this army ranged
for battle. which we have just passed in review. The di-

rector, according to the need of the person in retreat, presents to him as a defence in his combat, as a torch on his path, such a rule, such a meditation, such a method of conversing familiarly with God, as he judges best. The first manner of praying may be usefully taught to all; the second and third assist in making vocal prayer intelligently and experimentally. The meditations, of which St. Ignatius only indicates the principal points, referring to the Gospel for the developments, are made after the model traced at the beginning of each week. The rules of orthodox faith, written at the time when the pretended reform raised its standard against the Church, are not less useful to meditate on now than in former days. Nothing, again, can be more luminous, more profound, more practical, than these indications given by St. Ignatius for discerning the different spirits that act on ours, for the purpose either of saving or destroying us.

All these rules (whatever may be the modest name attached to them, such as "annotations or additions") are all penetrated by the spirit of the Gospel, by the doctrine of the Church, the traditions of experience, the teachings of the highest philosophy, enlightened and directed by faith. This may be illustrated by a single example. At the end of the second week we find the rule of "election." Here is the summary of the rules so deeply important in their object,—"the choice of a state." God can only make His good pleasure known to us through our senses by an act of His omnipotence, or to our understanding by a manifestation of His Word, or to our heart by an interior touch of His Spirit. The first voice is that heard by Matthew at his counter, by Paul cast to the earth on the road to Damascus. It has to be mentioned because the Lord sometimes employs it; but it is the farthest removed from the ordinary ways of Providence, and it would be presumption for us to wait for it to lead us to act. The third is the most frequently heard, and we learn to discern with certainty the move-

ments that the Spirit of God impresses on the heart of
His creature by consulting the rules for the discernment
of spirits. Finally, the second is manifest when the understanding, free from all the influences of the heart, examines and sees by reflection, by the study of its apti-
tudes, by the comparison between such and such a way,
that which in the present case is the most direct and the
most certain, in order to arrive at the final end of every
free being—salvation. After having discovered by this
method (which may be called the *analytical*) the advantages of such or such a choice, and the manifestation of
the Divine will by such or such an interior voice, St. Ignatius wishes that, for greater certainty, another mode
(which may be called the *synthetical*) should be employed.
Thus, if they wish to put the decision at which they
think they have arrived to the proof by the thought of
approaching death, of the judgment of Jesus Christ,
they ought to ask themselves, Have I chosen this course
solely with a view to the interests of my salvation?
Should I counsel this choice to one of my friends who,
in the same dispositions that I am, should ask my advice? Moreover, we must pray before, during, and after
the deliberation; and the director is at hand, not to suggest or give the impulse, but to smooth the way, set
aside the obstacles, dissipate the illusions, recall the
rules, lead us gently to observe them, and applaud the
choice made according to God's will.

Enlightened by lessons and advice equally wise, the
course, for any person who is able to fulfil the conditions
mentioned above, lasts for about thirty days. Each day
he devotes four hours (not consecutive) to meditation; almost every night he takes from his rest another hour for
this purpose. This hour at night is so silent, so profoundly
calm, so favourable to recollection, that those who during
their retreat have devoted it to the first exercise, have
praised the inspiration of St. Ignatius, and have con-
gratulated themselves on their courage. Two quarters

of an hour, one in the middle of the day, the other before
sleep, are given to examination of conscience. Some
chapters of the " Imitation," the narratives of the Gospel which develop the subject of meditation, are nearly
all the *reading*. He visits the church, assists at Mass,
he may see his director every day. According to the
needs of his soul, according to the mysteries meditated on,
he practises more or less penance; surrounds himself
with darkness, or enjoys the perfume of flowers and the
serenity of the heavens. The number of days of each
week is not fixed; each ends when its aim is attained.
The first, for a sinner not submissive to grace, may be
very long; for a soul already reconciled to God, it will
be much shorter; but it must never be omitted, even in
a retreat of eight or ten days. When the end of man
has been deliberately considered, we find in the book of
St. Ignatius meditations pointed out only for one day,
with this remark, however : if the spiritual profit of the
person require it, let him continue to meditate on the
consequences and the chastisements of sin. The second
week, when its object is the choice of a state of life, has
frequently to be prolonged. St. Ignatius has appointed
meditations for it for twelve or thirteen days, although
it may not reach that term, or may continue longer.
The third is only half as long as the second in its plan.
The fourth, like the first, is left entirely to the discernment of the director.

In tracing out this great and perfectly-arranged plan,
St. Ignatius has never for a moment lost sight of the infirmity of man, of the variety of his resources and his
wants, and of the multiform action of grace in the heart.
So, in opening this sublime course to elevated minds and
generous hearts, in directing their efforts towards the
highest perfection, in stimulating their emulation by the
most noble motives, in making, in short, the best use of
their capacity and strength, the author of the "Exercises"
has not forgotten the infinitely greater number of limited

capacities and feeble wills. One of the first rules that
this great man lays down for the director of a retreat is,
" that he adapt the exercises to the age, the capacity,
the strength of the person about to perform them ; that
he never impose too heavy a burden on an unenlightened
mind or a faint heart ; that he never propose any thing
to any one which is not in proportion to his present
strength and good-will." Thus a very few only of chosen
ones will be allowed to go through the whole course of
the exercises. Those of the first week, and the different
manners of praying, will suit a great number of persons;
but they may require to be modified even for them. It
will suffice for many to be taught how to examine their
consciences; to meditate half an hour every morning on
the commandments of God, or the capital sins; to confess
and communicate every week, and to practise the works
of mercy. One who is able to do more, but is much occupied, may, if he can spare an hour and a half every day,
receive from his director the developments of the subjects
disposed in their natural order, as well as the corresponding rules and methods. Every day, when he returns
home, he must devote an hour to meditation, returning
the next day and the day after to the same subject, so as
to supply by this double repetition the effect which the
continuation of the exercises would have produced.

Thus St. Ignatius makes himself "all to all men;"
he sacrifices to the utility of each the beauty and harmony of his plan; or, to express it better, his plan is to
carry to the highest state of perfection those who are
capable of it, and yet to be useful to more limited minds
and more imperfect wills. Magnificent as a whole, his
book is precious in its smallest details. The approbation
of the Holy See is remarkable in that it relates to every
part as well as to the entire work. We will cite these
remarkable words, which have far more authority than
any praise of ours : " After having examined" (says Paul
III. in his Bull *Pastoralis Officii*) " these Exercises and

Rules, and from the information and testimony of the examiners, we declare them full of piety and holiness, and that they are and will be very useful and advantageous to the edification and profit of the faithful. We wish also, as is suitable, to take into consideration the abundant fruits that Ignatius and his companions constantly produce through the whole world by the assistance of these spiritual teachings. Therefore, by our apostolic authority, by the tenor of these presents, and of our certain knowledge, we approve, praise, and fortify by all the authority of this writing, these teachings and spiritual Exercises, considered in the whole and in each part which they contain; earnestly exhorting all the faithful of both sexes throughout the world, each and every one, to be instructed in so good a school, and to profit by such holy lessons."

To this solemn approbation and confirmation the succeeding Pontiffs have added many spiritual graces in favour of those who perform the said exercises. Alexander VII., Benedict XIV., Gregory XVI., have granted a plenary indulgence to all the faithful who during eight days, or at least during five days, perform the exercises of St. Ignatius under the direction of a Father of the Society of Jesus. After having cited the testimony of the sovereign Pontiffs, we have no need to quote those of the Saints and the great Doctors of the Church.

May this book be the means of making the teachings of the holy founder of the Society of Jesus better appreciated; may it, together with this Society,—always combated by hell, always protected by its Divine head,—conduce to the greater glory of God, to the honour of our Lord and Saviour Jesus Christ, and the salvation of many souls!

PRAYER OF ST. IGNATIUS, " ANIMA CHRISTI,"

WHICH IS USED OFTEN DURING THE EXERCISES.

ANIMA Christi, sanctifica me.
Corpus Christi, salva me.
Sanguis Christi, inebria me.
Aqua lateris Christi, lava me.
Passio Christi, conforta me.
O bone Jesu, exaudi me :
Intra tua vulnera absconde me :
Ne permittas me separari a te :
Ab hoste maligno defende me ;
In horâ mortis meæ voca me,
Et jube me venire ad te,
Ut cum sanctis tuis laudem te
In sæcula sæculorum.   Amen.

SOUL of Christ, sanctify me.
Body of Christ, save me.
Blood of Christ, inebriate me.
Water out of the side of Christ, wash me.
Passion of Christ, strengthen me.
O good Jesus, hear me ;
Hide me within Thy wounds ;
Suffer me not to be separated from Thee ;
Defend me from the malignant enemy ;
Call me at the hour of my death,
And bid me come unto Thee,
That with Thy Saints I may praise Thee
For all eternity.   Amen.

I LOVE, I love Thee, Lord most high!
 Because Thou first hast lovèd me;
I seek no other liberty
 But that of being bound to Thee.

May memory no thought suggest
 But shall to Thy pure glory tend;
My understanding find no rest
 Except in Thee, its only end.

My God, I here protest to Thee,
 No other will have I than Thine;
Whatever Thou hast giv'n to me,
 I here again to Thee resign.

All mine is Thine,—say but the word;
 Whate'er Thou willest shall be done:
I know Thy love, all-gracious Lord;
 I know it seeks my good alone.

Apart from Thee all things are nought;
 Then grant, O my supremest bliss,
Grant me to love Thee as I ought;
 Thou givest all in giving this!

THE

Spiritual Exercises of St. Ignatius.

Spiritual Exercises.

————◆————

INTRODUCTION;

BEING INSTRUCTIONS FOR PERSONS MAKING A RETREAT, TEACHING
THEM WHAT THEY ARE ABOUT TO DO, AND THE RULES THEY
SHOULD OBSERVE DURING THE EXERCISES

1. BY *Spiritual Exercises* is understood certain operations of the mind and heart, such as the examination of
conscience, meditation, contemplation, mental and vocal
prayer, which are employed in order to free the soul
from its irregular affections, and so to put it in the
way of knowing and embracing the will of God towards it.

2. As it is the soul which is to be exercised in making a retreat, we must seek from our spiritual guide only
what is necessary to enable it to act with uprightness
and certainty. We must not expect from him many
words or long explanations, nor to hear long sermons or
interesting lectures. It is not the quantity of food, but
a healthy digestion, which nourishes the body; so it is
not the great amount of knowledge communicated, but
the manner in which the heart receives it, and is nourished by it, that satisfies the needs of the soul. More-

over, experience proves that the heart will receive with
delight, and with greater real profit, what it discovers
for itself, either by its own reflections, or by the light
shed upon it by Divine grace, than what is presented to
its intelligence by lengthened discourses.

3. These Exercises engage both the understanding
and the will of man. The understanding seeks by reasoning to obtain the full knowledge of the subject proposed to it; the will produces the various affections
which result from the knowledge acquired. In these
acts of the heart, wherein it approaches God and converses with Him, the faithful soul ought to be careful
never to forget the inward as well as the external respect
which the presence of the Divinity requires.

4. Although St. Ignatius has divided the Exercises
into four series or weeks, each consecrated to a special
work of reform, or a distinct study of our Lord Jesus
Christ, it must not be supposed that these weeks are
necessarily of seven days. Each one ends when its aim
is attained : this happens soonest to the most dili
gent, and those whom the grace of God influences
most quickly; later to those who, notwithstanding their
good-will, are longer tried by contending feelings.
Generally, the complete course of these Exercises re
quires about thirty days.

5. The person in retreat will find every thing easy,
and himself wonderfully assisted by grace, if from the
beginning he brings to God a large and generous heart;
if he abandons himself with all his wishes and all his
liberty to the action of his Creator; if he is disposed
to allow his Sovereign Lord to order him, and all that
concerns him, according to His good pleasure.

6. The rules which are given for the discernment of spirits will assist the soldier of Jesus Christ—sometimes consoled by Heaven as he will be, and sometimes a prey to desolation—to know and avoid the snares laid for him by his enemies. If he neither feels consolation, nor sadness, nor other movements of the heart, he must examine himself carefully on the manner in which he performs these Exercises. Does he perform them at the time prescribed, and in the manner pointed out? Does he observe the methods and rules traced out for him? In moments of temptation and dryness let him encourage himself; let him reassure himself with the hope of soon being consoled; let him, moreover, have recourse to the counsels of his spiritual director.

7. It is well for the person in retreat to concentrate his thoughts on the subject presented to him at the moment, without preoccupying himself at all about the day or the week which is to follow. Let him give an hour to each of the Exercises of the day; and as the evil one uses every means to make us shorten this time, let him take care to be able to reassure himself always with the thought that he has lengthened rather than shortened it. The time will appear short if it pass in the midst of consolation, but very long in moments of desolation and dryness. It is at these times that it would be well to prolong the Exercise, to conquer ourselves, and to show the enemy that his attacks are not only resisted, but turned to the advantage of our souls.

8. When consolation is abundant, no vow or promise should be made without having taken time to reflect and consult. When the soul, on the contrary, feels inclined towards things inferior or less perfect, every

effort must be made to elevate it and give it a contrary
direction.   To obtain this grace from the God of all
goodness, besides assiduous prayer, let other pious exercises be added; beg our Lord not to allow us to
obtain or keep any thing, whether honours, riches, or
happiness, until our irregular inclination for these things
has been reformed, and rendered subordinate to the interests of His service and glory.

9. That the director may guide with certainty the
soul placed under his care, and judge of its spiritual
progress, we must faithfully tell him, not precisely
our own thoughts and opinions, or our sins (the latter
will be told in confession), but the agitations and different movements which the Spirit of God, or the evil
spirit, may produce in us.

10. In order that the number, the length, and the
nature of the Exercises may be suited to the age,
capacity, and inclination of the person in retreat; that
no one may be overburdened, and all may have what
is suitable to their particular dispositions and wants at
the time,—each one will receive from his director, at
the beginning, a rule fixing the hours of rising, of meditation, of meals, and the other exercises and occupations
of the day.   His spiritual guide also will visit him as
often as he thinks requisite, setting him the employment
for each day as well as the directions, advice, and encouragement, which he judges to be suitable and useful.
The author of the Exercises, like the Apostle, made
himself all things to all men.   To strong, able, generous-
minded men, and to those who are masters of their time
and of their state of life, he recommends four meditations a day of an hour each; another meditation of an hour

in the middle of the night; an examination of conscience in the middle of the day, and another before going to rest. Some relaxation will be allowed these persons, if required, during this laborious course. Persons who unite all these conditions, except the time, and who cannot give more than an hour, or an hour and a half a day, the rest of their time being occupied in their ordinary avocations, will receive directions how to occupy themselves each day for an hour. By these means they will advance more slowly, but nevertheless in order, and will secure the continuity of the Exercises by one or two repetitions of each meditation. The Exercises of the first week are those which are suited to the capacity and devotion of the greater number. Such will come out of the retreat with a deeper fear of God, having made a good general confession, knowing how to examine their consciences well, and to approach the Sacraments more regularly. Others again must be satisfied with less. To these the commandments of God and the Church, and the method of examining their consciences and going to confession, will be explained; they will be instructed in the three methods of prayer which are mentioned further on. It is desirable that such persons should devote half an hour every morning to these Exercises, and that they should approach the Sacraments every week or fortnight.

11. But those who have their time at their disposal, and who wish to derive all the benefit possible from these Exercises, must perform them exactly as they are laid down. They must place before their eyes, either written or printed, the principal points of the Meditations, and the abridgment of the methods, that they may

not escape their memory. Their progress in the spiritual
life will be the more rapid according as they more com-
pletely separate themselves from their acquaintances
and friends, and from worldly thoughts and business.
Therefore such must, if possible, leave their homes and
retire to a more solitary room or house, and only come
out to assist at Mass and the Offices of the Church,
so as not to meet with interruptions. This solitude will
procure, amongst others, three great advantages: first,
in separating in this manner from friends, relations,
and worldly affairs, we shall obtain abundant grace
from Heaven. Then, as the mind is less distracted during this voluntary retreat, and not drawn off to other
subjects, the thoughts are more easily fixed and concen-
trated on the one thing necessary,—the service of God:
and the will follows the subject which the understanding
offers to it with all the liberty and energy of its nature.
In fine, the more the soul is disengaged and separated
from creatures, the more she is at liberty to follow and
attain to her Creator and Master, who only approaches
her to enrich her with the infinite gifts of His bounty.

12. That the relations between him who gives the
retreat and those who make it may be as agreeable and
as profitable as possible, neither must lose sight of this
advice: Every good and pious Christian must be disposed to receive in a favourable sense and to take in
good part every word susceptible of being so received
and understood, rather than to take it in a rigorous and
objectionable sense. If it happen that the expression is
not defensible, ask the person his intention in saying it,
and if he is really in error, point it out to him in a charit-
able manner, that he may set himself right on the point.

INTRODUCTION TO MEDITATION,

WITH THE RECOMMENDATIONS OF ST. IGNATIUS, CALLED THE
" TEN ADDITIONS."

MEDITATION consists in calling to mind some dogmatic or moral truth, and reflecting on or discussing this truth according to each one's capacity, so as to move the will and produce in us amendment.

Thus, if you have to meditate on the sin of the angels, you will call to mind how they, having disobeyed their Creator, forfeited grace and were cast out of heaven into hell. You will then reflect attentively on this subject, so as to feel confounded by and blush at the multitude of your sins, compared to this one single sin which ruined the rebel angels. In fine, you will conclude that you have often merited the same punishment as they, since you too have so often sinned.

To meditate usefully, observe well the following rules :

Before Meditation.

1. The subject should be divided into two or three points, that the meditation may be rendered more easy by a division which is natural and easy to remember.

2. Before beginning, we must by a preparatory prayer beg of God by His grace to direct all the powers and operations of our souls to His service and glory alone.

3. The heart having taken this proper and generous resolution, the faithful soul must impress the subject proposed on the mind, the imagination, and the will.

If the subject of the meditation is a history,—for example, that of the Prodigal Son,—the *memory* must recall the principal facts. This is the first prelude as generally used, particularly during the second and following weeks.

The *imagination* seizes its object by placing it in a certain spot which the mind represents to itself. This has caused the name of "composition of place" to be given to the second prelude. If the meditation is on some visible object, such as the birth of Jesus Christ, we must figure to ourselves the place where this mystery was accomplished,—the stable at Bethlehem, the manger, &c. If the mind is occupied by a truth purely intellectual,—for example, the misery of sin,—we may assist ourselves by a picture of a soul imprisoned in the body, banished among animals in this vale of tears. The object of this prelude is to give the soul the impression that would be produced upon it by the sight of a picture representing exactly the subject of meditation; or, still better, by the sight of the place where the mystery occurred. We must avoid in this, even more than in other points, all violent efforts of the mind, or loss of time. Since every person's imagination is not sufficiently lively and docile to succeed easily in this prelude, it must be set aside if it prove an embarrassment.

The *will* is exercised in soliciting a grace according to the mystery: for example, contrition, sorrow, joy, &c.

During the Meditation.

1. We must endeavour to understand and feel inwardly the truth on which we meditate, rather than think much on it.

2. If facility and consolation are experienced, we must beware of vain satisfaction. We must never make a vow lightly or without advice. Our reflections and sentiments must always be directed towards our own amendment.

3. In times of dryness and desolation we must be patient, and wait with resignation the return of consolation, putting our trust in the goodness of God. We must animate ourselves by the thought that God is always with us, that He only allows this trial for our greater good, and that we have not necessarily lost His grace because we have lost the taste and feeling of it.

4. Meditations should be ended by one or several *Colloquies.* These are familiar conversations in which we speak to God like a son to a father, a servant to a master, one friend to another, a criminal to a judge, sometimes acknowledging our faults, sometimes exposing our wants, sometimes asking graces. These colloquies are addressed to the Blessed Virgin, to our Saviour, or to God the Father, sometimes to all three successively. This is the part of the meditation requiring the most liberty and confidence, but also the most respect. They must be concluded either by the "Ave Maria," the "Anima Christi," or the "Pater," according to the person to whom they are addressed. These colloquies may take place not only at the end, but at the beginning, or in the course of the meditation, as devotion may inspire. When we address ourselves to Jesus Christ, and beg Him to intercede for us before God, it must be understood that we consider Him, not simply as God, but in His human nature as our Mediator and Advocate.

After Meditation.

When two meditations have been made, it is customary to repeat them once or twice. This method is very useful, for it often happens that the first view of a mystery offers food chiefly to the *curiosity* of the mind; but, this desire of knowledge once satisfied, the soul returns calmly to its first impressions, and can more easily give free course to its affections; for it is in the affections of the heart that the fruits of an exercise consist. In these repetitions we must avoid all long reasonings, and only replace before our eyes, and run over, so to say, our first thoughts, dwelling on them with our will and heart. The use of the colloquies should be more frequent during the repetitions than during the Exercises.

ADDITIONAL RECOMMENDATIONS

IN THE FORM OF RESOLUTIONS, WHICH WILL ASSIST US IN MAKING THE EXERCISES WELL, AND OBTAINING FROM GOD WHAT WE ASK OF HIM.

1. On lying down, before going to sleep, during the short time which will suffice for repeating the "Hail Mary," I will fix the hour of my rising, and review in my mind the points of my meditation.

2. On awaking, immediately excluding all other thoughts, I will apply my mind to the truth on which I am going to meditate; at the same time I will excite in my heart suitable sentiments. For example, before the Exercise on the "triple sin," I will say to myself while I dress, "And I, loaded with so many graces, the object of predilection to my Lord and King, I stand

convicted of ingratitude, of treason, of rebellion, before His eyes and those of His whole court." Before the Exercise on personal sins, "Behold me, a criminal deserving death, led before my Judge loaded with chains." These sentiments must accompany the act of rising, and will vary according to the subject of meditation.

3. Standing a few paces from the spot where I am going to make my meditation, I must recollect myself, raise my mind above earthly things, and consider our Lord Jesus Christ as present and attentive to what I am about to do. Having given to this preparation the time required to say the "Our Father," I will offer the homage of my soul and body to our Saviour, assuming an attitude full of veneration and humble respect.

4. I will then begin my meditation, if I am alone in my chamber or elsewhere without witnesses, in the posture most suitable to the end I propose to myself, sometimes with my face bowed to the earth, sometimes standing, sometimes sitting; only observing that if I obtain what I seek kneeling, or in any other attitude, I ought to remain so without seeking any thing better. In the same way, if any particular point causes me to experience the grace which I am seeking, I must remain there calmly until my devotion is satisfied, without caring for any thing more.

5. After having finished the Exercise, I will either walk about or sit still, and examine how it has succeeded. If it has not, I will ascertain the cause, sincerely repent, and make firm resolutions for the future. If the success has been satisfactory, I will make acts of thanksgiving, and resolve to follow the same method for the future.

6. I will lay aside during the first week all joyful thoughts, such, for instance, as the glorious resurrection of Jesus Christ. This thought would dry up the tears which I ought at this period to shed over my sins. I must rather call up thoughts of death and judgment, in order to assist my sorrow.

7. For the same purpose, I will shut out the daylight, only allowing sufficient light to enter my room to enable me to read and take my meals.

8. I will carefully avoid all laughter, or any thing which can lead to it.

9. I will not look at any one, unless obliged to salute them or say adieu.

10. The tenth "recommendation" will be found in the Second Part, under the title of "Rule of Penance"

PREPARATORY EXERCISE.

Veni Creator. Ave maris stella. Invoke St. Joseph, your ange guardian, and your patron saints. Then read attentively the subject of meditation which is to open the Exercises.

MEDITATION ON RETREAT.

FIRST CONSIDERATION.

What God has prepared for you in retreat.

GOD has prepared for you a superabundance of His graces in this retreat. It is the same in retreat as in the great solemnities of religion and in certain privileged sanctuaries of Mary. Jesus Christ has graces for every day; but He reserves His choicest ones for the days on which the Church celebrates the great mysteries of His life on earth. Mary is always our benefactress and our mother; but she has favourite sanctuaries, to which she attaches her greatest blessings and miracles. The privilege of a retreat is to draw down upon us all the graces of God in their greatest plenitude. "Behold, now is the acceptable time: behold, now is the day of salvation" (2 Cor. vi. 2).

Consider, with St. Bernard, that it has been in retreat that God has always pleased to signalise His greatest mercies towards men. It was in retreat on Sinai that Moses received the tables of the law; it was in the retreat of Carmel that Elias received the double

spirit which animated him; it was in the retreat of
the desert that John Baptist received the plenitude of
the Spirit of God; it was in retreat that the Apostles
received the gifts of the Holy Ghost; it was in retreat that God converted the most illustrious penitents, that He raised up the most fervent apostles of
the new law, that He inspired the founders of religious
societies; in fine, it was in the retreat of Nazareth that
Mary became the mother of God; and it may be said
that all the life of Jesus Christ was a retreat. "Solitude was witness of the vigils of Jesus; solitude heard
the prayers of Jesus; solitude saw Him come into the
world, preach, be transfigured, die, rise from the dead,
ascend into heaven" (P. de Celles).

Believe, then, and rest assured that all the graces
of God await you in this retreat.

Who are you who this day begin these holy Exercises? *Who are you?* A soul established in virtue?
You need renewing. The most solid virtue is a perfume which evaporates, a mirror which tarnishes, a
water which becomes impure in the midst of the world.
"Bless the Lord, O my soul, ... who satisfieth thy
desire with good things; thy youth shall be renewed
like the eagle's" (Ps. cii. 1, 5). To you the grace of
a retreat will be one of renovation.

Who are you? A soul divided in the service of
God? a soul embarrassed by a multitude of human
affections? You have now to detach your heart from
creatures. "How long do you halt between two sides?
If the Lord be God, follow Him" (3 Kings xviii. 21).
For you the grace of retreat will be a grace of detachment

Who are you? A soul given to worldly pleasures? one who does not pray, or prays badly? You must return to yourself and to God. "Return, ye transgressors, to the heart" (Is. xlvi. 8). "We ought always to pray" (Luke xviii. 1). For you the grace of retreat will be one of recollection and prayer.

Who are you? A soul struggling with long and violent temptations? You need strength to resist. "If you return and be quiet, you shall be saved : in silence and hope shall your strength be" (Is. xxx. 15). For you the grace of retreat will be one of firmness and perseverance.

Who are you? Lastly, are you a guilty soul? perhaps a soul grown old in sin, perhaps an impenitent soul, perhaps a soul struck with blindness and hardness? And if this question alone does not make you tremble, certainly you are a hardened soul. Ah! you require nothing less than all the graces of God ; and this retreat offers them to you,—the grace of light on your state, on the enormity of your faults, on the greatness of your losses for eternity, on the judgments of God which menace you; the grace of compunction; the grace of firm resolution; the grace of a real and solid conversion.

SECOND CONSIDERATION.

What God asks of you in this retreat.

God requires two things of you, on which depend all the graces of the retreat.

1. *Recollection of spirit.* You are in retreat to listen to God. "I will hear what the Lord God will

c

speak within me" (Ps. lxxxiv. 9). But the voice of God only makes itself heard in the repose and silence of the soul. It is true that the voice of God, having once fully penetrated the heart, becomes strong as the tempest and loud as the thunder; but before reaching the heart it is weak as a light breath which scarcely agitates the air. It shrinks from noise, and is silent amid agitation. "The Lord is not in the earthquake" (3 Kings xix. 11). Retire into your heart with God, to meditate, to pray, to weep, to speak to the Lord and to listen to Him. You will not be alone when you are with Him. "How can he be alone who is always with God?" says St. Ambrose. If you are deprived of the conversation of men, you will enjoy that of the saints, of the angels, of Jesus Christ.*

2. *Perfect docility of heart*. This comprises three things: fidelity to rules; application to the exercises; obedience to all the movements of grace. Be afraid of refusing any thing to God: however small the sacrifice may be, perhaps our conversion, our salvation, may depend on it. A single word of the Gospel converted St. Anthony; a word from a sermon converted St. Nicholas Tolentino; a fact of history, a reading, a conversation, began the conversion of St. Augustine, of St. Ignatius, of St. Francis Xavier. Can you tell to what sacrifice God may have attached the change of your heart? Enter, then, into the disposition of the prophet: "My heart, O Lord, is ready" (Ps. lvi. 8). Do not fear to be too generous with God, and do not be

---

* "I call to me whom I will: I possess the society of saints; a troop of angels accompany me: I enjoy converse with Jesus Christ Himself." *St. Jerome.*

afraid of the sacrifices He may ask of you; this sweet
experience will force you to cry out with St. Augustine,
" How sweet has it been to me to be deprived of the
miserable delights of a frivolous world! and what
incomparable joy have I felt after a privation once so
dreaded!" Cast yourself, therefore, at the feet of Jesus
Christ, and say to Him, "Lord, Thou hast given me a
soul capable of knowing and loving Thee; I return it
to Thee, not adorned with the grace and virtue that
Thou bestowedst on it in baptism, but covered with the
scars and wounds of sin; cure it, O heavenly Physician, and restore to it its pristine life and beauty.

" Lord, I offer Thee my understanding; enlighten
it with Thy brightest light. 'Enlighten my eyes, lest
I sleep in death' (Psalm xii. 4).

" Lord, I offer Thee my memory; blot out from it
the remembrance of the world, and leave in it only the
memory of Thy mercies to bless them, and of my sins
to weep for them.

" Lord, I offer Thee my heart; change it by Thy
grace. 'Create a clean heart in me, O God, and renew
a right spirit within me' (Psalm l. 12).

" Lord, I offer to Thee the senses of my body, the
powers of my soul, my whole being; dispose of them
for my salvation and for Thy greater glory. 'I have put
my trust in Thee, O Lord; I have said Thou art my
God; my lot is in Thy hand'" (Psalm xxx. 15).

Poter. A...

FIRST PART.

DEVELOPMENT OF THE MEDITATIONS AND CONTEMPLATIONS OF THE FOUR WEEKS' SPIRITUAL EXERCISES.

FIRST WEEK.

Introduction to considerations on the end of man.

1. THE consideration on the end of man serves as a commencement to the Exercises. It is called the *foundation*, because it is the basis of the whole spiritual edifice. It will be seen in the sequel, that the other meditations are only a consequence of this, and that it is upon this that all the success of the retreat depends.

It is necessary in this Exercise to know thoroughly the end for which God created us, to resolve generously to make sacrifice of every thing which can divert us from this end, to look with indifference on every thing but that which leads to it, and even to carry our heroism so far as to choose whatever brings us to it most surely and rapidly, be the cost ever so great.

2. The object of this study is not precisely to excite gratitude towards God by recalling the benefits of creation; it is rather to show us the end for which we were created, and to teach us to look upon the benefits of God as so many means for obtaining that end. Thus, even

in this first meditation, the mind must concentrate its thoughts on itself, and inquire what conduct has hitherto been observed, either with regard to the end or the means, the wanderings and errors into which we have been betrayed, and how those creatures that should have been the means of raising us up to God, have been abused so as to separate us from Him. But the principal point is to impress well upon our minds the truth of our final end; for as the foundation of an edifice supports the whole building, so this first truth may be said to support all the others, in such manner that the success of the other meditations will be in proportion to the success of this.

3. The time to be given to this consideration has not been determined; but to render the beginning easier, each one is at liberty to devote the time most suited to his strength and his devotion, unless his director should have laid down some rule for him.

PRINCIPLE OR FOUNDATION.

Man was created for a certain end. This end is to praise, to reverence, and to serve the Lord his God, and by this means to arrive at eternal salvation.

All the other beings and objects which surround us on the earth were created for the benefit of man, and to be useful to him, as means to his final end; hence his obligation to use, or to abstain from the use of, these creatures,* according as they bring him nearer to that end, or tend to separate him from it.

* By the word *creatures*, St. Ignatius here means, in general,

Hence we must above all endeavour to establish in ourselves a complete indifference towards all created things, though the use of them may not be otherwise forbidden; not giving, as far as depends on us, any preference to health over sickness, riches over poverty, honour over humiliation, a long life over a short. But we must desire and choose definitively in every thing what will lead us to the end of our creation.

DEVELOPMENT OF THE PRINCIPLE OF THE EXERCISES.

FIRST PART OF THE TEXT.

The end of Man.

Text of St. Ignatius: *Man was created for this end: to praise, reverence, and serve the Lord his God, and by this means to arrive at eternal salvation.*

This meditation comprises three great truths which are the foundation of all the Exercises: *I come from God; I belong to God; I am destined for God.* That is to say, God is my first principle, my sovereign Master, my last end.

First Truth: *I come from God.*

CONSIDERATIONS.

1. Where was I a hundred years ago? I was nothing. If I look back a hundred years, I see the world with its

all things which are distinct from God and ourselves; all we find in nature, in society, as well as in the supernatural order; all events, all states of life, all the situations in which man finds himself from time to time.

empires, its cities, its inhabitants; I see the sun which
shines to-day, the earth on which I dwell, the land
which gave me birth, the family from which I sprung,
the name by which I am known: but I,—what was I,
and where was I? I was nothing, and it is amidst
nothingness I must be sought. Oh, how many ages
passed during which no one thought of me! For how
can nothing be the subject of thought? How many
ages when even an insect or an atom was greater than
I! for they possessed at least an existence.

2. But now I exist. I possess an intellect capable
of knowing, a heart formed for loving, a body endowed
with wonderful senses. And this existence, who gave
it me? Chance?—Senseless word!—My parents? They
answer in the words of the mother of the Machabees:
"No, it was not I who gave you mind and soul; it was
the Creator of the world" (2 Mach. vii. 22). Lastly,
was I the author of my own existence? But nothingness cannot be the cause of existence. It is to God,
then, that I must turn as my first beginning. "Thy
hands, O Lord, have made me and formed me" (Ps.
cxviii. 73). "Thou hast laid Thy hand upon me"
(Ps. cxxxviii. 5). Thou hast taken me from the abyss
of nothing.

3. Consider, O my soul, the circumstances of thy
creation.

(1.) God created me out of His pure love. Had He
any need of my existence, or could I be necessary to
His happiness? "I have loved thee with an everlasting
love" (Jer. xxxi. 3).

(2.) God created me, and the decree of my creation
is eternal like Himself. From eternity, then, God thought

of me. I was yet in the abyss of nothingness, and God gave me a place in His thoughts! I was in His mind, and in His heart. "I have loved you with an everlasting love."

(3.) God created me, and in creating me preferred me to an infinite number of creatures who were equally possible to Him, and who will for ever remain in nothingness. O God, how have I deserved this preference! "I have loved thee with an everlasting love."

(4.) God created me, and by creation made me the most noble of the creatures of the visible world. My soul is in His image, and all my being bears the stamp, the living stamp of His attributes.

(5.) Lastly, God created me, and He has continued His creation during every moment of my existence. As many as are the hours and moments of my life, so often does He make me a fresh present of life.

AFFECTIONS.

Sentiments of *humility* at the sight of our nothingness. "My substance is as nothing before Thee" (Ps. xxxviii. 6).

Sentiments of *admiration*. "What is man, that Thou shouldst magnify him? or why dost Thou set Thy heart upon him?" (Job vii. 17.)

Sentiments of *gratitude*. "Bless the Lord, O my soul, and let all that is within me bless His holy name. Bless the Lord, O my soul, and forget not all He hath done for thee" (Ps. cii. 1, 2).

SECOND TRUTH: *I belong to God.*

CONSIDERATIONS.

1. I come from God; hence, I belong to God. God is my creator; hence, He is my Lord and my Master. To deny this consequence would be to deny my reason.

2. The Lord enters into judgment with me, and deigns to argue His rights at the bar of His creature. Is it not true that the master has a right to the services of his servants or of his slaves? Is it not true that the king has a right to the obedience of his subjects? the father, to the submission as well as the respect of his children? Is it not true that the workman has a right to dispose of his work as he chooses? And I, the creature of God, do I not belong more to God than the slave to his master, than the subject to his sovereign, the child to his father, the picture to him who painted it, or the tree to him who planted it? Does not God possess over me all the rights of men over the creatures, and in a higher degree, and by more sacred titles? What is there in me that does not belong to Him, and is not the fruit, so to say, of His own capital, and therefore His property? "What have you that you have not received?" (1 Cor. iv. 7.) What would remain to me if God took back all that He has given me? If God took back my mind, what should I be?—On a level with the brute animals. If He deprived me of life and motion, what should I be?—A little dust and ashes. If He took away my substance and my whole being, what should I be?—A simple nothing. O my God! all I have comes from Thee; it is just that all in me should belong to Thee. "O Lord, just art Thou, and glorious in Thy

power, and no one can overcome Thee. Let all creatures serve Thee : for Thou hast spoken, and they were made; Thou didst send forth Thy Spirit, and they were created" (Jud. xvi. 16, 17).

3. Consider, O my soul, the characteristics of the dominion of God.

(1.) *Essential dominion.* It was not necessary that God should draw me from nothing. But since God has created me, it is necessary that I should be His. He would cease to be God if, being my creator, He ceased to be my sovereign and my master.

(2.) *Supreme dominion.* I belong to God before every thing, and above every thing. Properly speaking, I belong to God alone, and men have no other rights over me except such as God has given them. Their rights, then, are subordinate to the rights of God; and their authority must be always subjected to the authority of God.

(3.) *Absolute dominion.* God can dispose of me according to His pleasure; He can give or take from me fortune, health, honour, life; my duty is to receive every thing from His hand with submission and without complaint.

(4.) *Universal dominion.* Every thing in me is from God; therefore all in me belongs to God. The dominion of the Lord extends to all the stages of my life, to all the situations in which I may be placed, to all the faculties of my soul, all the senses of my body, to every hour and moment of my existence.

(5.) *Eternal dominion.* The dominion of God is immortal, like myself; it begins with time, and continues through eternity; death, which deprives men of all their rights, is unable to do any thing against the rights of God.

(6.) *Irresistible dominion.* We may escape the dominion of men; but how escape the dominion of God? Willing or unwilling, we must submit to it; we must either live under the empire of His love, or under that of His justice; either glorify His power by free obedience, or glorify it by inevitable punishment.

" O man, who art thou that repliest against God? Shall the thing formed say to him who formed it, why hast thou made me thus?" (Rom. ix. 20.)

AFFECTIONS.

1. *Adoration.* "Thou art worthy, O Lord our God, to receive glory and honour and power; for Thou hast created all things" (Apoc. iv. 11). "Come, let us adore and fall down before the Lord that made us; for He is the Lord our God" (Psalm xciv. 6, 7).

2. *Regret.* "Is this the return thou makest to the Lord, O foolish and senseless people? Is not He thy father, that hath possessed thee, and made thee, and created thee? Thou hast forsaken the God that made thee, and hast forgotten the Lord that created thee" (Deut. xxxii. 6, 18).

3. *Submission.* "O Lord, I am Thy servant, I am Thy servant, and the son of Thy handmaid" (Psalm cxv. 16).

THIRD TRUTH: *I am destined for God.*

CONSIDERATIONS.

1. God is not only my creator and my master, He is also my last end. A God infinitely wise must have

proposed to Himself an end in creating me; a God infinitely perfect could only have created me for His glory; that is to say, to know Him, to love Him, and to serve Him.

2. O my soul! dost thou wish for a proof of this great truth?

(1.) *Ask thy faith;* it will tell thee that God made all for Himself: "The Lord hath made all things for Himself" (Prov. xvi. 4). That He is the beginning and the end of all things: "I am the beginning and the end" (Apoc. i. 8). That the greatest of the commandments is to adore, to love, and to serve God: "Thou shalt love the Lord thy God;" "Thou shalt adore the Lord thy God, and Him only shalt thou serve" (Matt. xxii. 37, iv. 10).

(2.) *Ask thy reason;* it will tell thee that there must be some proportion between the faculties of man and their object. Hence there is nothing but the infinite perfections of God which can be the objects of a mind and heart craving with an intense desire to know and to love.

(3.) *Ask the creatures;* they will tell thee, by their imperfection, their inconstancy, their weakness, in a word, by their nothingness, that they are far too insignificant to be the end of thy being. "Vanity of vanities, and all is vanity, except to love God and to serve Him alone" (Imit. of Christ, i. 1).

(4.) *Ask thy heart;* it will tell thee that thou art formed for happiness, and that thou requirest happiness without alloy, happiness without limits, an eternal happiness; that is, that thou requirest nothing less than God Himself.

(5.) *Ask thy own experience;* it will thee why it is

that, when thou hast been faithful in serving God, peace has dwelt within thy breast; why it is that, when thou hast separated thyself from Him, thou hast felt nothing but disgust, emptiness, and remorse. Peace of heart is the fruit of order faithfully kept, faithfully observed. "We were made, O Lord, for Thee, and our heart is restless until it finds peace in Thee" (St. Aug.).

3. Thus my end is to know God, to love God, to serve God; this, therefore, is all my duty, all my greatness, all my happiness.

(1.) *All my duty.* Yes, I must know, love, and serve God. I must understand well this word, O my soul. I must be convinced that it is a real *necessity.* It is not necessary that I should possess talents, fortune, pleasures, an honourable position in society; it is not necessary that I should have a long life; it is not necessary that I should exist; but, supposing that I do exist, it is necessary that I should serve God. An intelligent creature that does not serve God is, in the world, what the sun would be if it ceased to shine, what our body would be if it ceased to move. It would be in the order of intelligence what a monster would be in the order of the bodily frame.

(2.) *All my greatness.* I am not made for a mortal man; I am not made for myself; I am not made for an angel. An intelligent and immortal being, I am too great for a creature, however noble, to be my end. My end is that of the angel; is that of Jesus Christ; is that of God Himself. God does not exist, could not exist, except to know Himself and to love Himself; and I only exist, or could exist, to know and to love God.

(3.) *All my happiness.* I cannot serve God in time without possessing Him in eternity. I cannot give myself wholly to God without His giving Himself wholly to me. "I am thy exceeding great reward" (Gen. xv. 1). His glory and my happiness are inseparable. It is, then, a question of my eternal destiny, and I myself am the arbiter of it. O my soul! picture to thyself on one side Heaven, with its ineffable delights; on the other Hell, with its fires and its despair; one or other will be thy eternal heritage, according as thou shalt have served or offended the Lord on earth. It is for thee to choose. "I call heaven and earth to witness this day that I have set before you life and death, blessing and cursing. Choose, therefore, life, ... that thou mayest love the Lord thy God, and obey His voice, and adhere to Him, for He is thy life" (Deut. xxx. 19, 20).

AFFECTIONS.

1. *Sorrow for the past.* "O God, Thou knowest my foolishness, and my offences are not hidden from Thee" (Ps. lxviii. 6).

2. *Contempt for creatures.* "All those that go far from Thee shall perish: Thou hast destroyed all those that were disloyal to Thee. But it is good for me to adhere to my God" (Ps. lxxii. 27, 28).

3. *Love of God.* "What have I in heaven? and beside Thee what do I desire upon earth? Thou art the God of my heart, and my portion for ever" (ib. 25, 26).

CONTINUATION OF THE DEVELOPMENT OF THE PRINCIPLE OF THE EXERCISES.

End of Creatures.

Text of St. Ignatius: *All other beings or objects placed around man on earth have been created for him, to serve as means to assist him in the pursuit of the end for which he was created.*

FIRST CONSIDERATION.

Creatures are from God.

Creatures have the same origin as myself. They, like me, have been taken from nothing, and He who drew them from nothing was God; but what difference between their creation and that of man!

1. Like me, they occupied from all eternity the thoughts and heart of God; but they held only the second place. God loved me for Himself, because I was destined for His glory; He loved creatures for the sake of man, because they were destined for the use of man, and because they only have reference to God distantly and through the medium of man.

2. Like me, creatures have received a being which is in some sort the efflux of His august perfections; but they have not, like me, the honour of being the living image of God, and made in His likeness.

3. Like me, they were created for the glory of God : but they have neither the understanding to know Him, nor the heart to love Him; they are incapable of possessing Him; they can only glorify Him in a very inferior and imperfect manner, that is, by the services

which they render to His servants. "Know, O man,
thy dignity" (St. Leo).

SECOND CONSIDERATION.
Creatures belong to God.

Creatures cannot have the same origin as myself
without having the same master. They come, then,
from God, and belong to Him. God has the same dominion over them as over me. Hence conclude:

1. I must, then, make use of creatures with a spirit
of *dependence*, according to the order of the Divine will,
not as a master who disposes at his pleasure, but as a
steward who must render an account to his lawful superior.

2. I must make use of creatures with a spirit of
gratitude, like a poor man who of himself has no right
to the use of the things of this world, and who holds
every thing from the liberality of God to whom all
belongs.

3. I must also make use of creatures with a spirit
of *fear*; for on one side my corrupt nature constantly
inclines me to the abuse of created things, and on the
other God will rigorously punish this abuse, which overthrows all the economy of creation.

Let me look back at the past. In what spirit have
I made use of creatures up to this day? Has it not
been in a spirit of *independence?* Almost always without consulting the will of God; often even contrary to
the order of His adorable will. Has it not been with
a spirit of *ingratitude?* O my God, when have I
thought of raising my heart to Thee, and thanking Thee
for Thy gifts? Has it not been with a spirit of *sensu-*

ality and of *selfishness?* only seeking myself and my pleasure in creatures, without thinking of the Divine justice, which will not fail to ask of me an account of so criminal an abuse. Let us accustom ourselves henceforward to read on every creature these three words— " *Receive, give, fear ;*" as if it should say, " Receive the blessing I offer you; give thanks to thy Creator for it; fear the judgment which will be passed upon you according to the use you have made of me" (Rich. de St. Victor).

THIRD CONSIDERATION.

Creatures are for God through the medium of man.

Creatures were formed for an end as well as myself, and this end is the glory of God; for God could only create for His Glory. Creatures deprived of understanding are not made to glorify the Lord directly ; they are made to serve man, who, in exchange for their services, must lend his intelligence and heart to praise and love God, and thus make them to conduce to the glory of their common Creator. This, then, according to the light of faith and reason, is the order of my relations with God and with creatures. I am for God, and creatures for me. From this follows that I cannot, like worldlings, make creatures my end without making myself guilty and miserable.

To place my affections on creatures would be to render myself guilty,—

1. *Guilty towards myself;* for it would be to degrade myself. "Such as the love of man is, such is he himself. Dost thou love the earth? thou art earth.

D

Dost thou love God? What shall I say? thou art God" (St. Aug.).

2. *Guilty towards creatures;* for it would be to turn them away from their end, and do violence to their nature. The Apostle tells us that they groan and suffer because sinners make use of them against God (Rom. viii. 22); and a holy doctor represents them as raising their voices against the sinner, and demanding vengeance. " All created things cry out, each according to their manner, and say: This is he who abused us. The earth says, Why must I bear upon me this monster ? The water says, Why may I not instantly suffocate him ? The air says, Why do I not deprive him of my benefits ? Hell says, Why do not my flames devour and inflict on him a thousand tortures ?" (St. Bonav.)

3. *Guilty towards God.* Guilty of injustice, because I should thus use the beings which belong to Him contrary to His will ;—guilty of a species of idolatry, for I should take from Him the first place in my homage, and substitute the creature in my thoughts and heart;— guilty of a kind of impiety, for it would be to attack all His attributes,—His goodness, which I should abuse; His wisdom, the plans of which I should derange ; His power, which I should turn against Him.

To place my end in creatures would be to render myself miserable ;—miserable for eternity ; I should lose at once both God, from whom I should be for ever separated, and creatures, who would become my everlasting torment ; miserable in time,—for how can creatures constitute my happiness ? Creatures whose being is so limited,—what a void they would leave in my heart! Creatures so full of imperfections,—what a source of disappointment and disgust! Creatures so fragile and perishable,—what a source of regret! Creatures so inconstant, so unfaithful,—what a source of distrust and fear! Creatures become my end, made the enemies of God,—what a source of remorse!

FOURTH CONSIDERATION.

How creatures glorify God in leading man to God.

I was made to know, to love, to serve, and possess God: this is my end; now creatures teach me,—

1. *To know God.* The order of the world reveals to me His wisdom: the stars announce His power—"The heavens show forth the glory of God" (Psalm xviii. 1); the ocean declares His immensity; the fertility of the earth praises His providence; the flowers of the field recall His beauty; the existence of the wicked even is a homage to His patience and His mercy. "Thou hast given me, O Lord, a delight in Thy doings: and in the works of Thy hands I shall rejoice. O Lord, how great are Thy works! The senseless man shall not know, nor will the fool understand these things" (Psalm xci. 5-7).

2. *To love God.* It is the goodness of God which has bestowed them upon me; it is His love which works for me through each of His creatures; it is He who warms me by the light of the sun; it is He who nourishes me by the fruits of the earth; it is He who clothes me by the garments which cover me. A God who serves me by means of His creatures, and serves me with so much constancy and so much goodness,—what a motive to love Him! "The eyes of all hope in Thee, O Lord. All wait upon Thee that Thou give them their food in season. What Thou givest them, they gather

up; when Thou openest Thy hand, they shall be filled with good" (Psalm cxliv. 15, ciii. 27, 28).

3. *To serve God.* Consider, O my soul, how they do the will of their Creator. They do it with pleasure, says the Holy Spirit. "The stars have given light in their watches, and rejoiced : they were called, and they said, Here we are; and with cheerfulness they have shined forth to Him that made them" (Bar. iii. 34, 35).

They do it with *respect.* " He sendeth forth light, and it goeth; it obeyeth Him with trembling" (Bar. iii. 33).

They do it with *promptitude.* " Who walkest upon the wings of the wind; who makest His angels spirits, and His ministers a flaming fire" (Psalm ciii. 3, 4).

They do it with an immutable *constancy.* " By Thy ordinance the day goeth on, for all things serve Thee" (Psalm cxviii. 91).

Thus, O my soul, every creature serves the Lord. Shall I be the only one that refuses to serve Him? shall I be the least faithful of His servants, because I am of all others under the strongest obligation?

4. All creatures assist me in *meriting the possession of God;* for there is not one that may not be the occasion of some virtue, and therefore the subject of some merit. Thus :—

There are some creatures the use of which is indispensably necessary,—those, for example, which are destined to sustain my existence. What occasions for practising moderation and detachment!

There are some things to which we must submit, though nature shrinks from them,—for instance, sickness, poverty, humiliation, mortification, &c. What

opportunities of practising patience, humility, charity!
There are some things which from their nature lead us
to God—such as assistances of the supernatural order.
What opportunities of exercising faith and piety!
There are some things which withdraw our heart from
God. What an opportunity of sacrifice! Is it in this
light that I have considered creatures? Is it in this
way that I have used them?

AFFECTIONS.

Bless God in the name of all His creatures. "Bless
the Lord, O all ye works of the Lord" (Dan. iii. 57).

Grieve for having sought happiness from creatures.
"Vanity of vanities, and all is vanity. . . . . I have seen
every thing under the sun, and all is vanity and affliction of spirit" (Eccles. i. 2, 14).

Resolve to love God alone. "Who shall separate us from the love of Christ? shall tribulation, or
distress, or famine, or nakedness, or danger, or persecution, or the sword? . . . . I am sure that neither death,
nor life, ... nor any other creature shall be able to
separate us from the love of God, which is in Christ
Jesus our Lord" (Rom. viii. 35, 38, 39).

CONTINUATION OF THE DEVELOPMENT OF THE
PRINCIPLE OF THE EXERCISES.

THIRD PART OF THE TEXT.

Indifference with regard to Creatures.

Text of St. Ignatius: *We must, then, above all
things, endeavour to establish in ourselves a complete*

indifference with regard to all created things, even that of which the use is not forbidden us;—not preferring, as far as depends on us, health to sickness, riches to poverty, honour to humiliation, a long life to a short one; since order requires that we wish for and choose in every thing what will lead us most surely to the end for which we were created.

All creatures were given to man to lead him to this his proper end. How is it, then, that they so frequently draw him away from God, and are the cause and instruments of his eternal ruin? " The creatures of God are turned to an abomination, and a temptation to the souls of men, and a snare to the feet of the unwise" (Wisd. xiv. 11). This arises from the irregularity of our affections as regards creatures. It is because nature, degraded by original sin, seeks them or avoids them, according as they flatter or mortify our corrupt passions. The purpose of this meditation is to reform the disorder of our attachments or aversions, and to establish in us a perfect indifference. This indifference consists in neither seeking nor avoiding, with a free and deliberate will, any created thing for itself, *but solely as it may bring us near to or separate us from God.*

FIRST CONSIDERATION.
Motives for this indifference as regards God.

1. *The sovereign dominion of God requires this indifference.* Is it not true that I belong to God, and that He has an absolute and universal dominion over me? Is it not true that He created me for an end, and that He wills that I should tend to and arrive at this end? Without this indifference, it is evident that

I am acting contrary to the will of God, and that I withdraw myself from His dominion. I dispose of my affections according to my own will, not according to His adorable will. Amidst the various situations in which I may be, I choose, not that which He destines for me, but the one which pleases me. I make myself the arbiter and proprietor of myself. Is not this to usurp the right of God?

2. *The sovereign perfection of God requires this indifference.* God is so perfect and so amiable that He ought to be loved above all things, and that nothing ought to be loved except for Him. Faith and reason proclaim this truth. And without this indifference how should I love God? How should I love creatures? I should love the latter for themselves, for the pleasures they procure for me; soon perhaps I should love them above God Himself. Is not this, O my God, the great disorder of my past life? and is it not the want of this indifference that has enfeebled, and often almost destroyed Thy love in my heart?

3. *The providence of God requires this indifference.* Not only did God create me for Himself, but His providence never ceases to conduct me towards my end. I am in the hands of this providence so infinitely good, infinitely wise, infinitely powerful. Can I fear that this providence is unable or unwilling to procure my greatest good? Surely no. Without this indifference, then, in regard to creatures, I derange the whole plan of this providence. Perhaps God has deprived me of health, honour, fortune, pleasure; perhaps He has tried me by sickness, poverty, or tribulation. Of these two paths, the first would lead to my eternal loss, and

the second secure my everlasting happiness. If, then, by my own will I depart from the way in which He has placed me for my salvation, am I not guilty as regards His providence?

SECOND CONSIDERATION.

Motives for this indifference as regards myself.

1. *This indifference is requisite to acquire solid virtue.* Virtue is at bottom but the spirit of sacrifice; in abnegation consists Christian sanctity. "If any man will come after Me, let him deny himself and take up his cross daily, and follow Me" (Luke ix. 23). Where there is not indifference, can there be a spirit of sacrifice? Thus there will not be any virtues, or at least only natural virtues without merit for eternity;—virtues mixed with imperfections, sullied by self-love and natural desires;—virtues, fragile and inconstant, which will give way before the first breath of temptation?

2. *This indifference is requisite to ensure peace of heart.* Without this indifference, what fears, what disappointments, what remorse! On the contrary, with this indifference, what sweet assurance! "The Lord ruleth me; I shall want nothing" (Psalm xxii. 1). "The Lord is my light and my salvation, whom shall I fear? The Lord is the protector of my life, of whom shall I be afraid?" (Psalm xxvi. 1.) With this indifference, what joy even in the midst of tribulation! "I exceedingly abound with joy in all my tribulations" (2 Cor. vii. 4). With this indifference, what fullness of peace in the depths of the heart! "Oh, that thou hadst

hearkened to My commandments; thy peace had been as a river, and thy justice as the waves of the sea" (Isaias xlviii. 18).

3. *This indifference is necessary to ensure my salvation.* How many perils threaten thy salvation, O my soul!—perils from the world, perils from the devil, perils within thyself—from the imagination, the heart, the memory, the senses; perils without—from friends, from business, from pleasure, from occupation, from solitude, from society. "Lord, when wilt Thou look upon me? Deliver my soul from this malice: my only one from thelions" (Psalm xxxiv. 17). O my soul, all these perils are reduced to one—to the making a bad use of creatures. Force thyself, then, to arrive at a perfect indifference; thou hast no other danger to fear, and thy salvation is secured. Take example from the clay which allows itself to be formed at the will of the workman; which does not say to him, "Why dost thou form me into an ignominious vessel, and not into a glorious vase?" Raise thy thoughts still higher. Learn from the angels, who with the same submission and the same tranquillity stand before the throne of God to sing, without ending, the canticle of Sion: "Holy, holy, holy;" or to watch over an obscure mortal to conduct him through the pilgrimage of this life. Look still higher. Take example by Jesus Christ, who had no other food or life on this earth than the will of Him that sent Him: "My meat is to do the will of Him that sent me" (John iv. 34).

RULES FOR THE PRACTICE OF INDIFFERENCE.

Rule 1. In the use of creatures, only esteem and

desire what leads to God. All the rest is useless for
His glory and man's salvation.

Rule 2. In the use of creatures, firmly resolve to
fly from all that God forbids—mortal sin, venial sin,
and the occasions of both. " Fear God and keep His
commandments; for this is the whole of man" (Ecc.
xii. 13). "Without this," says St. Bernard, "man,
whatever he may be, is nothing."

Rule 3. In the case of indifferent creatures, that is
to say, of things which in themselves neither bring us
nearer nor lead us farther from God, we must cease to
feel indifference towards them only as it accords with
the rule of the will of God, and His good pleasure.

End by reciting the *Pater.*

EXERCISES ON THE PUNISHMENT OF SIN.

FIRST EXERCISE.

Sin punished in the rebel angels.

Preparatory prayer. Ask of God the grace to devote to His glory and service all the powers and operations of your soul.

First prelude. Represent to yourself the flames of
hell, and in the midst of the flames an innumerable multitude of fallen angels.

Second prelude. Ask of God sentiments of shame
and repentance, at the sight of these victims of sin. The
angels only sinned once; but you, how often have you
not committed even mortal sins?

FIRST CONSIDERATION.

The state of the rebel angels before their sin.

Consider—

1. *The excellence of their being.* They were pure spirits, free from the bonds of a mortal body; the living images of the perfections of God; the first-fruits and most perfect work of the creation.

2. *Their intelligence.* What lights respecting God, creatures, their own dignity! What wisdom, what breadth and depth of knowledge!

3. *Their will.* What innocence! What uprightness! What a powerful inclination towards good! What natural movements of heart towards God, their sovereign beatitude!

4. *Their dwelling-place.* It is Heaven, where they do not yet see the Lord face to face, but where their life is to think of Him and to love Him.

5. *Their future destiny.* A few moments of trial, and God reveals Himself to their eyes without a cloud. They will be, through all eternity, at the foot of His throne, enjoying the happiness of seeing Him, of loving Him, and possessing Him with all the powers of their being. "They shall be inebriated with the plenty of Thy house; Thou shalt make them drink of the torrent of Thy pleasures" (Psalm xxxii. 9).

6. *Their chief.* Lucifer, the prince of the celestial hierarchy, and whose perfections are described by the Holy Spirit in Ezechiel: "Thou wast the seal of resemblance, full of wisdom, and perfect in beauty. Thou wast in the pleasures of the paradise of God: precious stones were thy covering, gold was the work of thy

beauty. I set thee on the mountain of God, and thou didst walk in the midst of stones of fire. Thou wast perfect in thy ways from the day of thy creation until iniquity was found in thee" (Ezech. xxviii. 12, 13, 14, 15). O my God, what couldst Thou have added to the magnificence of Thy gifts to these sublime intelligences? and what was wanting to them except to remain faith ful to Thee?

SECOND CONSIDERATION.

The sin of the rebel angels.

These noble spirits were in possession of their liberty, and it was their ruin. God had given it to them that it might be a merit: they abused it and were lost. According to St. Bonaventure and some other doctors of the Church, they became dazzled by their own perfections, and their sin was a guilty complaisance and a kind of idolatry of themselves. According to St. Thomas, God had revealed to them the future grandeur of the Incarnation, and had commanded them to adore the Man-God; and their crime was a resistance to this command of the Lord. Lucifer first raised the standard of rebellion; he dared to declare himself the rival of God, and he drew a third of the angels into his rebellion. "Thou saidst in thy heart, I will ascend into heaven; I will exalt my throne above the stars of God; I will sit in the mountain of the covenant; I will ascend above the height of the clouds; I will be like to the Most High" (Isaias xiv. 13, 14).

Consider attentively all the circumstances of this sin, in order to understand its motive.

1. *A sin of revolt against God.* "Thou hast broken

My yoke, thou hast burst My bands, and thou saidst, I will not serve" (Jer. ii. 20). Is not this the character of your sins? Are they not revolts against God?

2. *A sin committed in Heaven.* "Thou wert in the delights of paradise, and thou didst sin" (Ezech. xxviii. 13, 16). And you, placed in the land of saints, in the heaven on earth, in the Church of God, how many times have you not committed mortal sin?

3. *A sin committed amidst great lights.* "Thou wert full of wisdom, perfect in beauty, and thou didst sin" (ibid.). And you too have sinned amidst the brightest lights of faith.

4. *A sin committed after great benefits received.* "Thou wert the seal, the image of God, and thou didst sin" (ib.). And you, loaded with all the gifts of nature and grace, have sinned. You have offended your benefactor by the abuse even of His own benefits.

5. *A sin of scandal.* "And behold a great dragon; and his tail drew the third part of the stars of heaven" (Apoc. xii. 3, 4). And how many souls have not your sins drawn down? Count the victims of your scandals.

THIRD CONSIDERATION.

The chastisement of the rebel angels.

No interval exists between the crime and its punishment; the justice of God strikes them like the thunderbolt. They are cast into the depths of hell, and in the midst of flames expiate through an eternity the crime of a moment. What a terrible revolution in their whole being;—in their intelligence, no thoughts but of crime! in their will, no love but for evil! in their abode, no other

palace but hell! in their ministry, no other occupation
than to pervert or torment souls! in their destiny, their
end, supreme misery, and that for eternity! Oh, terrible
fall! "How art thou fallen, O Lucifer!" (Is. xiv. 12.)
O my soul, tremble for thyself! If an angel is so
treated, what will it be with man! "Howl, thou fir-
tree, for the cedar is fallen, for the mighty are laid
waste" (Zach. xi. 20).

Reflect on this terrible vengeance of God. 1. His
justice has no regard to the number of the guilty; de
not assure yourself by the number who sin like you.
2. His justice has no regard for the dignity or excellence of the victims; do not trust to your dignity of
rank in the world or the Church. 3. His justice pays
no regard to the services which the angels might render
to His glory, if repentant and restored to grace; do not
therefore comfort yourself by the thought of the services
you might render to Jesus Christ and His Church. 4. His
justice has no regard to the place which the angels had
occupied until then in His friendship and in His heart;
do not therefore assure yourself by the past mercies of
our Lord. 5. His justice strikes without pity, and yet
it is the first sin of the angels, and their only sin. What
will, then, become of you who can and ought to say with
the prophet, My iniquities are gone over my head?
(Psalm xxxvii. 5.)

AFFECTIONS.

End, at the foot of the crucifix, by the sentiments
of humility, confusion, and repentance, which a great
saint and doctor suggests to you. "My God, Thou
hast imprinted upon me Thy own adorable image, and

for it I have substituted the frightful image of Satan. I see myself more horrible than Lucifer. He fell proudly, having no example of Divine vengeance before him; I, after beholding his chastisement, have sinned contemptuously. He was once established in innocence; I have often been restored. He rose up against Him who had bestowed upon him his being; I against Him who has repaired mine. He remains for ever, fixed in his malice, under eternal reprobation; I, a sinner, am ever fleeing from the mercy of God, who calls me back. He abandoned a God who lets him depart from Him; I fly from a God who comes to seek me. And if both have sinned, he yet sinned against a God who did not call him to repentance; I, on the contrary, against a God who died to save me" (St. Bonav.).

Colloquy with Jesus crucified. *Pater.*

SECOND EXERCISE.

Sin punished in Adam and his posterity.

Preparatory prayer. As before.

First prelude. Represent to yourself Adam driven from Paradise by an angel armed with a fiery sword, and not knowing where to hide his shame and his remorse.

Second prelude. The same as last.

FIRST CONSIDERATION.

Adam before his sin.

Consider—

1. *The excellence of his being.* Adam is not made from nothing by a single word, like other creatures:

"He spoke, and they were made" (Ps. lxviii. 5). The Three Persons of the adorable Trinity deliberated, as it were: "Let us make man" (Gen. i. 26). God gave him a soul made in His image: "And God created man to His own image" (Gen. i. 27). He formed his body with His hands, and animates it with the breath of His mouth: "And the Lord God formed man of the slime of the earth, and breathed into his face the breath of life" (Gen. ii. 7).

2. Consider the happiness and glory of his state. The lights of his mind: "He created in them the science of the spirit" (Ecclus. xvii. 6). The innocence of his heart: "He filled their heart with wisdom" (ib.). His empire over his passions and over all the senses of his body, the profound peace of his soul: "What was wanting to him who was guarded by mercy, taught by truth, governed by justice, borne in the arms of peace?" (St. Ber.)

3. Consider the place of his abode. God had placed him amidst the delights of the terrestrial paradise: "God took man and put him into the paradise of pleasure" (Gen. ii. 15). He made him the king over all nature: "And gave him power over all things that are upon the earth; He put the fear of Him upon all flesh" (Ecclus. xvii. 3, 4).

4. Consider his relations with God. The Lord had deigned to make an eternal alliance with him. He Himself revealed to him His commands and His greatness. Adam was honoured to hear His voice: "He made an everlasting covenant with them: and their eye saw the majesty of His glory, and their ears heard His glorious voice" (Ecclus. xvii. 10, 11).

5. Consider his future destiny. After a few years of happy life in the earthly paradise, he was to enjoy for an eternity the sight and possession of God.

O God, how great was man in the days of his innocence! "Thou hast made him a little less than the angels; Thou hast crowned him with glory and honour, and hast set him over the works of Thy hands" (Psalm viii. 6, 7). Why was it that he forgot his greatness? "Man, when he was in honour, did not understand; he hath been compared to senseless beasts, and made like unto them" (Psalm xlviii. 21).

SECOND CONSIDERATION.

Adam's sin.

God had forbidden Adam to touch the tree of knowledge of good and evil. He exacted obedience from the first man as a homage to His supreme dominion, and He exacted it under pain of death: "But of the tree of knowledge of good and evil thou shalt not eat. For in what day soever thou shalt eat of it, thou shalt die the death" (Gen. ii. 17). Adam did not obey. Eve, tempted by the serpent, tempted her husband, who, by his fatal complaisance, betrayed his trust: "And the woman saw that the tree was good to eat, and fair to the eyes, and delightful to behold; and she took of the fruit thereof and did eat, and gave to her husband, who did eat" (Gen. iii. 6).

Consider attentively the characteristics of this first sin, and in the history of Adam's fall recognise the history of all others.

1 *Imprudence.* Eve listened to the perfidious

E

counsels of Satan; Adam listened to the insinuations of
his spouse. And you? What has been the cause or
your falls? Has it not been a temptation imprudently
listened to?

2. *Sensuality.* The beauty, the apparent sweetness
of the forbidden fruit seduced our first parents: "they
saw it was good to eat and fair to the eyes." And
have not all your faults, at least your more grave ones,
been sins of the senses?

3. *Cowardice.* With the lights of his intelligence,
with the rectitude and good inclinations of his heart,
with a conscience so upright and delicate, it was
easy for Adam to remain faithful. And you, formed
by religion, by a Christian education, what resources
against temptation have you not found in your faith, in
your conscience, in your heart, where grace has planted
such holy inclinations?

4. *Contempt of God.* Nothing arrests Adam,—
neither the bounty of God, which has surrounded him
with benefits; nor the authority of God, of which his
reason loudly proclaimed the rights; nor His justice, of
which the threats were so express and so formidable.
And have not you, when you committed sin, had as
little regard to the benefits, the authority, or the threat-
ened judgments of the Lord?

5. *Blindness.* Our first parents believed the word
of the tempter, and they did not believe that of God.
On the faith of Satan they persuaded themselves that
they should not die, that they should be like gods:
"You shall not die the death, you shall be as gods"
(Gen. iii. 4, 5). And their eyes were only opened when
the sin was committed: "And the eyes of them both

were opened" (Gen. iii. 7). Is not this the exact picture of your past blindness? In the moment of temptation have you not sought to deceive yourself by foolish reasonings on the justice of God, and on His mercy? Have you not sought to persuade yourself that sin is not so great an evil,—that God is too good to punish you? And is it not true that it was only after the sin that your blindness ceased, and that your eyes were opened to the light?

THIRD CONSIDERATION.

Adam after his sin.

1. Meditate well on the terrible sentence of God on guilty Adam. Because thou hast eaten of the forbidden fruit, the earth shall be cursed; it shall only bring forth thorns; thou shalt eat thy bread in the sweat of thy brow until thou returnest to the earth from which thou didst come out; for dust thou art, and unto dust thou shalt return (Gen. iii. 19).

2. Consider the accomplishment of the Divine sentence. A German prince, wishing to inspire his son with a great horror of war, ordered a painter to represent the different scenes of a bloody battle, and to write these words at the bottom of the picture: " Behold the fruits of war !" Imitate this prince, you who meditate at this moment on the fall of our first parent; represent to yourself all the evils which have followed it, and say to yourself: *Behold the fruits of sin.*

Consider the soul of Adam deprived of grace and original justice, and disfigured by sin: *Behold the fruits of sin.*

Consider his faculties wounded, as it were, wounded mortally; his mind given up to doubt, ignorance, error, his heart, without inclination for good, the sport of a thousand passions; his conscience, which has lost its peace, and is tormented by remorse : *Behold the fruits of sin.*

Consider the revolution which took place in nature : the inclemency of the seasons, the revolt of the animals, the sterility of the earth, which of itself only produces thorns and thistles: *Behold the fruits of sin.*

Consider the tribulations of Adam : the sweat of his daily work; the sorrows of sickness and infirmity; his desolation at the death of the innocent Abel; all the troubles of his heart and spirit; and after nine hundred years of penitence, the final trial of death: *Behold the fruits of sin.*

Consider the anger of God in pouring vengeance for this first sin on all the descendants of the first culprit; represent to yourself the miseries of men in all ages, —contagions, wars, disasters, violent deaths; so many tears shed, so many crimes committed, so many children for ever deprived of the sight of God, so many souls cast into hell. See here the consequences of one sin : *Behold the fruits of sin.*

3. End by turning back on yourself, and comparing the sin of Adam with your own personal sins. On the side of Adam a single sin, a sin committed before the Incarnation, a sin committed before he had any experience of Divine justice; above all, a sin which he repented of immediately, and which he expiated by nine centuries of penitence : and on your part so many sins, sins committed in a nature sanctified by Jesus Christ; sins com-

mitted in the face of the Cross and in the sight of hell; sins, perhaps, which you have never expiated; sins, perhaps, of which you have scarcely repented. "O God, what have I not to fear from Thy justice?"

AFFECTIONS.

Fear. "Who knoweth the power of Thy anger, and for Thy fear can number Thy wrath?" (Ps. lxxxix. 11.)

Confusion. "All the day long my shame is before me, and the confusion of my face hath covered me" (Psalm xliii. 16).

Regret. "There is no health in my flesh because of Thy wrath : there is no peace for my bones because of my sins" (Psalm xxxvii. 4).

Beg the mercy of God. "Have mercy on me, O God, according to Thy great mercy" (Psalm l. 1).

THIRD EXERCISE.

Personal sin punished in man.

Preparatory Prayer.

First prelude. Represent to yourself the flames of hell in which thousands of condemned souls are burning.

Second prelude. The same as last.

CONSIDERATIONS.

Consider that at this very moment, when you on earth are meditating on the malice of sin, there is perhaps in the depths of hell a soul that God has for ever condemned for one single mortal sin.

1. *Consider what this soul was before its sin.*

For a long time, perhaps, it had received much less grace than you who now meditate on its misery; and yet it may have persevered in virtue through many years; its childhood may have been sanctified by innocence and piety; in youth it may have remained pure in the midst of the strongest passions and most violent temptations. It had preserved its baptismal innocence, perhaps, up to the fatal moment which witnessed at once its fall, its death, and its reprobation. It may have lived many years in the friendship of God; practised great virtues, and given great examples of piety; perhaps received the spirit of prayer, like St. Louis Gonzaga; the spirit of mortification, like St. John of the Cross; the spirit of zeal, like St. Francis Xavier. Perhaps it had received a great gift of prayer, like St. Theresa; perhaps the gift of miracles, like Judas before his crime. Think what acts of virtue, what victories, what sacrifices, what merit in such a life, what titles to eternal glory! What are you in comparison with this soul? Compare your faults with its virtues;—the corruption of your heart with its innocence; your sensual life with its mortifications; your dissipation and forgetfulness of God with its habits of prayer, &c. And yet you may, if you choose, be one of the elect; and this is a reprobate soul, and will remain so through all eternity. "How is the gold become dim, the finest colour is changed!" (Lament. iv. 1.)

2. *Consider what this soul has become since its sin.*

It committed but one single mortal sin—one mortal sin after ten, perhaps twenty years of a holy life, full of good works. A single mortal sin! And if this unhappy man fell with the knowledge and consent necessary to constitute a mortal sin, yet he perhaps only sinned from weakness; perhaps was carried away by some strong passion; perhaps after long temptation, perhaps after long resistance. Are your faults of this kind? And if, during your life, you have only committed one such sin, do you not believe yourself almost innocent?

Yet the justice of God overtook this unhappy soul, without leaving any interval between the mortal sin and death.

All is over with it after the first crime; no grace, no repentance, no pardon; it is lost for all eternity. "How incomprehensible are His judgments, and how unsearchable His ways!" (Rom. xi. 33.)

If God had struck this soul a few hours earlier, death would have found it in a state of grace; this soul would have been saved; it would have possessed God. And now that it has entered eternity with mortal sin, it is for ever deprived of the sight and the possession of God, who is its end and its whole felicity. It would have been in the highest heavens and in the society of angels; and now it is in the depths of hell and in the company of demons. It would have been clothed with glory; and now it is surrounded with flames. It would have been inundated with peace and the joys of paradise; and now it is torn with remorse, and condemned to never-ending tears and despair. It would have lived in heaven for ever, to love and bless God; and now it lives in hell but to blaspheme Him, to curse Him, to hate Him, through all eternity. O God, what a fearful catastrophe! *And this is the work of one single sin!*

3. *Consider what this soul might have been if God had allowed it time to acknowledge and expiate its sin.*

After the first burst of passion, who knows if it would not have returned to itself; if reason would not have regained its empire, conscience made its reproaches heard, faith shown the depth of the abyss into which it had fallen, grace solicited the heart, the habit of prayer brought it back to the foot of the cross? The goodness of its heart could not have resisted the voice of Jesus Christ: "Why persecutest thou Me?" (Acts ix. 4.) For is not this what passes within you after each of your falls? Who knows whether a few hours after his sin, absolution—or perhaps even before absolution, perfect contrition — might not have restored him to the friendship of God, to his innocence, and to all his merit? Perhaps he might have spent the rest of his life in weeping over this one fault; perhaps he might have made this one sin the subject of constant repentance; he might, like Magdalen, like Augustine, have made the memory of this fault a motive for more fervent love. Now his mortal career would be ended, he would be at the feet of Jesus and Mary in heaven; and we might perhaps be invoking him on earth as a model of penitence and holiness, as an illustrious example of the power of grace and Divine mercy. But this time for repentance, which might have been so well employed, was refused by God; and this soul is lost, and for ever. *O the depth!*

To inspire yourself with a still greater horror of sin, ask yourself what this God is who thus punishes a single mortal sin. Has He ceased to be a God of wisdom? No; in punishing in this manner He always acts according to the immutable rules of His infinite wisdom : " O the depth of the wisdom of God !" (Rom. xi. 33.) Has He ceased to be a God of goodness and mercy? No. At the moment that His vengeance overtook this soul, He had no hatred but for the sin; and guilty as that soul was, He loved it as His creature, as the price of His blood, better than you love the work of your hands, better than a mother loves her only son : " For Thou lovest all things that are, and hatest none of the things which Thou hast made, because they are Thine, O Lord, who lovest souls" (Wisd. xi. 25, 27). Has He ceased to be a just God? No; the angels in heaven applaud the equity of His judgments; and in hell this condemned soul itself is obliged to render homage to the justness of the sentence which condemned it : " Thou art just, O Lord; and Thy judgment is right" (Psalm cxviii. 137). What an evil must one mortal sin not be, and who would not fear to offend a God who punishes so rigorously? " Who shall not fear thee, O King of nations ?" (Jer. x. 7.)

Now return to yourself.

(1.) How long is it since you committed mortal sin the first time?

(2.) Why did not God strike you dead after this first sin, as He foresaw that you would make use of your life to sin again and again, and with so much malice?

(3.) Why has God spared you until now, when every thing demanded your condemnation,—the interest of His perfections, which you have outraged; the interest of His graces, which you have trampled under

foot; the interest of souls, whose loss you have caused
by your scandals?

(4.) What was there in you to inspire God with so
much mercy towards you? If He considers the past,
—your baptismal innocence lost, a guilty childhood, a
youth given up to pleasure; if He considers the present,
—a heart attached to sin, rebellious against graces,
resolved not to make a sacrifice of its passions; if He
should consider the future,—iniquities multiplying with
years, infidelities growing with graces.

And yet God has left you life, and with life grace
to return to Him, to repent, to merit heaven! What
mercy on His part! You ought to look upon yourself
as a soul saved from hell by a singular privilege of
Divine goodness; you should say, Lord, if Thou hadst
called me before Thy tribunal on such a day, at such an
hour, and after such a fault, I should now be in hell
among the lost; in hell I should shed useless tears over
my sin. I will shed them on earth, that they may become efficacious and meritorious for heaven. In hell I
should have performed a useless and hopeless penance,
on earth I will perform a useful penance, in the hope of
obtaining my pardon;—in hell I should see all creatures
armed against me for my torment; I will detach my
heart from all earthly creatures for Thy love;—in hell I
should have no other occupation than blaspheming and
hating Thee; I will spend my life on earth in blessing
and loving Thee.

AFFECTIONS AT THE FOOT OF THE CRUCIFIX.

Sorrow and Shame. "My God, I am confounded,
and ashamed to lift up my face to Thee: for our iniquities

are multiplied over our heads, and our sins are grown up even unto heaven" (Esdras ix. 6).

Gratitude. "I have sinned, and have offended, and I have not received what I have deserved" (Job xxxiii. 27). "It is because of the mercies of the Lord that we are not consumed" (Lament. iii. 22).

Fidelity for the future. "I will praise Thee, O Lord my God, with my whole heart, and I will glorify Thy name for ever : for Thy mercy is great towards me, and Thou hast delivered my soul out of the lower hell" (Ps. lxxxv. 12, 13).

COLLOQUIES WHICH MUST BE FREQUENTLY REPEATED DURING THE FOLLOWING MEDITATIONS.

The first will be addressed to Mary the Mother of our Saviour, our Lady and our Queen; we shall supplicate her to intercede for us with her Son, and to obtain for us the three graces which are most necessary for us : first, a full knowledge, a true detestation, and a lively feeling of our sins; then a reformation of ourselves such as God expects of us, and such as this thorough knowledge and profound horror of our past disorders should produce; finally, the happiness of profiting by this sad experience of the sinfulness of the world, which we bitterly deplore, by renouncing for ever the world and its vanities. This colloquy will end by an *Ave Maria.*

The second will be addressed to Jesus Christ our Lord and Mediator. We shall beg of Him to obtain for us these three graces from the Eternal Father. We shall recite at the end the prayer *Anima Christi.*

The third will be addressed to God the Father, that He may deign to grant us this threefold favour, and we shall end by saying the *Pater*.

FOURTH EXERCISE.

On the infinite malice of mortal sin.

Preparatory Prayer.

First prelude. Present yourself before God as a criminal appearing before his judge, and about to hear his sentence.

Second prelude. "I groan in Thy sight as one guilty; shame hath covered my face, because of my sin; spare me, a suppliant, O my God."*

FIRST CONSIDERATION.

A God offended by man.

Consider attentively the greatness of the God who is offended; the nothingness of the sinner; the matter and the motive of the sin.

1. *The greatness of the God who is offended.* What is God? Who is like to Him in greatness? Nations before Him are as a drop of water; the universe as a grain of sand; the whole human race as nothing. " Behold the Gentiles are as a drop of a bucket, and are counted as the smallest grain of a balance. Behold the islands are as a little dust; all nations are before Him as if they had no being at all" (Isaias xl. 15, 17).

----

* " Ingemisco tanquam reus:
    Culpa rubet vultus meus:
    Supplicanti parce, Deus."   *Dies Iræ.*

Who is like God in power? He created all by a
word: "He spoke, and it was made." He preserves all
by His will: "Upholding all things by the word of His
power" (Heb. i. 3). One word of His can chain the
ocean: "Hitherto shalt thou come, and shalt go no
further" (Job xxxviii. 11). One look of His makes
the earth tremble: "He looketh upon the earth, and
maketh it tremble; He toucheth the mountains and
they smoke" (Ps. ciii. 32). And before His face the
mountains melt: "The mountains melted like wax at
the presence of the Lord" (Ps. xcvi. 5).

Who is like to Him in holiness? In His eyes the
just, the very saints, appear defiled: "The Heavens are
not pure in His sight" (Job. xv. 15). He even finds
sin in His angels: "And in His angels He found wickedness" (Job iv. 18). Who is like Him in justice, in
wisdom, in goodness? "Thy justice is as the mountains" (Ps. xxxv. 7). "Of His wisdom there is no
number" (Ps. cxlvi. 5). "All things are naked and
open to His eyes" (Heb. vi. 13). "The Lord is sweet
unto all, and His tender mercies are over all His
works" (Psalm cxliv. 9).

Finally, who is like to God? He has lived from all
eternity: "But Thou, O Lord, endurest for ever"
(Psalm ci. 13). Behold His name: "I am who am"
(Exod. iii. 14). His empire is heaven and earth:
"Heaven is My throne, and the earth My footstool"
(Isaias lxvi. 1). His palace is the light: "He inhabit-
eth light inaccessible" (1 Tim. vi. 16). His vestments
are beauty and glory: "Thou hast put on praise and
beauty" (Psalm ciii. 1). His carriage the clouds and
the wings of the wind: "Who makest the clouds Thy

chariot, who walkest upon the wings of the winds"
(Psalm ciii. 3). His subjects and His ministers are
the angels: "Who makest Thy angels spirits, and
Thy ministers a burning fire" (Psalm ciii. 4). And
this is He whom the sinner has dared to offend: "Be
astonished at this, O ye heavens" (Jer. ii. 12).

2. *The nothingness of the sinner.* Who art thou, O
man, that darest to measure thyself with God? "Who
art thou that repliest against God?" (Rom. ix. 20.)
Thou art but flesh full of impurities: "Unclean flesh"
(Ezech. iv. 14). Behold the corruption of thy nature:
as dried grass ready to fall beneath the scythe: "All
flesh is grass" (Isaias xl. 6). Behold thy weakness:
a leaf the sport of the wind: "A leaf that is carried
away with the wind" (Job xiii. 25). Behold the inconstancy of thy heart: a vapour scarce formed, and
already dissipated in the air—this is thy life: "It is a
vapour which appeareth for a little while, and afterwards shall vanish away" (James iv. 15). A little
dust and ashes; behold thy origin and thy end upon
earth: "Dust and ashes" (Eccles. x. 9). And it is
thou who darest to raise thyself up against God: "Thou
hast lifted thyself up against the Lord of Heaven, and
thou hast said, I will not serve" (Dan. v. 23; Jer. ii. 20).

3. *The matter of the sin.* That is to say, a law of
God transgressed;—a law infinitely pleasant, a law infinitely wise, a law the accomplishment of which was so
easy, a law to which were attached such consoling promises, such terrible threats for time and eternity: "And
thou saidst, I will not serve."

4. *The motive of the sin.* "To whom have you likened
Me? said the Lord" (Isaias xlvi. 5). To a passion at

which you blush, to a pleasure which passed so quickly to a little gold which melted in your hands. Did you not find in Me all you vainly seek in creatures? "With Me are riches and glory; glorious riches and justice" (Prov. viii. 18). Why, then, drink these corrupt waters? "And now what hast thou to do in the way of Egypt, to drink the troubled water?" (Jer. ii. 18.) These waters which only increase your thirst: "Whosoever drinketh of this water shall thirst again" (John iv. 13). "Be astonished, O ye heavens, at this: They have forsaken Me, the fountain of living water, and have digged to themselves cisterns, broken cisterns that can hold no water" (Jer. ii. 12, 13).

SECOND CONSIDERATION.

A God offended by man, and offended in all His attributes.

What is it you do when you are so unhappy as to commit a mortal sin? By this single sin you outrage God in all His titles, and in all His perfections.

You outrage God the Father in profaning this supernatural being, this participator of His Divine nature which He gave you in baptism: "Partakers of the Divine nature" (2 Peter i. 4).

You outrage the Word Incarnate. You dishonour Him in rendering subservient to the devil your soul, His spouse; you trample His blood under foot, and make His sufferings and death useless; you renew His passion and crucify Him again in your heart: "Crucifying again to themselves the Son of God" (Heb. xxvi. 6).

You outrage the Holy Ghost. You grieve this Holy Spirit (Eph. iv. 30). You do more, you resist Him: "You always resist the Holy Spirit" (Acts

vii. 51). You do more, you stifle Him within you: 'Extinguish not the Spirit" (1 Thess. v. 19).

You outrage God in all His titles. As creator, in revolting against His supreme dominion; as legislator, by violating His laws; as redeemer, by despising His grace; as your friend, by provoking His enmity; as your father, by braving His authority; as your king, by banishing Him from your heart, which is His throne.

You outrage His unity. You make divinities of your passions, which have your heart for an altar, your thoughts and affections as a homage, your soul and your eternity as a sacrifice.

You outrage His infinite perfections. To Him you prefer a creature full of imperfections, who is a mere nothing, and whom death will soon take from you; and you prefer serving the devil, who is deformity itself, at the risk of falling into hell, rather than serve God, who is perfect beauty, and promises you heaven.

You outrage His wisdom. By sin you reverse the order of His providence; you turn creatures away from their end, and you destroy the harmony of the universe.

You outrage His holiness. You dishonour His features in your soul, and you cast His image down in the mire of your passions and vices.

You outrage His immensity. If men were to witness your sin, their presence would recall you to your duty; you know that God is every where present, that you commit iniquity under His eyes, and as it were in His bosom; and yet the presence of God, thrice holy, does not deter you from crime.

You outrage His justice. If sin could destroy your

fortune or your reputation, you would not commit it; and because it exposes you only to the anger of God, to the rigour of His judgment, you commit it without fear, and as if you had nothing to dread from His justice.

You outrage His patience. If God left no interval between the crime and the punishment of the culprit, would you dare to offend Him? Is it, then, the longanimity of God which inspires you with the boldness to sin?

Finally, and to say all in one word, you go still farther, and are *guilty of deicide:* " Sin, as far as it is possible to it, destroys God" (St. Bern.). It is true you cannot actually destroy God; but you do so in your heart. *Why?* Because the contempt you offer to His perfections occasions Him such lively displeasure that He would die of it if, by His nature, He were not impassible and immortal. *Why?* Because, in preferring a vile creature before Him, you take from Him the very essence of His being, that sovereign amiability which deserves to be loved above all things. *Why?* Because, in consenting to sin, you deprive God of the life He lived in your soul; you make Him die within you; it may truly be said that your heart is His grave. " Be astonished, O ye heavens, at this" (Jer. ii. 12).

THIRD CONSIDERATION.

A God offended by man, notwithstanding the many motives which should induce him not to offend.

Consider how many reasons there are to induce you to remain in submission to your God.

F

1. *Your respect for your fellow-creatures.* You are so small, so humbly submissive before your masters; in presence of a sovereign, of an enemy, of a powerful protector; you bow down before their most unreasonable notions, their most absurd caprices;—how is it that you are daring only against God, the first of masters, the most powerful of protectors, the most formidable of enemies?

2. *What you exact from others.* You are so tenacious of your authority; you are so jealous of your honour and your rights; you insist with so much eagerness that all should give way before your ideas and your will;—how is it, then, that you respect so little the authority, the rights, the honour of your God?

3. *The sacrifices you make for the world.* When the world speaks, nothing stops you; you obey at every risk, at the price of your repose, of your pleasure, of your liberty, of your passions; sometimes even of your life. Why, then, when the Lord commands, is He not obeyed in the same manner? Why is it that then alone sacrifices are difficult and appear impossible?

4. *The promises you have made to God.* You glory in respecting your pledged word; you would rather die than fail in your oath. Why do you feel a horror of perjury only when it regards men? Why does it no longer appear infamous when it regards God? Did not God receive your vows in baptism, on the day of your first communion, often in the holy tribunal? Has, then, the oath, which is so strong to bind man to man, no strength to bind man to God?

5. *The benefits you have received from God.* You hold every thing from God;—intelligence, imagination,

heart, senses, talent, fortune, authority, birth, rank, youth, life. You can only sin by making use of His gifts. What black ingratitude is it, not only to forget your benefactor, but to return Him evil for good, to make use of His own gifts to insult Him, to force Him to act against Himself, and to turn against Himself His own bounty and power, which preserve you. "'Thou hast made Me to serve with thy sins, thou hast wearied Me with thy iniquity" (Isaias xliii. 24).

AFFECTIONS.

Place yourself at the foot of the crucifix, like a perjured friend at the feet of his friend, like a rebel subject at the feet of his king, like a parricide son at the feet of his father. Humbly ask of our Lord Jesus Christ the pardon of your sins.

Pater. Ave.

FIFTH EXERCISE.

The effects of mortal sin on the soul of the sinner.

Preparatory Prayer.

First prelude. Present yourself before God like a criminal loaded with chains, brought from the dungeon of a prison and placed before the tribunal of his judge.

Second prelude. Beg of our Lord that He will vouchsafe to show you the sad state of a soul which has been so unhappy as mortally to offend God: "Give me, O Lord, that I may see" (Luke xviii. 41).

FIRST CONSIDERATION.

By mortal sin we forfeit the friendship of God.

When you were in a state of grace, God dwelt in your soul: "If any man love Me, My Father will love him, and We will come to him, and will make Our abode with him" (John xiv. 23). The most august bonds united you to Him. He called you His people: "Thou art My people" (Osee ii. 24). His friend: "I have called you friends" (John xv. 15). His spouse: "Thou hast wounded my heart, my sister, my spouse" (Cant. iv. 9). His children: "Behold what manner of charity the Father hath bestowed upon us, that we should be called, and should be, the sons of God" (1 John iii. 1). Another self: "I have said ye are gods" (Psalm lxxxi. 6). But what a change since mortal sin entered into your soul! That moment God left your heart: "Woe to them, when I shall depart from them" (Osee ix. 12). To His friendship has succeeded hatred: "Thou hatest all the workers of iniquity" (Psalm v. 7). You have ceased to be His people: "Ye are not My people, and I will not be yours" (Osee i. 9). In His eyes you are now an enemy on whom He has sworn vengeance: "I live for ever; I will render vengeance to My enemies" (Deut. xxxii. 40, 41). He no longer recognises you as His spouse: "I know you not" (Matt. xxv. 12). In you He no longer sees any thing but the child of Satan: "Ye are of your father the devil" (John viii. 44). He has no longer any thing for you but maledictions: "If thou wilt not hear the voice of the Lord thy God, cursed shalt thou be in the city, cursed in the field, cursed shall be the fruit of thy womb. And all these curses shall come upon thee, and shall pursue and overtake thee, until thou perish" (Deut. xxviii. 15-17, 45). He arms every scourge against you: "Death and bloodshed, strife and the sword, oppressions, famine, afflictions, scourges; — all these things are created for the wicked" (Ecclus. xl. 9, 10). O guilty soul, consider what thou hast been, and what thou now art, in the eyes of thy Lord; and sigh deeply at the sight of thy misery. "Thou wast the spouse of Christ, the temple of God, the sanctuary of the Holy Ghost; and as often as I say ' thou wast,' I must needs groan, because thou art not what thou wast" (St. Aug.).

SECOND CONSIDERATION.

Mortal sin deprives us of all the gifts of grace.

1. *It destroys the beauty of the soul.* A soul in a state of grace attracts the looks and ravishes the heart of God: "I will fix my eyes upon thee" (Psalm xxxi. 8); "Behold thou art fair, O my love" (Cant. i. 14) But mortal sin destroys all trace of this beauty: "All her beauty is departed" (Lament. i. 6); and covers the soul with a hideous leprosy, which makes it an object of horror to God and His angels.

2. *It deprives the soul of all merit.* Even if you united in yourself all the merits of all the saints together, all their alms, all their prayers, all their austerities, all their sacrifices,—a single mortal sin would be enough to destroy all: "If the just man turn himself away from his justice, and do iniquity, all his justices which he hath done shall not be remembered" (Ezech. xviii. 24).

3. *It deprives the soul of all power of meriting.* Yes; if you are in mortal sin, all your good works are useless to obtain heaven.   Spend all your goods in alms; embrace the most rigorous austerities; convert the whole world, if it be possible; give your body to the flames,—St. Paul assures you that all this is useless for salvation if there be a single sin in your heart: "If I have not charity, I am nothing" (Cor. xiii. 2).   To what can I compare you, O unhappy soul?   "To what shall I compare thee, or to what shall I liken thee, O daughter of Jerusalem?" (Lam. ii. 13.)   To a vine loaded with fruit suddenly destroyed by the storm; to a temple unexpectedly overthrown; to a ship that the tempest suddenly sinks with all her treasures; to a rich city which fire has reduced to a heap of burning ashes: "To what shall I equal thee, that I may comfort thee? . . . . Who shall heal thee?" (Lam. ii. 13.

THIRD CONSIDERATION.
Mortal sin deprives us of our liberty.

When you are in a state of grace, you are free: "Where the Spirit of the Lord is, there is liberty" (2 Cor. iii. 17).   You enjoy the sweetest, the most honourable liberty; the only liberty that no power in the world can deprive you of, liberty conquered for you by the blood of Jesus Christ: "The freedom wherewith Christ has made us free" (Gal. iv. 31); which consists in freedom from every yoke except that of God, which we cannot lose without degrading ourselves.   But have you had the unhappiness to sin mortally?   You have become a slave: "Whosoever committeth sin is the servant of sin" (John viii. 34).   You are given over to sin: "Sold under sin" (Rom. vii. 14). The devil reigns as master in your heart, which is your prison: "He hath built against me round about, that I may not get out" (Lam. iii. 7). Each day he tightens his chains about us: "He hath made my fetters heavy" (Lam. iii. 7). Every thing within you is enslaved, your faculties, your senses, your talents, your fortune. Is it not true that, in this sad state, you have often wished to return to God, to pray, to confess, to avoid the occasions of sin, to break through the habit of sin? Did the devil permit it? Has he not treated you as the centurion in the Gospel treated his soldiers: "I say to one, Go, and he goeth; and to another, Come, and he cometh; and to my servant, Do this, and he doeth it" (Luke vii. 8). Has he not always said to you, "Bring, bring" (Prov. xxx. 15):— again this passion; again this sin. Has he not always been obeyed? Finally, is it not the story of your slavery that St. Augustine tells with so much force when he describes the servitude of his own passions: "I sighed, chained as I was, not by iron, but by my own will, stronger even than iron. My own will held me bound; and it was of it that the enemy of salvation made use to enchain me, and surround me on all sides by inextricable bonds" (*Conf.* book viii. c. 5).

FOURTH CONSIDERATION.

Mortal sin robs us of peace of heart.

A soul which belongs to God knows no trouble or fear: "The just is bold as a lion" (Prov. xxviii. 1). The heart of the just is like an eternal festival: "A secure mind is like a continual feast" (Prov. xv. 15).

Even in the midst of tribulation he tastes ineffable joys
" I exceedingly abound with joy in all my tribulations"
(2 Cor. vii. 4). But how different is it with the sinner;
every where he carries a trembling heart, a heart a prey
to sorrow: "If you will not hear the voice of the Lord,
He will give thee a fearful heart, and a soul consumed
with pensiveness" (Deut. xxviii. 15, 65). Tribulation
and anguish penetrate the depths of his soul: "Tribulation and anguish upon every soul of man that worketh
evil" (Rom. ii. 9). Remorse is in the conscience like
an arrow which lacerates it: "I am turned in my anguish whilst the thorn is fastened" (Psalm xxxi. 4).
And his life is like the waves of the sea tossed by a
storm : "The wicked are like the raging sea" (Isa. lvii.
20). God has no need to arm the hand of man against
the sinner; his conscience pursues him incessantly, and
is at once witness, judge, and executioner; it accuses,
condemns, and tortures him. Sometimes it pursues him
in the midst of serious occupations, like David,—"I
walked sorrowful all the day long, there is no peace
for my bones because of my sins" (Psalm xxxvii. 4, 7):
sometimes amidst pleasures, like Baltassar; sometimes
amidst the pains of sickness, like Antiochus; almost
always in silence and solitude, like Cain. To some it
reproaches the pleasure of a moment purchased by a
long repentance: "What fruit, therefore, had you then
in those things of which you are now ashamed?" (Rom.
vi. 21.) To others it shows all the bitterness of iniquity :
"Know thou, and see that it is an evil and a bitter
thing for thee to have left the Lord thy God" (Jer ii.
19). To some it recalls incessantly the ingratitude and
malice of their sin: "Thy own wickedness shall reprove

thee, and thy apostasy shall rebuke thee" (Jer. ii. 19).
To others it shows the sword of God's justice suspended
over their heads: " Looking round about for the sword
on every side" (Job xv. 22). It causes cries of vengeance to be heard around them: " The sound of dread
is always in his ears" (Job xv. 21). It disturbs their
sleep with threatening visions: " Thou wilt frighten me
with dreams, and terrify me with visions" (Job vii. 14).
"O sinner, what misery is yours! How much are you
to be pitied if your conscience thus pursues you! Yet
you are still more so if your conscience leaves you in
peace" (St. Aug.). For this peace of a guilty conscience is the certain sign of the great wrath of God.

FIFTH CONSIDERATION.

Mortal sin destroys the soul.

The soul is the life of the body, and God is the life
of the soul. Thus sin kills our soul in separating it
from God: " The soul that sinneth, the same shall die"
(Ezech. xviii. 20). Look at the man who has mortally
offended the Lord; he walks, he sees, he speaks, and you
think he lives. Ah! what lives in him is the body, the
soul has ceased to live. " The most noble part is extinct;
the house stands, but the inhabitant is dead. O Christian, there is no longer any feeling of piety in your
heart if you weep over the body from which the soul
has departed, and yet shed no tear over the soul from
which God has departed" (St. Aug.).

And what difference is there between a corpse and
a soul in mortal sin? A corpse has lost the use of all
its senses. Is not this a faithful image of the sinner?

1. *A dead man no longer sees.* Every thing ought to strike the eyes of the sinner;—the state of his soul, the grave ready to open for him—judgment, hell, eternity; and the sinner sees nothing!

2. *The dead no longer hears.* Every thing speaks to the sinner;—conscience, grace, events, ministers of religion; and the sinner hears nothing!

3. *The dead are insensible.* Neither insults nor honours, neither the attentions of men nor their contempt, can touch them. God moves heaven and earth to touch the sinner; He endeavours to rouse him, sometimes by benefits, sometimes by afflictions; and the sinner remains insensible!

4. *The dead exhale an infectious odour.* A corpse, if not placed in the grave, spreads around it a fatal contagion. The sinner exhales an odour of corruption; the contagion of his scandals spreads death around him, and the infection of his vices makes him an object of horror to just men, to angels, and to God.

O fatal death! O death which deprives us, not of the life of nature, but of the life of grace; that is to say, of the life of God! Who will give us tears to bewail thee? "Who will give water to my head, and a fountain of tears to my eyes? and I will weep day and night for the slain of the daughter of my people" (Jer. ix. 1).

AFFECTIONS AT THE FOOT OF THE CROSS.

"Bless the Lord, O my soul, and forget not all that He hath done for thee; . . . . who healeth all thy diseases; who redeemeth thee from destruction" (Ps. cii. 2-4).

Pater. Ave.

SIXTH EXERCISE.

On the number and greatness of our sins.

Preparatory Prayer.

First Prelude. Present yourself before God like a criminal who appears at the tribunal of justice, and is about to hear his sentence.

Second prelude. " I groan in Thy sight as one guilty ; shame hath covered my face, because of my sin ; spare me, a suppliant, O my God,"

FIRST POINT.

Recall all the sins of your life.

1. *The sins of childhood.* Since the first dawn of reason, of what have I thought? To whom did I give the first movements of my heart? What use did I make of my first moments of liberty? Alas, Lord, I seek in vain any time, any place, which has seen me without iniquity! When I was still young, I was already a sinner before Thee (St. Aug.).

2. *Sins of youth.* Where shall I not find memories of sin? I find them every where : in the shelter of my father's house, in the schools where I went in search of learning, in the various scenes of my plays and diversions, in the societies formed around me by a common education, in the places even where sin should never enter,—in the sanctuary of Thy temples, O my God, and even at the foot of Thy altar!

3 *Sins of riper age.* Interrogate, O my soul, the course of years which succeeded those of early youth. Where was the day that had not its sin? Examine those societies, those affairs, those employments; what do they recall but grave and frequent falls? Examine

all the laws of the Lord; is there one which you have
not transgressed? Examine past temptations; how
many are there before which you did not fall? Examine
all your faculties; which is there that has not been
guilty? Examine all your senses; which of them is
there which has not served as an instrument of sin? O
my God, I confess I have sinned beyond all measure: "I
confess to Almighty God that I have sinned exceed-
:ngly."

SECOND POINT.

Consider the malice of all your sins in themselves.

What deformity in my sins, O my God! They must,
indeed, be of an infinite ugliness, since they are opposed
to Thee, O Lord, who art infinite beauty.

What ingratitude in my sins! All I had was from
Thee, and I have dared to say: Go from me; depart
from my senses, which only live through Thy power;
depart from my lips, which only received movement to
praise Thee; depart from my mind, which receives light
from Thee alone, and from my heart, which only received feeling from Thee in order to think of Thee and
to love Thee; depart from my being, which Thou only
gavest that by it I might serve Thee.

What audacity in my sins! I have dared to say, I
will not obey: I have said this to Thee, and on the
brink of the tomb, on the brink of hell, above which Thou
holdest me suspended by the slender thread which I
call life.

What folly in my sins! I have left Thee, my Father,
my Supreme Beatitude! and for whom? for a perfidious
master, for a hateful tyrant, for the most cruel of exe
cutioners, for Satan.

Finally, *what malice* in my sins! I have sinned, carried away by passion; I have sinned deliberately; I have sinned publicly, and with scandal; I have sinned and remained at rest in my sin, notwithstanding so many lights, so many good examples, so many instances of Thy justice, so many exhortations from Thy ministers; notwithstanding the counsels and prayers of virtuous parents; notwithstanding the calls of conscience and remorse. " I confess that I have sinned exceedingly."

O my God! if a man had once treated me as I treat Thee every day of my life, I should hate him for ever,—what do I say? If I had treated a man as I have treated Thee, I should hate myself, and I should never forgive myself the malice of my heart. " I confess that I have sinned exceedingly."

THIRD POINT.

Consider who you are that have so offended God.

What are the angels before God? What are all men, compared to the angels? What am I, compared to the whole of mankind? Like one leaf in the midst of an immense forest, a drop of water in a stream, a grain of sand on the shore of the ocean, an atom in the immensity of the universe; and it is I, vile and worthless dust, who have not feared to declare myself a rebel against God: " Thou saidst, I will not serve" (Jer. ii. 20).

FOURTH POINT.

Consider who God is, whom you have offended.

Against whom have I rebelled, O my God, when

I committed sin? I, weakness itself, revolted against strength. I, lowness itself, revolted against sovereign greatness. I, evil itself, revolted against infinite goodness. I, who am only corruption and darkness, revolted against wisdom and sanctity itself. I, who am nothing, revolted against the Being of all beings. "Be astonished, O ye heavens, at this, and, ye gates thereof, be very desolate" (Jer. ii. 12).

FIFTH POINT.

Conclude by a fervent address to God and His creatures.

Be astonished that, after so many iniquities, all creatures should not have armed themselves against you, that they should have continued to serve you, when you were incessantly insulting their God and yours. Be astonished that God has not withdrawn His gifts from you; that He has left you this fortune, this credit, these ta-'ents, this mind, this heart, this life, which you abuse to offend Him.

Then ask pardon of all the perfections of God which you have offended. Pardon, O justice of my God, for having so long braved Thy thunder! Pardon, O holiness of God, for having so long stained the purity of Thy sight by my crimes! Pardon, O mercy of God, for having so long despised Thy voice! "Show mercy to a poor penitent, whom Thou hast so long spared in his impenitence" (St. Bernard).

COLLOQUY.

Return thanks to the mercy of God, and solemnly promise at the feet of Jesus Christ never more to offend Him.

FIRST EXERCISE ON HELL.

Preparatory Prayer.

First prelude. Imagine to yourself the height, the breadth, and the depth of hell.

Second prelude. Ask of God a lively fear of the pains of hell, so that, if ever you are so unhappy as to lose the grace of the love of God, at least the fear of punishment may deter you from sin.

FIRST CONSIDERATION.

The habitation of the damned.

It is hell. But what is hell? The Holy Spirit calls it the place of torments (St. Luke xvi. 28). A prison, where the condemned shall be imprisoned by the justice of God, to be tormented through ages of ages : "They shall be shut up there in prison" (Isaiah xxiv. 22). A region of misery, a darkness where an eternal horror dwells : " A land of misery and darkness, where the shadow of death and no order, but everlasting horror dwelleth" (Job x. 22). A lake of fire and brimstone : " They shall have their portion in the pool burning with fire and brimstone" (Apoc. xxi. 8). A deep valley, where a torrent of sulphur rolls, lighted by the breath of the Lord : " For Topheth is prepared from yesterday, prepared by the King, deep and wide ; the nourishments thereof are fire and much wood ; the breath of the Lord, as a torrent of brimstone, doth kindle it" (Isaias xxx. 33). A burning furnace : " Thou

shalt make them as an oven of fire" (Psalm xx. 10).
The depths of an abyss: "He opened the bottomless
pit" (Apoc. ix. 2); the smoke from which darkens the
sun like the smoke from a vast furnace: "And he
opened the bottomless pit; and the smoke of the pit
arose as the smoke of a great furnace" (Apoc. ix. 2).
Finally, the anger of the Almighty is like a wine-press,
in which an angry God will trample upon and crush
His enemies: "And He treadeth the wine-press of the
fierceness of the wrath of God the Almighty" (Apoc.
xix. 15); "I have trampled on them in My indigna-
tion, and have trodden them down in My wrath"
(Isaias lxiii. 3).

SECOND CONSIDERATION.

The company of the damned.

In hell a triple society will form the torment of the
condemned.

1. The society of his body, which, to the infectious
corruption of a corpse, will unite all the sensibility of a
living frame, and every member of which will have its
torment and its pain.

2. The society of devils. "There are spirits that
are created for vengeance, and in their fury they lay
on grievous torments" (Ecclus. xxxix. 33). Damned
themselves, they have no other occupation but to torture the damned. Not being able to revenge their reprobation on God, they revenge it on man, His image;
they pursue God in the condemned, and they pursue
Him with all the hate and fury that can enter the
hearts of demons.

3. The society of an infinite number of wretched

creatures damned like himself. Represent to yourself an assembly so hideous, that even in the galleys and prisons of human justice you could not find any thing like it; an assembly of all that the earth has borne of licentious men, of robbers, of assassins, of parricides. Imagine to yourself all these wretches bound together, according to the expression of the Holy Spirit, like a bundle of thorns—" As a bundle of thorns they shall be burnt with fire" (Isaias xxxiii. 12); or a heap of tow cast into the midst of the flames—" The congregation of sinners is like tow heaped together, and the end of them is a flame of fire" (Ecclus. xxi. 10). Represent to yourself in this horrible reunion the accomplices or the victims of the damned bound and chained with him to burn in the same fire : " They themselves being fettered with the bonds of darkness, and a long night" (Wis. xvii. 2). What torment for the unhappy man, not to be able to separate himself from the companions of his reprobation, who never cease to accuse him of their misfortune, and who find a horrible consolation in tearing him to pieces! " They have opened their mouths upon me, and reproaching me they have struck me on the cheek; they are filled with my pain. (Job xvi. 11).

THIRD CONSIDERATION.

The punishment of the reprobate through the powers of his soul.

1. *Torment of the imagination.* The imagination of the damned presents his misery to him with incredible clearness. It represents to him all the pleasures of his past life. See how happy thou wert on

earth; thy life was but one tissue of delight and joy; all that is passed and can never return: "All those things have passed away" (Wis. v. 9). It shows him all he has suffered, all that he has yet to suffer. Oh, what years thou hast burnt in hell, and yet thy eternity is not begun! Oh, what ages and millions of ages will pass, and thou wilt have no other occupation but to burn! It shows him heaven, with all its felicity. How happy thou wouldst be near Mary, near Jesus Christ. Listen to the songs of the blessed; behold those souls which love and possess God for all eternity. All that is lost for thee. "The wicked shall see, and shall be angry, he shall gnash with his teeth and pine away; the desire of the wicked shall perish" (Psalm cxi. 10).

2. *Torment of memory*. The memory of the damned will recall all his sins: "What fruit, therefore, had you in those things of which you are now ashamed?" (Rom. vi. 21.) It recalls all the trouble taken for advancement in this world: "What doth it profit?" (Wis. v. 8.) It recalls all the graces received —faith, a Christian education, the example of so many virtuous persons, the instructions of the ministers of Jesus Christ, the Sacraments of the Church. "And have been able to show no mark of virtue" (Wis. v. 13). It recalls the warnings that were given on earth. How often has he not heard that it is terrible to fall into the hands of the living God, that there is no mercy in hell! Why didst thou not listen to these wise warnings? "Did I not protest to thee by the Lord, and tell thee before?" (3 Kings ii. 42.)

3. *Torment of the understanding*. The under

standing of the reprobate never ceases to show him
the deformity of sin, the greatness and beauty of God,
the justice of the punishment of hell. Thou wert made
for God; why hast thou refused Him thy heart? God
is so great, He is so perfect, He is so good; who deserved thy love and service as He did? Ungrateful!
thou hast abandoned thy benefactor. Perjured! thou
hast dared to break thy oaths. Parricide! thou hast
wished to kill thy Father. Begone! suffer for all eternity; an eternal hell is not too much to punish thy
crime. "Thou art just, O Lord, and Thy judgments
are right" (Psalm cxviii. 137).

4. *Torment of the will.* Represent to yourself how
the condemned soul is tormented. *By its regrets:* It was
so easy to save myself. Oh, why did I abuse the time
and the grace of God? *By its remorse:* Woe to me!
I was mad, a wretch; I am lost through my own fault.
By its jealousy: Why was such a one saved? He
had committed greater sins than I; he had received
fewer graces than I; he is happy in heaven, and I
burn in hell. *By its desires:* Oh, that I might return to the earth, that I might receive a few years of
life; I would frighten the world by the rigours of my
penance. *Its reaching after God:* Oh, that I might
yet see Thee, Lord; that I might love, that I might
possess Thee! *Its imprecations:* My prayer, then, is
useless. Malediction upon me! perish the day of my
birth! destruction fall on my body, on my soul, which
the anger of God pursues! perish this unpitying God,
who has nothing but vengeance for me! "The wicked
shall gnash his teeth and pine away; the desire of the
wicked shall perish" (Psalm cxi. 10).

FOURTH CONSIDERATION.

The torment of the damned in all his senses.

1. *Torment of sight.* The aspect of this dreary prison,—of the damned, the companions of his misery,—of the demons, the executioners of the vengeance of God,—of the cross of Jesus Christ printed on the vaults, —of these terrible words engraved on the gates of hell, "*ever, never,*"—of those flames which roar around him.

2. *Torment of hearing.* The groans of so many millions of the damned,—the howls of their despair,—their blasphemies against God and against the saints, —their imprecations on themselves,—their cries of rage as they invoke death or annihilation,—the reproaches they address to themselves, — the maledictions with which they load their accomplices,—the noise of the flames devouring so many victims.

3. *Torment of smell.* The horrible infection which exhales from so many bodies, which preserve in hell all the corruption of the grave : "Out of their carcasses shall rise a stink" (Is. xxxiv. 3).

4. *Torment of taste.* A maddening hunger,— "they shall suffer hunger like dogs" (Ps. lviii. 7,— the violence of which shall compel the damned to devour his own flesh: "Every one shall eat the flesh of his own arm" (Is. ix. 20). A devouring thirst, and not one drop of water to refresh his parched tongue,— no drink but wormwood and gall : "Their wine is the gall of dragons and the venom of asps, which is incurable" (Deut. xxxii. 33). For refreshment, a chalice which the anger of God has filled with fire, with sul-

phur, and the spirit of tempests: "Flames and brimstone and storms of winds shall be the portion of their
cup" (Ps. x. 7).

5. *Torment of touch.* The damned will be enveloped
in flames as in a garment. The fire will penetrate al'
the members of his body,—and what a fire! Not
fire like that on earth, which is a gift of the divin᾽
bounty, but a fire created by justice to punish sin; not
a fire lighted by men—and yet what terrible power in
a fire which calcines marble, melts metals!—but a fire
lighted and kept up by the breath of God, who avenges
His offences, and avenges them without mercy, and
avenges them according to the extent of His justice
and His power; a fire which does not consume the
victim, but which at one and the same time exhausts
and renews that sensibility, and thus renders the pain
eternal; a fire armed with the attributes of God;—
His anger to punish, His knowledge to distinguish the
senses which have been the most guilty, His wisdom
to proportion the chastisement to the degree of crime;
a fire so penetrating that it in a manner so identifies
itself with its victim, that it boils in the veins and in
the marrow,—that it escapes and re-enters by all the
pores,—that it makes of the damned a burning coal in᾽
the midst of the furnaces of hell; a fire which unites
in itself every torment and every pain, which infinitely
surpasses any thing man can suffer from sickness,—all
that tyrants ever made the confessors of Christ to en-
dure: "Which of you can dwell with devouring fire,
which of you can dwell with ᾽verlasting burnings"
(Is. xxxiii. 14).

FIFTH CONSIDERATION.

Torment of eternity.

How many years or centuries will the damned be chained in this prison? *For ever.* How many years or centuries will he groan in tears of regret and despair? *For ever.* How many years or centuries will he be condemned to the society of demons? *For ever.* How many years or centuries will he burn in flames? *For ever.*

Will God, then, never have pity on his misery? *Never.* Will there not be any interruption of his torment? *Never.* Will he not at any time receive any mitigation of his pains? *Never; always, never.* Stretch your imagination,—add years to years—ages to ages; multiply them like the leaves of the forest, the sand of the sea-shore, the drops of water in the immensity of the seas;—you will not yet conceive the meaning of those two words, *ever, never.* "What number of years can equal eternity, since it is without end?" (St. Aug.)

COLLOQUY.

Cast yourself at the feet of Jesus Christ. Represent to yourself this innumerable multitude of souls that sin has precipitated into hell. Return thanks to our Saviour, who has preserved you from this dreadful eternity, and has hitherto followed you with His mercy and His love.

Pater. Ave.

SECOND EXERCISE ON HELL.

Preparatory Prayer.
First and second prelude. Same as last.

APPLICATION OF THE SENSES.

1. *Application of the sight.* Consider in your mind the vast fire of hell; souls shut up in bodies of fire, as in an eternal prison; wicked spirits constantly employed in tormenting them.

2. *Application of the hearing.* Listen to the groans, the howls, the cries of rage, the blasphemies against Christ and His saints, the mutual maledictions of the damned.

3. *Application of the smell.* Imagine you smell the fire, the brimstone, the infection which exhales from so many hideous corpses.

4. *Application of the taste.* Taste in spirit all the bitterness, the tears, the regrets, the remorse of the damned.

5. *Application of the touch.* , Touch in imagination those devouring flames which in hell consume not only the bodies of the reprobate, but the souls themselves. What do you think of them? Could you inhabit these eternal furnaces for a few hours? "Which of you shall dwell with everlasting burning?" (Is. xxxiii. 14.)

End, at the foot of the crucifix, by addressing to yourself the following questions:

1. *What are those souls that suffer in hell?* Souls created, like yours, to love and possess God,—souls for whom God had given His heart, His blood, His life;

upon whom He wished to bestow His glory for all etc.
nity.

2. *What do they suffer?* Pains truly infinite; for,
except in the being of the sinner, the infinite is every
where;—in the offence which is avenged, in the wisdom which invented the pain, in the justice which decrees it, in the power which applies it and which makes
it eternal.

3. *Why do they suffer?* For mortal sins, perhaps
less enormous or less multiplied than yours.

4. *What led them to hell?* The way which you
perhaps have followed until this day,—the way of self-
love, of sensuality, of tepidity.

COLLOQUY.

And now converse with Jesus. At the foot of the
cross recall to mind that all the reprobate are so, either
for having refused to believe in His coming as a saviour,
or for not obeying His precepts;—the crime of men before
His coming on earth, of the condemned of His time, and
of those who have come after Him. Attach yourself
to Him, then, with heart and mind, that He may save
you from eternal death. Finish by acts of lively grati
tude that He has not allowed you to fall into this frightful abyss, following you even to this day, not with
maledictions, but with unspeakable goodness and infinite
mercy.

Pater. Ave.

FIRST EXERCISE ON DEATH.

Preparatory Prayer.

First prelude. Transport yourself in thought to the bedside of a dying man, beside a grave open to receive a coffin, or to the middle of a churchyard.

Second prelude. Ask of our Lord a salutary fear of death, and the grace to be ready at any moment.

FIRST CONSIDERATION.

What is death ?

1. To die is to bid farewell to every thing in this world;—a farewell to your fortune; farewell to your titles and your rank; farewell to your pleasures, to your friends ; farewell to a part of yourself, your body; and, saddest of all, farewell for ever to this world.

2. To die is to be abandoned by all whom you leave behind; by **your friends** and acquaintance, who think no more of **you**; by your heirs, who will perhaps scarcely speak of you except to dispute your property; by your dearest relatives, who will soon weary of shedding tears, or even bestowing a thought upon you.

3. To die is to leave your house for a deep narrow grave; it is to wait the day of judgment under a stone, in a coffin six feet under ground, without any other garment than a shroud, without other society than reptiles and worms, without other titles than an inscription, which few will read and which time will soon efface.

4. To die is to pass into the most humiliating state, the nearest to nothingness; it is to go where your

bodily senses will no longer act; where you can see nothing, not even your own destruction; where you will no longer hear any thing, not even the work of the worms which devour you; where you will become the prey of corruption and the food of the most hideous reptiles; where you will slowly fall to pieces; where you will decompose into an infectious corruption. "Under thee shall the moth be strewed, and worms shall be thy covering" (Is. xiv. 11). "I have said to rottenness, thou art my father; to worms, my mother and my sister" (Job xvii. 14).

5. Lastly, to die is for your soul all at once to leave this world, and enter in a moment into an unknown region called Eternity; where it goes to hear from the mouth of the Lord in what place it must make that great retreat which will last for ever; whether it is to be in heaven or in the depths of hell.

SECOND CONSIDERATION.

Must I die?

Most certainly. But what assures me of it? *Reason*, which tells me that a body constantly undermined by time must finally fall to dust. "A mountain falling cometh to naught, and a rock is removed out of its place. Waters wear away the stones, and with inundation the ground by little and little is washed away. How much more shall they that dwell in houses of clay, who have an earthly foundation, be consumed?" (Job xiv. 18, 19; iv. 19.) *Faith* tells me that a sentence of death has been pronounced against all men: "It is appointed unto men once to die" (Heb. ix. 27). *Experience* shows me in all places and at all hours man

cast down and trampled under foot by that terrible
king called Death : " Destruction treads upon him like
a king" (Job xviii. 14). Man has raised doubts on
all truths; but who has ever doubted the certainty
of death? "There is no man that liveth always, or
that hopeth for this" (Eccles. ix. 4). To almost all
the questions that might be asked about you the answer would be "*perhaps.*" Shall you have a large
fortune, great talents, a long life? *Perhaps.* Will
your last hour find you in the friendship of God?
Perhaps. After this retreat, shall you live long in a
state of grace? *Perhaps.* Shall you be saved? *Perhaps.* But shall you die? *Yes, certainly.* Will a
day arrive when to health shall succeed sickness, then
agony, then the last sigh? *Yes.* Will there be a day
when the bell will toll for your burial, when your name
will be inscribed in the register of the dead, when your
coffin and your tombstone will be ordered, and when
your servants will carry you from your apartments to
your grave? *Yes.* Shall you be laid in the bosom of
the earth to moulder away, to be eaten by worms, and
to crumble into dust? *Most certainly, yes.* "It is
appointed" (Heb. ix. 27).

Take every precaution you please,—use the most
wholesome food, surround yourself with the most delicate attentions, consult the ablest physicians,—you will
not escape this decree of death. Say, where are the
generations which have preceded you? Where are the
monarchs who ruled your fathers, the generals who
commanded their armies, the magistrates who admi-
nistered justice? Where are your fathers? Those
whose name and title you bear,—where are they? In

the grave,—in eternity! Know that you will one day
have the same end as they, and that to-morrow, perhaps, it will be your turn to fall under the stroke of
death: "Yesterday for me, and to-day for thee"
(Ecclus. xxxviii. 23).

THIRD CONSIDERATION.
Shall I die soon?

Consider that the measure of your life is this time,
of which the days, the hours, the moments, press upon,
and as it were swallow up each other. How, then, can
you flatter yourself that death is far off when it has
already begun for you? From the moment of your
birth to this hour, what have you done but die? Count
all the years, the weeks, the days, the hours, which
united make up what you call your age,—what are they
but so many steps towards the grave? You are like
the candle, which is consumed in giving light, and gives
light in being consumed; like it you live in dying, and
in living die. An action continued without interruption is soon accomplished. All other human actions
have some cessation—business, study, pleasures, sleep,
every thing, in fact, has some interval. There is but one
action which is never interrupted, and this action is
death; death which began with your first sigh, ano
will end with your last. How can you be long before
you die, when you began to die at your birth, and are
dying every moment of the day and night?

What is your age? Is it twenty, thirty, forty, or
are you still older? What do these past years appear
to you—years already passed into eternity like waves
into the ocean? How quickly they are gone! Be per

suaded that your future years will pass as quickly, if even there are years before you. Death will take from you the future, as it took from you the past, with the rapidity of lightning. And this is the life of all; the Holy Spirit says it is like the track of a ship on the ocean, the flight of a bird through the air, or an arrow shot by a vigorous hand; it is like the froth on the edge of a stream, like a little dust on the plain, like a vapour which a breath of wind dispels for ever.

FOURTH CONSIDERATION.

When shall I die?

" It is not for you to know the times or moments, which the Father hath put in His own power" (Acts i. 7). " Watch, for you know not the day or the hour" (Matt. xxv. 13). It is not for us to penetrate the secrets of God; but it is for us to watch, that we be not surprised. For how many terrible uncertainties are there not in death! (1.) At what age shall you die? In old age, in middle age, or in youth? " *Watch, for you know not.*" (2.) What kind of death shall you die? Will it be a sudden death, without time to prepare yourself? Will it be after a long illness, which will deprive you of the use of your senses, the use of time, of grace, of the sacraments? Will it be after violent pain, which will render it out of your power to attend to your everlasting salvation? Will it be from a fall, from fire, from the weapon of an enemy? " *Watch, for you know not.*" (3.) In what place shall you die? Will it be in your own house, or in that of strangers? At table, at play, at the theatre, at church? Will 't be in vour bed, or in a prison, or on the scaffold ? "*Watch, for you know not.*" (4.) What day shall you die? Will it be in ten years ? Why not this very year? Why not this month, this week? Why not even this day ? "*Watch, for you know not.*" (5.) During what action shall you die ? There is not one action that may not be your last. You pray—why should not death strike you while you pray? You study—why should not death strike you in the midst of this study? You sleep—why should not this sleep be eternal ? Not one of your words, not one of your movements, which may not be followed by the silence and stillness of death. "*Watch, for you know not.*" (6.) In what state shall you die? Will it be in a state of grace, or in a state of sin? Again the same uncertainty. All that we know is that death is the echo of life, and that we almost always die as we have lived. "*Watch, for you know not.*"

FIFTH CONSIDERATION.
How often shall I die?

Once only. "It is appointed unto men once to die" (Heb. ix. 27). This is what is most terrible in death : in this great and decisive action all errors are irreparable ; the misfortune of a bad death is an eternal misfortune. If you could die twice, you might reassure yourself as to the risks of your eternal salvation. If you were lost the first time, you might be saved the second : but it is not so ; you have but one life, one soul, one death. Once lost, you are lost for all eternity.

And on what does a good or a bad death depend ? On a single moment ! What is required to consent to temptation? A moment! What is required mortally to offend the Lord? A single instant! Consider well that no more is necessary to decide your eternity; one moment is enough to ensure your damnation. On this moment depends eternity!

If you had died such a year, such a day, such an hour of your life, when you were the enemy of God, where would you be now? You would be lost, and lost for ever; for it is written, "If. the tree fall to the south, or to the north, in what place soever it shall fall, there shall it be" (Eccles. xi. 3). Are you not seized with terror at the thought of the danger to which you have voluntarily exposed your soul? Resolve to live more carefully for the future, and hasten to assure yourself of the sanctity of your death by the sanctity of your life.

AFFECTIONS.

Fear. "Enlighten my eyes, that I never sleep in death, lest at any time my enemy say, I have prevailed against him" (Ps. xii. 4, 5).

Desire. "Do with me according to Thy will, and command my spirit to be received in peace" (Tob. iii. 6).

Resolution. "All the days in which I am now in warfare, I wait until my change come. Thou shalt call me, and I will answer Thee" (Job xiv. 14).

COLLOQUY.

Represent to yourself our Lord dying on the cross, and recommend to Him the hour of your death.

Pater. Ave.

SECOND EXERCISE ON DEATH.

FIRST CONTEMPLATION.

Your agony.

Preparatory Prayer.

1. *Application of the sight.* Contemplate—(1) Your apartment faintly lighted by the last rays of day, or the feeble light of a lamp; your bed which you will never leave except to be laid in your coffin; all the objects which surround you and seem to say, You leave us for ever! (2) The persons who will surround you: your servants, sad and silent; a weeping family, bidding you a last adieu; the minister of religion, praying near you and suggesting pious affections to you. (3) Yourself stretched on a bed of pain, losing by degrees your senses and the free use of your faculties, struggling violently against death, which comes to tear your soul from the body and drag it before the tribunal of God. (4) At your side the devils, who redouble their efforts, to destroy you; your good angel, who assists you for the last time with his holy inspirations.

2. *Application of the hearing.* Listen to the monotonous sound of the clock which measures your last hours, and says at each movement, Behold yourself a second nearer to the tribunal of God; the sound of your painful laboured breathing, and that terrible rattle, the forerunner of death; the stifled sobs of those who surround you; the prayers of the Church recited in the midst of tears: "From an evil death, from the pains of hell, from the power of Satan, deliver him, O Lord." "Depart, Christian soul, in the name of God Almighty, who

created you,—in the name of Jesus Christ, Son of the living God, who died for you,—in the name of the Holy Ghost, who sanctified you. Deliver, Lord, the soul of Thy servant from the perils of hell, as Thou didst deliver Noe from the deluge, Abraham out of Chaldea, Job from his sufferings." And from time to time the priest will suggest to you these words, which the Church places in his mouth: "Lord Jesus, receive my spirit. Mary, mother of grace, mother of mercy, protect us from the enemy and receive us at the hour of death." Meditate well on these words now, which sickness will not allow you to meditate upon at the hour of your death.

3. *Application of the taste.* Represent to yourself all the bitterness of the dying agony: "Doth bitter death separate in this manner?" (1 Kings xv. 32.) For the *present*, what bitterness in this separation from your possessions, your rank, your pleasures, your friends, your relatives, your body; in the weariness, the sadness, the fears, which precede the last moment! For the *past*, what bitterness in the memory of your whole life, in which you perceive so many infidelities, so many graces not corresponded with, so many grave sins, so many scandals! For the *future*, what bitterness in the thought of the judgment you have to undergo, when you must give an account of all your works, when you will hear the decisive sentence of your eternity! "O death, how bitter is the remembrance of thee!" (Ecclus. xli. 1.)

4. *Application of the touch.* Imagine yourself holding in your feeble hands the crucifix, which the priest presents to you; imagine yourself touching your own

II

body, which will soon be only a corpse. How cold your feet! Your arms, shrivelled by sickness, begin to stiffen. How painfully your chest labours with your unequal breathing, which soon will cease! Your heart, which beats with a scarcely perceptible movement, your face hollowed by fever and covered with cold sweat,—is it not in this state you have seen friends, near relatives, dying? It is in this state your friends and relatives will see you before long. Make these reflections to-day, which your agony will soon inspire in those who witness it.

End by a colloquy with our Lord dying: "Into Thy hands, O Lord, I commend my spirit" (Psalm xxx. 6).

Pater. Ave.

THIRD EXERCISE ON DEATH

SECOND CONTEMPLATION.

Your state after death.

Preparatory Prayer.

First and second preludes. The same.

Application of the *sight.* Consider—1. A few moments after your death. Your body laid on a funeral bed, wrapped in a shroud, a veil thrown over your face; beside you the crucifix, the holy water, friends, relatives, a priest kneeling by your sad remains, and reciting the holy prayers, " De profundis clamavi ad te, Domine;" the public officer who writes in the register of the dead all the particulars of your decease,—such a death, such a year, such a day, such an hour,—the servants all occupied with the preparation for your funeral.

2. The day after your death. Your inanimate body enclosed in a coffin, covered with a pall, taken from your apartment, sadly carried to the foot of the altar, received by the priest of Jesus Christ; deposited before the Lord present in the Tabernacle; then, the Holy Sacrifice over, laid in its last home, the grave. Consider well the dismal field where the eye sees nothing but tombs; this open grave where they are laying your body, the priest who blesses you for the last time, your relatives and friends who contemplate the spectacle with fear, the grave-digger who ends the scene by throwing earth on your coffin.

3. Some months after your death. Contemplate this stone already blackened by time, this inscription beginning to be effaced; and under that stone, in that coffin which is crumbling bit by bit, contemplate the sad state of your body; see how the worms devour the remains of putrid flesh; how all the limbs are separating; how the bones are eaten away by the corruption of the tomb! See what remains of the body you have loved so much!— a something which has no name in any tongue, and on which we cannot think without disgust.

Application of the *hearing*. Go through again the different scenes where you are the spectacle. Listen —(1.) To the dismal sound of the bells which announce your death, and which beg the prayers of the faithful for your soul. (2.) The prayers which they recite at the foot of your bed: " Saints of God, come to its assistance. Angels of God, come to its help;

receive his soul. Eternal rest give unto him, O Lord;
and let perpetual light shine upon him."   (3.) The
remarks of the servants who speak of you.   (4.) Your
friends and relatives, who communicate to each other
their reflections on your death, and mutually console
each other for your loss.   (5.) The assistants called
in to arrange your funeral, who speak of you with cold
indifference.   (6.) The chants of the Church during
the funeral service : " Deliver me, Lord, from eternal
death in that dreadful day when the heavens and the
earth shall tremble, when Thou shalt come to judge
the world by fire ;—that day, a day of wrath, of calamity, and of misery ; that great and very bitter day."
(7.) The conversations of the persons whom duty,
friendship, or civility call to your funeral.   (8.) What
is said of you in society after your death.   Examine
well all these circumstances, and conclude by making
a resolution to detach yourself from creatures, and belong to God alone.

Application of the *smell* and the *touch*. Imagine
yourself respiring the odour your body exhales when
the soul is departed ; the infection it would give out, if
it were taken from the coffin a few months after your
death.   Imagine you touch this damp earth, where
they have laid you ; this shroud in which they have
wrapped you, and which is now in rags ; this bare
skull, once the seat of thought ; these dismembered
limbs, which once obeyed all the orders of your will;
—in fine, this mass of corruption, which the sepulchre
has enclosed a few months, and the sight of which is
horrible.   In presence of this terrible scene, ask your-

self what aré health, fortune, friendship of the world, pleasures of the senses, life itself : " Vanity of vanities, all is vanity" (Eccles. i. 2).

End by a colloquy with our Saviour dying : " Into Thy hands I commend my spirit, O Lord."

Pater.   Ave.

EXERCISE ON THE PARTICULAR JUDGMENT.

Preparatory Prayer.

First prelude. Represent to yourself the tribunal of Jesus Christ, and your soul brought into the presence of its Judge to give an account of all its works.

Second prelude. "Remember, O most loving Jesu, that for me Thou didst humble Thyself to this mortal life. Let me not be lost, I beseech Thee, on that great day."*

FIRST CONSIDERATION.

The time and the place where the judgment will be held.

The time will be that at which you breathe your last sigh. Represent to yourself your relatives and friends examining your lips and heart to find a breath or a beat which may yet give token of life. While they are still asking whether you belong to time or eternity, you are already before the tribunal of your Judge. And where is this tribunal? In the room where you have just expired, beside your death-bed, before your corpse, before those who surround your inanimate remains, and who assist at this terrible scene without desiring it, and probably without thinking of it.

SECOND CONSIDERATION.

The accused.

It is your soul, but your soul alone with its works:

* "Recordare, Jesu pie,
Quod sum causa tuæ viæ;
Ne me perdas illâ die."

"Their works follow them" (Apoc. xiv. 13). Your soul suddenly illuminated by the lights of eternity, embracing at one glance the extent of its obligations, all the consequences of the graces it received, all the circumstances of the sins it committed: "In Thy light we shall see light" (Ps. xxxv. 10). Your soul in the presence of God, without the power to escape this awful sight. What a situation for the sinner! A worldling in the presence of that God he has never truly loved; a voluptuary in the presence of a thrice holy God, who has witnessed all his excesses, and is about to punish them; a careless man in presence of that God of whom he thought as little as if He had not existed!

THIRD CONSIDERATION.

The accusers.

1. *The devil.* Satan will stand before the tribunal of Jesus Christ repeating the words of your consecration to the Lord. He will recall your baptismal vows. He will say, "You were asked, 'Do you renounce the world, the flesh, and the devil?' and you replied, 'I do renounce them.' How, then, have you kept your promise?" Then turning towards our Lord, "I did not sweat blood for him; I was not crowned with thorns for him; I never shed a drop of blood for him; I was not suspended to the cross one moment for him. And yet he did not serve *you*, but *me*. I never gave my life for this soul; and yet it was not to you he gave himself, it was to me. Pronounce the sentence, then, and let him belong to me through sin, since he would not belong to you by grace."

2. *The angels.* Your guardian angel will reproach
you with rejecting his inspirations, despising his counsels, sullying his looks by your sins which he witnessed.
" Arise, O God, and judge Thy own cause" (Psalm
lxxiii. 22). The angels charged with the souls of your
brethren will reproach you with your scandals, and demand vengeance for your fatal example, which perhaps
caused their loss: "*Arise, O God, and judge.*" The
angels who watch before the holy altars will reproach
you with that indifference which kept you from the holy
table, or even from the temples of Jesus Christ; those
irreverences which have so often outraged the holiness
of sacrifice or prayer; the word of God listened to with
worldly dispositions; the Sacraments rendered useless
by tepidity, perhaps profaned by sacrilege. "*Arise, O
God, and judge.*"

3. *Your own conscience.* Your conscience will place
your whole life before your eyes; it will show you all
your works, which will say: Do you know us? we are
your works: "It was thou who didst us; we will not
leave thee" (St. Bern.). At each accusation of the
devil or the angels, it will bear witness against you:
" It is true thou art guilty of this iniquity; it was such
a day, at such an hour, thou didst commit this sin."

FOURTH CONSIDERATION.

The Judge.

It is Jesus Christ, once your father, your spouse,
your friend, your brother; but who now, forgetting all
these titles, is only your judge,—and what a judge! A
Judge *infinitely holy;* He has an infinite horror of every

sin, however small. A Judge *thoroughly omniscient;* there is no sin so small, so secret, that He does not know it and reveal it. A Judge *infinitely just;* there 's no sin that He leaves without vengeance. A Judge *without appeal;* whose sentence it is impossible to revoke. A Judge *all-powerful;* how can man escape the chastisements of His justice? Behold, then, the Judge before whom you will appear to give an account of His graces, and His blood shed for you! What will become of your soul in presence of such a Judge? "What shall I do when God shall arise to judge?" (Job xxxi. 14.)

FIFTH CONSIDERATION.

Your defence at the judgment of God.

If you appear before the tribunal of God in mortal sin, what will you answer to your accusers? "All iniquity shall stop her mouth" (Psalm cvi. 42). Will you excuse yourself by your ignorance? But they will oppose to you the lights of your conscience and of the Gospel, and the instructions of the Church and its ministers. Will you excuse yourself by your weakness? But they will oppose to you the strength of grace. Will you excuse yourself by your temptations? They will oppose the means God gave you to overcome them —prayer, the Sacraments, &c. Will you excuse yourself by the scandals which led you away? They will oppose all the holy examples which ought to have strengthened you in virtue. Finally, leaving all excuses, will you have recourse to the intercession of holy Mary and of the Saints, to the mercy of Jesus Christ? The Blessed Virgin, the Saints, can no longer do any thing for you·

and Jesus is now the God of justice, not the God of mercy: "My eye shall not spare them, neither shall I show mercy" (Ezech. viii. 18).

SIXTH CONSIDERATION.

The sentence.

To the just it will be said, "Come, ye blessed of My Father, possess the kingdom prepared for you from the beginning." To the wicked it will be said, "Begone, ye cursed, into everlasting fire, prepared for Satan and his angels" (Matt. xxv. 34, 41). Begone: that is to say, every tie between us is broken; go far from Me, wandering sheep, I am no longer your shepherd; go far from Me, faithless spouse, I am no longer thy spouse; go far from Me, unnatural child, I am no longer your father; begone, you shall have no part in My friendship, in My kingdom, in any thing belonging to Me. My Mother is no longer your mother; My angels are no longer your guardians; My saints no longer your protectors. Begone, ye cursed, cursed in every sense, which has each its punishment,—cursed in thy mind, which shall never have one good thought; cursed in thy heart, which shall be given up to despair without end. Begone to everlasting fire,—to that fire where thou wilt have a furnace for thy dwelling, flames for thy food, burning coals for thy couch, devils for thy society, tortures for thy repose; to that fire which will last as long as I am God. Begone to the fire prepared for Satan. I take heaven and earth to witness it was not prepared for thee. I protest before angels and men that I neglected nothing to save thee from this eternal fire. Behold My angels, to whose care I committed thy soul. Behold My Mother, whom I gave thee for thy mother and patroness. Behold My wounds, and My heart open and pierced for thy salvation. But since thou wouldst not have My graces and My friendship, begone from Me, and begone for all eternity : "Depart from Me, ye cursed, into everlasting fire."

AFFECTIONS.

Colloquy, first, at the feet of Jesus crucified:

"O most just Judge, bestow upon me, I beseech Thee, the gift of pardon before that day of reckoning. Behold, I groan in Thy sight as one guilty; shame covereth my face because of my sin. Spare me, a suppliant, O my God."*

Second, at the feet of an image of Mary:

"O Mary, at once the Mother of God and the mother of the sinner, mother of the Judge and of the criminal, let not God your Son condemn your son the sinner."

Pater. Ave.

* "Juste Judex ultionis,   Ingemisco tamquam reus:
Donum fac remissionis,   Culpa rubet vultus meus:
Ante diem rationis.   Supplicanti parce, Deus."

ON VENIAL SIN.

Preparatory Prayer.

First prelude. Represent to yourself the fires of purgatory, and a soul in these fires expiating the sins it committed on earth.

Second prelude. Ask of God the knowledge and the hatred of venial sin.

FIRST CONSIDERATION.

The malice of venial sin.

Venial sin is essentially an offence against God. It is consequently a contempt of the majesty of God, an ingratitude towards His goodness, a resistance to His will, an injury to all His perfections;—a slight injury if compared to that which mortal sin offers to God, but very serious if considered in itself; for it is an offence against Infinite Majesty by a vile creature, and for a vile motive.

Venial sin is, then, really the evil of God. Meditate well on these words: *An evil against God;* that is to say, an evil so great that it surpasses all the temporal and even eternal evils of creatures.

The destruction, or above all the damnation, of the whole human race would be a great evil; and yet it would be a sin to wish, if we had the power, to save the human race from destruction or hell at the price of one venial sin.

It is an evil so great that all the sacrifices and virtues of creatures render less glory to God than one venial sin takes from Him.

It is an evil so great that neither the mind of man can comprehend it, nor his will hate it as it deserves to be hated, nor any expiation of his suffice to repair it. For it requires nothing less than the mind, the will, and the atonement of a God.

SECOND CONSIDERATION.

The effects of venial sin.

Venial sin, it is true, does not destroy in us habitual grace; but, nevertheless, how deplorable are its effects in the soul!

1. It imprints a stain which tarnishes its beauty. It is to the soul what an ulcer is to the body.

2. It weakens the lights of the spirit and the fervour of the will; and from that arise languor in prayer, in the use of the Sacraments, and in the practice of Christian virtues.

3. It deprives the soul of the superabundance of graces—choice graces, which God only gives to purity of heart.

4. It deprives the soul of a greater degree of grace and glory which it would have acquired by its fidelity, and which is lost by its fault. A God less glorified eternally, less loved, and less possessed,—such are the consequences of venial sin to the soul.

5. It leads to mortal sin as sickness leads to death; for the repetition of venial sins insensibly weakens the fear of God, hardens the conscience, forms evil attachments and habits, gives fresh strength to the temptations of the enemy of our salvation, nourishes and develops the passions. Hence the Holy Spirit says, " He that

contemneth small things, shall fall by little and little"
(Ecclus. xix. 1); and that of our Saviour, "He that is
unjust in that which is little, is unjust also in that which
is greater" (Luke xvi. 10).

THIRD CONSIDERATION.

The punishment of venial sin.

Even in this life God has often inflicted most rigorous vengeance for venial sin. Moses and Aaron
were excluded from the promised land in punishment
of a slight distrust; the Bethsamites were struck dead
for an indiscreet look at the Ark; seventy thousand
Israelites were carried off by a destructive scourge in
punishment of the vain complaisance of David in the
numbering of his subjects.

But it is above all in the next life that venial sin
is punished with the most alarming rigour. Enter in
spirit this blazing prison, where the justice of God pu-
rifies His elect, and meditate attentively on the following circumstances:

1. *What is the victim suffering in purgatory?* It
is a predestined soul; a soul confirmed in grace, and
that cannot lose it; a soul so dear to God that He is
impatient to give it the most magnificent testimony of
His love, that is to say, the possession of Himself.

2. *What does it suffer?* Pain which man cannot
conceive; that is, fires which differ in nothing from
those which devour the damned—it is the opinion of St.
Augustine, confirmed by St. Thomas, "The same fire
forms the torment of the damned and the purification
of the just;" and the privation of God, which delivers

up the soul to all that is most agonising in regrets and desires.

3. *Why does it suffer?* For some of those faults which almost every moment are committed from the weakness of our will.

End by looking into your conscience. Examine the faculties of your soul and the senses of your body. Call to mind how far divine faith regulates the use of them with regard to God, your neighbour, and yourself. Examine all the venial faults you commit each day in these different points, through ignorance, levity, or weakness—perhaps even with malice and reflection. Humble yourself before God, and say with the prophet: "For evils without number have surrounded me; my iniquities have overtaken me, and I am not able to see. They are multiplied above the hairs of my head, and my heart hath forsaken me. Be pleased, O Lord, to deliver me" (Psalm xxxix. 13, 14).

Colloquy with the Blessed Virgin and our Saviour

Pater. Ave.

FIRST EXERCISE.

The prodigal son.

Preparatory Prayer.

First prelude. Represent to yourself the prodigal son returning to his father after long wanderings.

Second prelude. Ask of our Lord the grace to imitate the repentance of the prodigal, and, like him, obtain pardon for your past sins.

THE WANDERINGS OF THE PRODIGAL SON.

" A certain man had two sons; and the younger of
them said to his father, Father, give me the portion
of substance that falleth to me.   And he divided unto
them his substance.   And not many days after, the
younger son, gathering all together, went abroad into
a far country, and there wasted his substance, living
riotously.   And after he had spent all, there came a
mighty famine in that country, and be began to be in
want.   And he went and cleaved to one of the citizens
of that country.   And he sent him to his farm to feed
swine.   And he would fain have filled his belly with the
husks the swine did eat: and no man gave unto him"
(Luke xv. 11-16).

Consider well all the circumstances of this history.

1. *He is young.*   The passions of youth : here we
see the cause of his error.   Youth is the age of illusions : the prodigal promised himself a happy and brilliant life away from the paternal mansion.   Youth has
a passion for pleasure : the prodigal sighed after gaieties
of the world;   he envied other youths of his age the
pleasures of idleness, the noisy joys of their amusements,
the success of their mad passions.   Youth is, above all,
jealous of its independence : the prodigal is weary of
the constraint his father's presence imposes on him; he
wishes to be the master of his liberty, and the arbiter of
his destiny.   Look within yourself : what have been the
causes of your errors, if not the illusions of the world,
the passion for pleasure, the fatal love of independence?

2. " *Father, give me the portion of substance that
falleth to me.*"   He asks of his father that portion of

the heritage which comes to him. *What ingratitude!*
The name alone of father, ought it not to have recalled
to him all the benefits bestowed by paternal tenderness, the cares which surrounded his infancy, the lively
affection of which he received fresh testimonies every
day? *What unjust pretensions!* This substance which
he claims belongs to his father, who received it from
his ancestors, or who perhaps owes it to a long series
of labours or to prudent economy. By what right does
he take it during his father's lifetime? and what title
has he to exact the division of a fortune not yet belonging to him? *What foolish temerity!* This property
once in his hands, what will become of it? Scarcely
will he be master of it before he will dissipate it in
luxury and debauchery. Apply these reflections to
yourself. Is not God your Father in the order of nature and in the order of grace? When you left Him
to serve the world, did you not act like the prodigal,
ask for your portion of the heritage, that is, the free
disposal of yourself, as if you were not the property of
God, who created you and redeemed you, as if you
could for a moment become master of yourself without
making yourself miserable? What ingratitude in you.
departure from God! what injustice! what folly!

3. *"And not many days after he went abroad into
a far country."* Being now master of his property, the
prodigal goes into a distant country. If he remained
in the neighbourhood of his father's house, too many
memories would trouble him in the midst of his pleasures; he would be in constant fear of the remonstrances
of his father's friends, the presence perhaps of this
father himself, the reproaches of his own heart. To

give himself up to pleasure with less trouble and more
liberty, he goes into a distant country. An image this
of your wanderings, when you gave yourself to the
world. You dreaded the exercises of piety, prayer,
frequenting of the Sacraments; the society of good people; even meeting the ministers of Jesus Christ, whose
zeal might have brought you back to Him; your own
reflections and the reproaches of your own conscience;
—all these you feared. You fled as far from yourself and
as far from God as possible, for fear that grace should
find you out and restore you, even against yourself, to
your Father and God.

4. "*And there wasted his substance, living riotously.*" Away from his father, the prodigal child has
soon dissipated his fortune. He does not consider that
it is the fruit of his father's toil; that it is his sole resource for the future; that this fortune, however brilliant it may be, must come to an end in the expenses of
luxury and sin. A few months are scarcely passed,
and there remains to him nothing of his riches, nothing
but dread poverty: " He wasted his substance." And
what treasures of grace have you not dissipated, far
from God! Recall to mind all these losses, and weep
for them with tears of blood,—loss of the friendship of
God; loss of your past merits; loss of those holy inspirations, which you have continually despised; loss of
those good examples rendered useless; loss of that
Christian education of which you have abjured the
principles; loss of those happy dispositions of nature,
of that taste for virtue, that uprightness of heart, of
that delicacy of conscience, of those favourable tenden-
cies to piety; loss of your talents, which you have pros-

tinted to the service of pleasure and sin; loss of your
reason, of your faith, of which you have perhaps even
smothered the light. What a sad use of the gifts of your
God! " He wasted his substance in riotous living."

5. " He began to be in want, and he cleaved to one
of the citizens ; and he sent him into his farm to feed
swine." Sad consequences of the profusion and liber-
tinism of the prodigal!—want, slavery, degradation,
and infamy.

Want. A great famine falls upon the country
where the prodigal has gone; and, his riches wasted in
luxury, he is left in shameful poverty. In vain he addresses himself to the companions of his excesses, to the
friends on whom he had bestowed pleasure and fortune; he is left alone without resource, and forced to
beg his bread from the pity of a stranger. This country a prey to famine is the world. This hunger is the
devouring hunger of the passions, which incessantly cry
from the depths of the guilty heart, " Bring, bring"
(Prov. xxx. 15). This indigence is the emptiness of a
soul tormented by the want of happiness, and begging
it in vain from creatures, which only offer him agitation,
regret, disgust, weariness, and afflictions without end.
O my God, how true it is that in losing You the sinner
loses all ! " What can be more lost than what is out of
God ?" (St. Bernard.) " What do you possess if you
possess not God ?" (St. Aug.)

Slavery. What a sad change! This young man so
jealous of his liberty obliged to take service with a
hard and unfeeling master! he who was such an enemy
of all restraint reduced to the lowest occupations! he
so haughty confounded with the vilest slaves! And

is not this the humiliating state of the sinner? Like the prodigal, he is the slave, not of one master, but of innumerable tyrants ;—slave of Satan, who reigns over his mind, his imagination, his heart, his senses ; slave of his inclinations, which every moment require the sacrifice of his repose, his conscience, his reason ; slave of the world, and so must respect its judgments, applaud its maxims, spare its susceptibility, humour its caprices, satisfy its exigences, dissimulate, and suffer without complaint all its ingratitude and injustice ; slave of habits, which become a sort of necessity and second nature, and which defy all the efforts of grace, all the reflections of reason, all the remorse of conscience. What a slavery! "Such is the fate of whoever refuses himself to his Father" (St. Chrysol.).

Degradation. The prodigal reduced to feed unclean animals, and even envying them their degrading food. What disgrace! It is that of the sinner away from his God. There is no pleasure, however gross and brutal, from which he does not seek happiness ; he even descends to envy the lowest libertines their most shameful excesses, their most monstrous debauches. He even envies the stupid condition of the brutes, wishing to have like them no law but instinct, no other destiny than the gratification of sense : "Man, when he was in honour, did not understand : he hath been compared to senseless beasts, and is become like to them" (Ps. xlviii. 13).

SECOND EXERCISE ON THE PRODIGAL SON.

Preparatory Prayer.

First prelude. Represent to yourself the prodigal son returning to his father after long wanderings.

Second prelude. Ask of our Saviour the grace to imitate the repentance of the prodigal, and to obtain from Him the pardon of your past wanderings.

THE RETURN OF THE PRODIGAL.

The prodigal returning to himself, said, " How many hired servants in my father's house abound with bread, and I here perish with hunger. I will arise and will go to my father, and say to him: Father, I have sinned against heaven and before thee: I am not now worthy to be called thy son; make me as one of thy hired servants. And rising up, he came to his father. And when he was yet a great way off, his father saw him and was moved with compassion; and running to him, fell upon his neck and kissed him. And the son said: Father, I have sinned against heaven and before thee; I am not now worthy to be called thy son. But the father said to his servants: Bring forth quickly the first robe, and put it on him, and put a ring on his hand and shoes on his feet; and bring hither the fatted calf and kill it, and let us make merry : because this my son was dead, and is come to life again ; was lost, and is found" (Luke xv. 17-24).

Consider two things: the conversion of the prodigal, and the welcome which he receives from his father.

1. The conversion of the prodigal.

(1.) *The misfortunes of the prodigal are the beginning of his conversion.* He had forgotten his father when he was rich and happy; miserable and poor, all his thoughts turned to this father so unjustly abandoned. Acknowledge the value of affliction; God always visits with His grace those whom He visits with tribulation.

(2.) *The prodigal, thus cast off by the world, returns to himself, and begins to reflect on his unhappiness and his sins.* The injustice, ingratitude, and perfidy with which the world recompenses our services, will they not make us also return to ourselves? What subjects of reflection does not a soul that has left God for creatures find in itself! O God, what have I gained by leaving Thee? What rest, what happiness have I found in the world? Was it requisite, Lord, to take from Thee my heart, renounce Thy grace, lose my peace of conscience, risk my salvation and my eternity, for pleasures so fleeting, so empty, so degrading?

(3.) *Returning to himself, the prodigal compares his state to that of his father's servants:* "How many hired servants in my father's house abound with bread, and I here perish with hunger!" Unfaithful soul, what a difference between your state and that of the servants of God! what peace in their souls! what interior joy! what fullness of consolation, even in the midst of their sacrifices! In your heart, on the contrary, what troubles! what bitterness! what agonies! What a difference between you and them! Recall what even your heart was under the empire of the Divine grace; see what it is become under the empire of sin; and by the troubles of your present state learn to regret the happiness of your past condition: "Who will grant me that I might be according to the months past, according to the days in which God kept me?" (Job xxix. 2.)

(4.) *The prodigal arms himself with a noble and courageous resolution:* "I will arise and go to my father." He does not stop at words and wishes only He does not put off his change to a distant future. He is not afraid of the talk and the raillery of the world at the change. He does not draw back before the sacrifice of his attachments and his passions. What an example of true conversion !

(5.) Finally, *It is by the humble avowal of his faults that the prodigal wishes to return to his father's favour:* "I will say to him, Father, I have sinned against heaven and before thee." Let that be the first step also of your conversion. Go, throw yourself at the feet of Jesus Christ, present in the person of the priest, and say to Him, I have sinned against heaven and before Thee; against heaven by the scandal of so many iniquities committed in the light of day; before Thee by so many secret sins, which, though buried in my heart or hidden in darkness, are not less clear to Thy invisible eye. Ah! I am not worthy to be called Thy child—too happy if Thou wilt deign to admit me among Thy servants: "I am not now worthy to be called thy son : make me as one of thy hired servants."

2. The welcome the prodigal receives from his father.

(1.) "*When he was yet a long way off, his father saw him, and was moved with compassion.*" His father perceived him at a distance, and was immediately moved with compassion. So, when feelings of repentance arise in your heart, God looks upon you with pity. He forgets every thing,—your revolt against His will, your having despised His mercy and His justice, your having resisted His grace, your obstinacy and hardness in sin; He no longer remembers that you were ungrateful and rebellious, He only sees in you your misery and your penitence.

(2.) " *He ran to him, fell upon his neck, and kissed him.*" Does it not seem as if the prodigal's father ought to have waited for his son; then, restraining his tenderness, leave him for some time at his feet, and only grant pardon to the importunity of his prayers? Far from that, this father runs to meet him, throws himself on his neck, and clasps him to his heart. See in this description the goodness of God: you abandoned Him; and now that creatures abandon you, ought He not to withdraw Himself in His turn? Does He not owe it to His honour to reject your heart as creatures do? to His holiness, not to encourage sin by so easily forgiving a sinner like you? to His justice, by treating you as He has treated so many unhappy ones, whom He punishes in hell without pity for the same crimes you commit so boldly? And yet He seeks you; He does not wait for you to ask pardon, He offers it to you; He does not allow you to remain at His feet, He embraces you and presses you to His sacred heart: " Thus does this Father judge, thus does He chastise, thus does He give His erring son, not the rod, but a kiss. I ask you, then, where is there room for despair?" (St. Chrysost.)

(3.) *"Bring forth quickly the first robe, and put it on him, and put a ring on his hand."* To pardon the repentant son seems little to this tender father; he wishes to restore to him all the marks, and at the same time all the rights, of his first condition. No reproaches for the past, no trial for the future; immediately he reinstates him in all the prerogatives of his birth. Thus the Lord treats the soul which returns to Him. In restoring to him His friendship, He restores all that sin had deprived him of; and He restores it without delay : "Our Father does not know what it is to make us wait for pardon" (S. P. Chrysol.). With pardon what will you not regain? innocence, peace, your merits, your rights to the glory of heaven, your title to the esteem of the good, all your dignity as man and Christian; and all this you regain in a single moment : "At this very moment I may, if I desire, become the friend of God" (St. Augustine).

(4.) *"Bring hither the fatted calf, and let us eat and make merry."* Finally, the prodigal's father orders a splendid feast to celebrate the return of his son; and he wishes all his friends and his servants to take part in the joy of this feast; "For," said he, "my son was lost, and is found ; he was dead, and is alive again." So the heavenly Father celebrates your return by a solemn festival, where He gives you the body of His Divine Son, who is every day offered, in order to be given to us at the Eucharistic table. He invites just men and angels to rejoice at our spiritual resurrection; He wishes that the day of our conversion should be a feast-day for all the family, that is to say, for his Church. After this, why do we delay returning to the arms and the heart of this good Father?

COLLOQUY.

Cast yourself at the feet of Jesus Christ, like the prodigal child at his father's feet, and solemnly promise never more to forsake Him.

Anima Christi.

SECOND WEEK.

THE aim of the first week is to know how far we have
wandered from the path which leads to our last end, to
deplore so great an error, and to conceive an ardent
desire to return to this path, never more to quit it.

The purpose of the second week is to propose to ourselves Jesus Christ as the true way, as He Himself says:
"I am the way, the truth, and the life; no man cometh
to the Father but by Me" (John xix. 6). Jesus Christ
is, in fact, the Divine model whose example must reform and regulate our lives. And as the life of our
Saviour is the very perfection of holiness, it follows that
the more faithfully we imitate Him, the more perfect
our lives will be; and as perfection is our end, to approach nearer to our end, is to be nearer repose and
happiness. Thus, the more our life resembles that of
Jesus Christ, the happier it will be.

The recommendations proper to this week are—

1. To undertake the Exercises with great courage
and a sincere desire to follow the way of God, as it
shall be manifested to us. This disposition is so necessary for the fruit of the Exercises, that it would be better
to interrupt them than to continue them with an undecided will.

2. After the meditations, any spare time may be employed in reading some useful work, but one more cal-

culated to nourish piety than give rise to curiosity—such as some of the works of St. Bernard, of Louis of Granada, the Imitation of Christ, the Lives of the Saints, and the Holy Gospels. It must be observed, however, in order to avoid distraction, that if the work treats of the mysteries of our Saviour, we must not stop to dwell upon any other mystery than the one on which we are to meditate then or during the day.

3. In the observance of the additions there must be the following modifications:

(1.) On waking you must recall the subject of meditation, and excite in yourself a great desire to know more particularly the mystery of the Word incarnate, that you may love Him with more ardour, and serve Him with more fidelity.

(2.) During the day you must frequently recall some event in the life of our Saviour, from the time of His incarnation to that of the mystery which is the subject of the present meditation.

(3.) In the time of meditation, make use of light, or of obscurity, according as the one or the other appears most suitable to the sentiments and affections we desire to excite in ourselves. With regard to corporeal mortifications, they must be regulated according to the mystery we are meditating on; for some of the mysteries should excite us to penitence, some to other virtues.

When meditation has for its immediate object the mysteries of Jesus Christ, it naturally takes the form of contemplation. It is therefore necessary here to trace out the method of contemplation and the application of the senses.

CONTEMPLATION,

OR MANNER OF MEDITATING ON SENSIBLE OBJECTS.

In this Exercise, where the mysteries of our Saviour are the object, we fix on persons, listen to words, consider actions ; and from each of these we endeavour to draw some fruit for the soul.

I. BEFORE THE CONTEMPLATION.

The same thing is to be observed as in the meditations, only adding a prelude. It is a sort of representation of the mystery intended to be meditated upon, and which consists in recalling the history in brief. This prelude should be placed after the preparatory prayer, and before the construction of place.

II. DURING THE CONTEMPLATION.

1. Consider first, the persons, with whatever they present in themselves of good or bad.

2. The words, interior or exterior, the thoughts, the affections.

3. The actions, praiseworthy or blamable, going back to their cause in order to draw more spiritual profit from them.

Each of these points we must consider as regards ourselves, and apply the reflections suggested by the different objects contemplated. We may also meditate on the mysteries, reflecting on all the circumstances, the causes, the end, the effect, the time, the place, the manner of their accomplishment.

End by one or more colloquies and the *Pater*.

III. AFTER THE CONTEMPLATION.

The same review as after the meditation.

ON THE REIGN OF CHRIST.

CONTEMPLATION.

Preparatory Prayer.

First prelude. Represent to yourself the synagogues, villages, cities of Judea, and the different places, the scenes of the preaching of Jesus Christ.

Second prelude. Ask of God the grace not to be deaf to the calls of His divine Son, but prompt to obey Him and follow Him.

I.

Let us suppose that the bounty of Heaven has sent on earth a monarch who unites in himself all the moral and Christian virtues, all the heroic qualities, every title of legitimacy, all the gifts of valour and fortune that can render a general or a king formidable to his enemies and dear to his subjects ;—a prince wiser than Solomon, greater than Charlemagne, more pious than St. Louis, more fortunate in war than Bonaparte in the days of his greatest prosperity ;—a sovereign to whom the Lord has given in an authentic manner, and acknowledged by all Christian people, the title of universal monarch, which Henry IV., Charles V., and Napoleon aspired in vain to be ; in fine, a king to whom all the princes of Europe would willingly become tributary, and who had incontestable rights over the states of the infidels. Suppose, moreover, that this great man, this invincible general, this supreme monarch, should one day call around him all these princes,—formerly independent, but now considering themselves more fortunate in being his generals and his officers,—and should speak to them thus : " Kings, my friends and my subjects, who enjoy with so much happiness the peace that reigns throughout Christian Europe, you are not ignorant of the evils that weigh on a part of humanity still barbarous and savage. In one place absurd divinities exact and receive human sacrifices, in another place cannibals feed on the hearts of their enemies, or even on the yet living flesh of their parents. Elsewhere, unhappy widows are obliged to burn themselves on their husband's funeral pile; officers and courtiers are buried alive with their dead prince. There are chiefs of tribes who punish with death any unfortunate being who should by chance cross their shadow, or cast a single look on them. Almost every where, the child who is too great a burden on its parents is condemned to perish at its birth, and the Chinese seas daily swallow up thousands of children. There and elsewhere the laws of natural morality, of the rights of man, of modesty, of humanity, are unknown or violated. Nowhere is there liberty, security, instruction, order, or true prosperity. By the announcement only of our approach, by the mere view of our armies, by the reputation of knowledge, wisdom, and strength that Europe has acquired in the world, these unhappy people will feel that their subjugation will be their happiness, and will submit to us without striking a blow. As they are our subjects by the order of divine power, we must spare their blood as we should spare that of our own soldiers. Thence we must take more precautions and run more perils ; but I will be there at your head to set you the example of clemency and bravery; in so splendid an enterprise, I wish to undergo myself the greatest part of the privations and sufferings. No one in the army shall have any thing to do, or to suffer that I have not done and suffered before him. This, then, is the condition I impose on those who wish to take part in this great expedition; to accompany me in the midst of hazards and dangers, or rather to follow me into them, suffer with me, but always less than myself. And behold the prize that I promise to the conquerors, and which shall be proportioned to the services rendered : I shall soon have a great number of crowns to distribute; the smallest reward I shall give to my brave and faithful companions will be a throne,— a throne to occupy for the liberation, the civilisation, the happiness of a whole people.''

With what enthusiasm would this discourse be re-ceived! with what unanimous applause! The enterprise is so glorious; the end proposed so noble, so useful; the example of the monarch so encouraging; the rewards promised so magnificent! What generous ambition would fire every heart, and how on every lip would be heard the cry of our fathers marching to the conquest of the Holy Sepulchre, " *God wills it, God wills it!*" And if it happened that one of these princes, preferring an ignoble repose to this glorious labour, should dare to reply, without dying of shame, " For me, I prefer remaining in the midst of my idleness, enjoying the delights of the court," what a general hoot, what exclamations of disapprobation and contempt, would follow this cowardly and indolent refusal !

II.

And now compare with this great monarch and his noble expedition another monarch,—the King of kings, Jesus Christ, and the enterprise which brought Him from heaven upon earth.

1. Son of God, Creator and Saviour of all mankind, King of the whole earth, He received all nations as His inheritance; He is the way, the truth, and the life, and no one arrives at the Father but through Him; there is no salvation possible to mortals but in Him and through Him alone. Full of grace and truth, He unites in Himself all virtues, all perfections, divine and human. And this is the discourse He addresses to all those who have become His subjects by baptism, and His soldiers by confirmation : " My will, the most just of all wills, is from the height of My cross to draw all to Me ; to enter into the possession of My domain, the world ; to subjugate all My enemies for their salvation; and as a peaceful conqueror and master, universally obeyed by all the earth, to introduce with Me into the glory of My Father all these men redeemed by My blood. Let those who would share My crown accompany Me, follow Me; their eternal reward will be proportioned to their labours and their efforts."

2. Let us reason and understand that it would be folly to refuse to Jesus Christ the generous and fervent offer of our entire selves. Let us, moreover, conceive that we must not only offer to follow Him in bodily works and fatigues, but that we owe Him a more worthy and precious service;—the struggle and the victory against our flesh, our senses, our self-love, the

K

love of the world. Let us say, weighing all the circumstances of this sublime vocation :

(1.) *Who is it that calls us?*   It is a God who has
every right to our submission. *The right of His infinite perfections.* We cannot belong to ourselves; we
must belong to God or to our passions. We have only
the choice of the one yoke or the other. Which appears the most honourable? *The right of creation.*
What are we? what have we? All that we are, all
that we have, comes from God, and consequently belongs
to God.   Shall we disown, violate, towards Him alone
that right of property which reason and justice consecrate in human society ? *The right of redemption.* A
thing belongs to us if we buy it with our money, still
more if we purchase it by long and hard labour; yet
more would it appear so if bought with our blood. But
what are we with regard to Jesus Christ? We are the
price of all His wealth, the price of all His sufferings,
the price of His blood and His death : " Know you not
that you are not your own? For you are bought with
a great price" (1 Cor. vi. 19, 20). *The right of our
vows and promises.* What more sacred than an oath dictated by gratitude and justice, sworn in the fullness of
liberty and reflection, renewed so often and so solemnly
in the face of heaven and earth? This is the oath which
binds us to Jesus Christ.

(2.) *To what enterprise does Jesus Christ call us?*
To the most noble and most heroic that can be proposed.
In this enterprise all is great. Consider : *The enemies
to be combated ;*—the devil, the world, our own hearts.
The weapons ;—faith, prayer, humility, patience, self-
denial charity, zeal. *Our companions in the battle;*

—the most illustrious that the world ever saw; the apostles, the martyrs, the penitents, in one word, all the saints. *Our leader;*—Jesus Christ Himself; but Jesus Christ who combats in us by His grace, and who, already a conqueror in so many saints, wishes to conquer in each one of us and in the hearts of all mankind. Lastly, *the motive and end of the combat;*—to bestow on all the captives of Jesus Christ liberty, glory, happiness; to restore them to the way, the truth, and the life.

(3.) *What are the conditions of the enterprise?* To partake in the labours of Jesus Christ, that we may afterwards partake of His glory. But let us remark well, that *the sacrifices which Jesus asks of us He has first accomplished Himself.* If He asks humility of us, He first humiliated Himself; if He asks renouncement of us, He first renounced Himself. He has done more, He has gone beyond what He asks of us; He humbled Himself even to annihilation; He renounced Himself even to the cross. *The sacrifices which Jesus Christ demands are sweetened by the unction of His grace.* The cross has been without alleviation for Him alone; for His servants He lightens the weight by consolations. He alone could say in the full force of the words, "My soul is sorrowful even unto death" (Matt. xxvi. 38); He enables His servants to say, "I exceedingly abound with joy in all our tribulations" (2 Cor. vii. 4). *The sacrifices that Jesus Christ asks of us are only passing.* A short period of combat, an eternity of reward.

(3.) Let us consecrate ourselves generously to the service of so great and magnificent a master, and say to Him: "Behold me at Thy feet, supreme Monarch of the universe. Without doubt I am unworthy to march

after Thee; but full of confidence in Thy grace and
protection, I consecrate myself to Thee without reserve.
All that I am and all that I possess I submit to Thy
holy will. I declare before Thy infinite goodness, in
presence of the Virgin-Mother of my Saviour, and of
all the heavenly court, that my desire, my unalterable
resolution, my determined will, is to follow Thee as
nearly as possible, detached in spirit from the things
of the earth, and, if Thou shouldst will it, really poor;
humble of heart, and, if that also is Thy will, partaking
all Thy humiliations and all Thy ignominies; living
and dying at the post where the interests of Thy glory
and my salvation and Thy divine call may have placed
me." "As the Lord liveth, and as my lord the king
liveth : in what place soever thou shalt be, my lord
king, either in death or in life, there will thy servant
be" (2 Kings xv. 21).

FIRST EXERCISE ON THE INCARNATION.

MEDITATION.

Preparatory Prayer.

First prelude. Recall the mystery—" The ange. Gabriel was sent from God into a city of Galilee called Nazareth, to a virgin called Mary. The angel being come in, said unto her : Hail, full of grace, the Lord is with thee ; thou shalt bring forth a Son, and thou shalt call His name Jesus. Mary said, Behold the hand-maid of the Lord, be it done to me according to thy word" (Luke i. 26-38).

Second prelude. Represent to yourself Nazareth, and the humble house of Mary, where the mystery of the Incarnation was accomplished.

Third prelude. Ask the grace of knowing well the infinite charity of the Word incarnate, that you may love Him with more ardour and serve Him with greater zeal.

FIRST POINT.

Consider the state of the human race before the Incarnation of the Word. With the exception of a few faithful souls, men lived in a profound forgetfulness of their last end. The devils had altars among all the people ; pride, voluptuousness, love of riches, reigned in all hearts ; the knowledge of God disappeared gradually from their hearts : " Truths are decayed from among the children of men" (Ps. xi. 2). The Jews themselves were, for the most part, scarcely nearer to God and salvation than idolatrous nations.

Witness the reproaches addressed to them by the Baptist,—" Ye brood of vipers, who hath showed you to flee from the wrath to come?" (Matt. iii. 7.) And after him our Lord,—" You are of your father the devil" (John viii. 44). In a word, God was scarcely any longer known, or loved, or served on earth. And souls fell into the abyss every day in such numbers that hell was obliged to enlarge its precincts,—" Hell hath enlarged her soul, and opened her mouth without any bounds" (Is. v. 14).

Could man in this state of degradation and misery reasonably hope that God would deign to pity him and save him? For should not God thrice holy, God infinitely just, turn away His eyes with horror from the human race, of whom it is written, "To God the wicked and his wickedness are hateful" (Wis. xiv. 9)? "Thy eyes are too pure to behold evil, and Thou canst not look on iniquity" (Hab. i. 13). Should He not treat man as He had treated the rebel angels, and deliver him up for ever to all the rigours of His vengeance?

Did not God, infinitely great, owe it to His glory not to pardon criminals, whose ingratitude He foresaw, and who would only receive His mercy with indifference, contempt, resistance, and hardness? Where would mankind be, where should we be, if God had only consulted the interests of His greatness or His justice? Let us, then, recognise the infinite need we have of His mercy, and return thanks to Him for not having abandoned us in our misery.

SECOND POINT.

Consider the intention of the eternal Word in the Incarnation. His design is to repair the glory of the Father by bringing man back to his end,—that is, to the knowledge, love, and service of God.

1. *The Word became man to bring men back to the knowledge of God.* Consider that the Incarnation is the plainest proof of the Divine perfections. It reveals to us the grandeur of God, which cannot be worthily adored except by a Man-God;—His wisdom, which knew how to invent this wonderful union of Divine and human nature for His glory and our salvation;—His holiness, the offence to which can only be repaired by the satisfactions of a God;—His mercy, which, instead of abandoning guilty man to eternal reprobation, takes pity on him and saves him;—His love, which, not content with the gifts bestowed on man in the order of creation, wishes also to present him with a God as a Saviour.

2. *The Word becomes incarnate to recall men to the love of God.* Consider that creatures, instead of leading man to God, usurped all the affections of his heart. What does the Divine Word do to restore this heart to the empire of charity? Because man is under the dominion of his senses, He appears in a sensible form; because he is smitten with the love of creatures, He makes Himself one of them,—He becomes man; and that He may more irresistibly captivate the human heart, He gives the first example of the love He asks. Recall the great precept of charity, "Thou shalt love the Lord thy God with thy whole heart, with thy whole

soul, and with thy whole mind, and with thy whole strength" (Mark xii. 30). Recall also the whole life on earth of the Word incarnate. See Him bestowing on our redemption all His thoughts, all His affections, all His works, His humanity, His entire divinity;—and say, has He not fulfilled the precept of charity in its full extent towards man?

3. *The Word became incarnate to recall man to the service of God.* Consider that precepts no longer sufficed to teach man how God should be served. It was because of this that the Divine Word came to instruct us, not only by words, but by example. His whole life is only a practical lesson of devotion to His Father's service. What do we see in it in fact? (1) A Man-God, who, from the first moment of His conception, offers Himself to His Father. This is to teach us that there is not a single moment of our lives that does not belong to God. "When He cometh into the world He saith: Sacrifice and oblation Thou wouldest not; but a body Thou hast fitted to Me; then said I, Behold I come to do Thy will, O God" (Heb. x. 5-9). (2) A God who fulfilled all the details and observances of the law, which could not bind Him. This was to teach us that He wishes to be served with a religious obedience to all His commandments. (3) A God who devotes Himself to every sacrifice, even to death upon the cross. This is to teach us that God merits to be served, however much it may cost to nature.

Meditate attentively on the great end that the Word proposed to Himself in the Incarnation, and ask of Him the grace to correspond to it faithfully.

THIRD POINT.

Consider how the Incarnation of the Word was accomplished. An angel is sent to Mary, a virgin, the spouse of a poor artisan. He comes to announce to her that the Word has chosen her for His mother, and to ask her consent to the great mystery which was to be accomplished in her. Meditate on each of these circumstances.

(1.) *A God who incarnates Himself*; that is to say, a God who makes Himself man, who makes Himself flesh, who unites Himself so closely to this vile flesh, subject to so many infirmities, which is common to us with the beasts, and which He assumes in a state of feebleness and humiliation in the state of infancy. From this annihilation of the Son of God learn the necessity and excellence of humility.

(2.) *A God who becomes incarnate in the womb of a virgin mother*. Admire the privilege of virginity : it is to it that the greatest honour is granted that God could do to a creature, the honour of the Divine maternity. From this conduct of God, who chose a virgin for His mother, and the purest of virgins, learn the necessity and the value of purity.

(3.) *A God who becomes incarnate in the womb of a poor mother*. The Son of God could have chosen a rich mother, and one of elevated rank according to the world. He fixes His choice on the spouse of a poor artisan. Engaged by His promises to be born of the race of David, He waits to be born of her until this royal race had fallen into obscurity and almost indigence. Learn from this the necessity and value of detachment

(4.) *A God who makes His incarnation depend on the consent of His creature.* Learn from this the dignity and power of Mary. God willed that men should, as it were, owe Jesus Christ, and with Jesus Christ their redemption, to the free-will of this blessed Virgin. Conceive, then, a great respect and confidence for the Mother of God, and never forget that the Word incarnate having only come into the world through Mary, it is only by Mary that we can go to Him.

COLLOQUY WITH THE THREE PERSONS OF THE ADORABLE TRINITY.

Adore the infinite charity of God, who deigns to save men, notwithstanding their unworthiness and their ingratitude. Render thanks to the Word incarnate. Address yourself to Mary, and beg of her to obtain for you the grace of a tender love and faithful imitation of her divine Son.

Anima Christi.   Pater   Ave.

SECOND EXERCISE ON THE INCARNATION.

CONTEMPLATION.

Preparatory Prayer

First prelude. Recall the mystery,—" The angel Gabriel," &c., as in the first Meditation.

Second and third preludes also as before.

1. Contemplate the persons.

(1.) Men spread over all the universe, almost all

opposed in manners, characters, passions, interests, and yet almost all agreeing on one point; that is, in forgetting their last end, in offending God, in serving the devil, in dying as sinners and reprobates, and precipitating themselves for ever into hell.

(2.) The holy Trinity, which suffices to itself, which finds its happiness in its own perfections, without having need of creatures, and which, instead of overwhelming criminal men with its justice, casts upon them looks of pity and mercy.

(3.) The blessed Virgin Mary, retired in the humble house at Nazareth, and absorbed in prayer.

(4.) The angel Gabriel descending from heaven and saluting Mary, as Mother of God, full of grace, blessed among women.

Practical reflections and affections

2. Listen to the words.

(1.) On earth and among men words of hatred, of scandal, imprecations, blasphemies.

(2.) In heaven, words of clemency and charity ;— the august Trinity, which decrees the incarnation of the Word; the Word, who offers Himself to the Father for His glory and the salvation of man.

(3.) At Nazareth, the words of the angel Gabriel to Mary : "Hail, Mary, full of grace; the Lord is with thee; blessed art thou amongst women. The Holy Ghost shall come upon thee, and the power of the Most High shall overshadow thee. And therefore the Holy which shall be born of thee shall be called the Son of God" (Luke i. 28, 35). The answer of Mary, who humbly submits to the will of the Lord : " Behold the handmaid of the Lord, be it done to me according to thy word" (Luke i. 38).

Practical reflections and affections.

3. Consider the actions.

(1.) On earth. The diverse crimes of men;—the sacrilegious worship paid to idols and demons; the disorders of their plays, feasts, pleasures; their endeavours to supplant and even to destroy each other.

(2.) In heaven. The charity of the three Divine Persons towards man; with what love the Father gives us His own Son; the Word consents to become incarnate; the Holy Ghost forms the union of the Divine and the human nature.

(3.) At Nazareth. The respect of the angel in the presence of the Blessed Virgin; the trouble of Mary on hearing the words of Gabriel; her love for virginity, which she prefers to the honour of the Divine maternity; her humility and obedience to the will of Heaven.

Practical reflections and affections.

COLLOQUY WITH THE THREE PERSONS OF THE ADORABLE TRINITY.

Adore the infinite charity of God, who deigns to save men, notwithstanding their unworthiness and ingratitude. Render thanks to the Word incarnate. Address yourself to Mary, and beg of her to obtain for you the grace of a tender love and faithful imitation of her Son.

Anima Christi. Pater. Ave.

ON THE BIRTH OF JESUS CHRIST.

MEDITATION.

Preparatory Prayer.

First prelude. " It came to pass that in those days there went out a decree from Cæsar Augustus that the whole world should be enrolled. And all went to be enrolled, every one into his own city. And Joseph also went up from Galilee out of the city of Nazareth into Judea, to the city of David, which is called Bethlehem, to be enrolled with Mary his spouse. And she brought forth her first-born son, and wrapped him in swaddling-clothes, and laid him in a manger; because there was no room for them in the inn" (Luke ii. 1-7).

Second prelude. Represent to yourself the road from Nazareth to Bethlehem,—its length, its windings, its roughnesses. Then this cave where the Saviour was born, representing it according to your imagination, as wide or narrow, on a level with the road or in a hollow, as commodious or incommodious, &c.

Third prelude. The same as in the preceding meditation.

Since the fall of our nature by sin, a triple disorder keeps the heart of man away from his final end,—*pride, love of riches, attachment to the pleasures of sense.* The birth of Jesus Christ opposes to these disorders His *humility,* His *poverty,* His *sufferings.*

FIRST POINT.

The humility of Jesus Christ in His birth.

1. He humbles Himself, even to acknowledging Himself the subject of an idolatrous prince. To obey the edict of Augustus,—an edict dictated by pride,—He wills that His holy Mother should take Him to a strange country, where at His birth He should be in poverty and want.

2. He is the Messiah promised to the world; foretold by the prophets many ages before; expected by the people; whose coming the earth has sighed after, and to Whom it has cried, " Oh, that Thou wouldst rend the heavens and come down !" (Is. lxiv. 1.) And at His coming He would remain unknown ; He allows His people to treat Him as a stranger, and that His own should deny Him like a mendicant who begs for public charity : "He came unto His own, and His own received Him not" (John i. 11).

3. He intentionally hides the greatness of His birth; He who is of the royal race and of the blood of David wills to be born as the son of a poor artisan ; nay, He wills to be born as even the children of the poor are not born,—in a stable, in a manger, in the society of vile animals.

4. Not only does He hide His divinity under the guise of humanity, but He debases His humanity itself to the infirmities and weaknesses of infancy. What a humiliation ! This God-Man become like little children ; like them, deprived of the use of speech, of the liberty of movement; dependent in every thing on the will of those around Him !

Let us look in upon ourselves. How opposed are the maxims of the world, and the maxims of our corrupt nature, to the example of Jesus Christ! Let us beg of the Divine Infant to change our hearts by His grace; let us ask of Him that we may understand and love the way of humility.

SECOND POINT.

The poverty of the birth of Jesus Christ.

1. He is born in a strange country, out of His mother's house, where He would have found what is never wanting even to the most neglected of poor children, a roof to shelter Him and a cradle to rest in.

2. He is born in the most miserable place in the little city of Bethlehem. Whilst the poorest around Him have an asylum, He is banished to a wretched building, open to the wind and rain.

3. His cradle is a little straw in a manger, so that His birth resembles that of the lowest animals. He is reduced to such misery that He can say with truth even now, "The foxes have holes, and the birds of the air nests; but the Son of Man hath not where to lay His head" (Luke ix. 58).

4. Every thing around Him participates in His poverty;—His parents, who scarcely possess a few coarse garments to clothe Him with; the poor shepherds, who at the voice of the angels leave their flocks to come and adore Him.

Consider that this wretchedness of the Son of God was not necessary and compulsory, like the poor in the world; it is free and of His own choice. Conceive a high idea of this poverty, which appeared so precious to our Lord, that to espouse it He quitted heaven and His glory. Above all, understand the necessity of detachment, and be persuaded that disengagement from creatures is the only true way which leads to God.

THIRD POINT.

The sufferings of Jesus Christ from His birth.

Consider that the sufferings of Jesus commenced with His life; that they begin in His cradle, never more to leave Him but with His last sigh on the cross.

1. He suffers in His sacred body; for He is born in the depth of winter; at the hour when the cold is the most piercing; in a place where He is exposed, thinly clothed, to all the inclemency of the weather.

2. He suffers above all in His soul, which has the full exercise of its faculties. He suffers from the rebuffs He experiences in His tribe, and even in His own family, where none know Him. He suffers yet more for the troubles of Mary and Joseph, whom He sees repulsed with contempt from all the houses in Bethlehem, and inconsolable not to find any other asylum for Him but a stable.

3. He suffers, with the intention of suffering during His whole life, toil, hunger, thirst, perpetual poverty, the most profound humiliations, the scourges, and the cross; and *all this for me.* Let me, then, seek to penetrate the motives which induce Him to suffer so much for love of me, and seek it for my instruction, and above all, for my edification.

COLLOQUIES WITH JESUS, MARY, AND JOSEPH.

Adore Jesus Christ in His cradle; beg Him to be

born in our hearts; ask Him to come to us with the virtues He teaches us in the manger,—with humility, detachment, spirit of sacrifice. Beg the powerful intercession of Mary and Joseph to support our prayer.

Anima Christi. Pater. Ave.

ON THE BIRTH OF JESUS CHRIST.

CONTEMPLATION.

Preparatory Prayer.

First prelude. The same as in the preceding meditation.

Second prelude. Represent to yourself a ruinous stable, and at the end of it a manger, where Mary and Joseph are adoring the Son of God, who is lying in it between two animals.

Third prelude. Ask a grace conformable to the present mystery, and to your spiritual wants; for example, humility or detachment.

FIRST POINT.

Contemplate the persons.

The Holy Virgin, St. Joseph, Jesus Christ our Lord, who is just born, the angels who surround the manger, the shepherds who have hastened to the crib of the newborn Child. Represent to yourself the Divine beauty of the Saviour; the modesty, meekness, and humility imprinted on the features of Mary; the simplicity and recollection of Joseph; the rapture of the angels; the joy of the shepherds. Imagine that you are beside the

L

manger with Mary and Joseph, to contemplate Him, to
serve Him. Consider what spiritual fruit you ought
to draw from this sight; and to this end ask yourself.
Who is this that is just born? Why did He choose for
Himself, and for all that were dearest to Him in the
world,—that is, Mary and Joseph,—humiliation, poverty, pain? What is that treasure of graces which
God has hidden in detachment from all things? &c.

SECOND POINT.
Listen to the words.

1. The conversations of Joseph and Mary during
the journey from Nazareth to Bethlehem;—how they
beg an asylum at the inns, and in what terms they are
refused; what they say to each other at the sight of
the stable where they are obliged to take shelter; their
effusion of heart beside the crib where Jesus reposes.

2. The words of the angels. One of them says to
the shepherds, "I bring you tidings of great joy that
shall be to all people; for this day is born to you a
Saviour in the city of David." And the others sing
in concert, "Glory to God in the highest; and on earth
peace to men of good will" (Luke ii. 10-14).

3. The conversation of the shepherds among themselves: "Let us go over to Bethlehem, and let us see
this word that is come to pass" (ib. v. 15); their ex-
pressions of faith and admiration at the sight of Jesus
Christ; their conversation with Mary and Joseph.

THIRD POINT.
Consider the actions.

1. In Joseph and Mary:—The fatigue of the journey; the contempt and the rebuffs they suffer at Beth-

lehem, their solicitude and trouble to find an asylum; their cares to provide a more convenient and worthy cradle for the Divine Child: and in all this the admirable virtues which they practise;—their patience, their interior peace, their union with God, their lively faith, and their ardent love towards the Saviour.

2. In the shepherds:—The contrast of their docility with the hardness of the inhabitants of Bethlehem; their adoration, and their homage to the new-born Child.

3. Above all, in Jesus Christ:—The extreme deprivation in which He chooses to be born; in which henceforth we shall see Him live and die. If we again ask ourselves, why these deprivations of the Son of God?—ah! it is for us; for our instruction, and for our salvation.

Colloquies with Jesus, Mary, and Joseph, as in last meditation.

ON THE SAME MYSTERY—APPLICATION OF THE SENSES.

PRELIMINARY REMARKS.*

1. By the imagination, the soul can render an object present, and as it were see it, hear it, taste it, &c. So that to apply this faculty of the soul and the five senses to a truth of religion (according as it is suscep-

* These remarks or explanations are given here because they are so placed by St. Ignatius, and because, though the application of the senses is employed from time to time during the first week, it becomes of daily use in the second.

tible of it), or to a mystery of our Lord Jesus Christ, is what is called *application of the senses.*

2. The application of the senses differs from meditation in this : that in the one the intelligence proceeds by reasoning, discoursing on the attributes of God, and the causes and effects of mysteries; while in the other, it is confined solely to sensible objects—to what can be seen, heard, touched, &c. It is not that the application of the senses, in order to be useful, does not require some reasoning and reflections, but they should be short, simple, and rapid.

3. This exercise generally contains five points; or four only, when the senses of smell and taste are joined together. The following is the method:

First point. Represent to yourself the different persons, together with all their circumstances, and endeavour to draw some spiritual fruit from each.

Second point. Listen to their words, or to what it may be supposed they say.

Third point. Taste interiorly the sweetness, or bitterness, or any other sentiment, of the person you are considering.

Fourth point. Respire, as it were, the perfume of the virtues, or the infection of the vices, the sulphur of hell, the corruption of dead bodies, &c.

Fifth point. Touch interiorly the objects; for example, the eternal flames, the vestments of our Saviour; kiss His footsteps, the manger, &c.

After two meditations or contemplations, it is usual to repeat the two together twice, and then to follow with the application of the senses on the same truths or mysteries

APPLICATION OF THE SENSES ON THE BIRTH OF
JESUS CHRIST.

The *preparatory prayer* and the three *preludes* as in the preceding meditation.

1. *Sight.* Contemplate the stable which is falling in ruins; the manger where Jesus Christ reposes on a little straw; the coarse swaddling clothes in which He is wrapped; the animals which warm Him with their breath; the Divine Infant Himself, who fixes His eyes on us, and extends His arms to us; Mary and Joseph praying before the manger; the shepherds coming to adore the new-born Child whom the angel has announced to them; all heaven attentive to the great event which is being accomplished at Bethlehem; and, at the same time, the profound indifference of the rest of men to the coming of the Son of God. Practical reflections and affections.

2. *Hearing.* Listen to the discourse of the strangers going to Bethlehem; to the conversations of Mary and Joseph during the journey; to the words of the inhabitants of Bethlehem, who repulse them; to Jesus Christ, who speaks to His heavenly Father, who speaks to us by His cries and His tears; to the angels singing in the heavens, "Glory to God in the highest, and on earth peace;" to the shepherds making inquiries from the holy family about the birth of Jesus. Practical reflections and affections.

3. *Taste.* Taste interiorly the bitterness of the hearts of Mary and Joseph; the peace of their souls; their joy at the sight of the new-born God. Unite yourself in spirit to the abasement, the tears, the poverty,

the prayer, all the virtues of our Saviour in His birth. Practical reflections and affections.

4. *Touch.* Kiss respectfully the walls of the stable, the straw in the manger, the swaddling clothes, the sacred hands and feet of Jesus Christ. Practical reflections and affections.

Colloquies as in the preceding contemplation.

Anima Christi. Pater. Ave.

THE HIDDEN LIFE OF JESUS AT NAZARETH.

MEDITATION.

Preparatory Prayer.

First prelude. Jesus having been found in the Temple by Mary and Joseph, left Jerusalem and returned with them to Nazareth, and was subject to them; and He advanced in wisdom and grace with God and man (Luke ii. 51, 52).

Second prelude. Represent to yourself the humble house at Nazareth, the workshop of St. Joseph, &c.

Third prelude. Ask of God a grace conformable to the present mystery and to your wants; for example, the love of a retired life, of retreat, of labour, of prayer, of obedience, &c.

The Gospel only teaches us three things regarding the life of Jesus at Nazareth:—1. That He obeyed: " He was subject to them" (Luke ii. 52). 2. That He worked with His hands, and at the work of an artisan: " Is not this the son of the carpenter" (Mark vi. 3). 3. That " He grew in wisdom, in age, and in grace before God and. before men" (Luke ii. 52).

FIRST POINT.

At Nazareth Jesus obeyed.

Consider the obedience of Jesus Christ in all its circumstances.

1. *Who is He that obeys?* It is He who is reason by essence; He whose will is sovereignly wise and independent; it is the WORD OF GOD.

2. *Whom does He obey?* His creatures. He obeys Joseph and Mary, whom He infinitely surpasses in lights and in sanctity; who derive, and can only derive, light and holiness from Him. He obeys even strangers, who command Him like a mercenary; that is to say, He submits His will, the most noble and most upright that ever was, to wills full of weakness, of ignorance, of caprice—wills only made to obey Him.

3. *In what does He obey?* In every thing that was commanded Him; consequently in the most trifling things, even in the meanest things;—for example, in all the details of care required by a poor household, and the station of a mechanic who earns his bread by the sweat of his brow.

4. *How long does He obey?* For thirty years, that is, not only during His childhood, when obedience is both a necessity and a duty for man, but also in the strength of age, when, according to the ordinary laws of nature and society, every man is arrived at the time when he has a right to govern himself.

5. *How did He obey?* In the most perfect way that can be conceived. By obedience of action, which executes promptly and to the letter; obedience of mind, which does not reason on the motives of the order or

its nature; obedience of heart, which submits with love to the orders of man as to the orders of the Divine will.

Let us examine ourselves, our thoughts, our feelings, our conduct, with regard to obedience. Let us beg our Lord to teach us by His example the value, the necessity, the practice of this virtue.

SECOND POINT.
At Nazareth Jesus worked.

Represent to yourself what passes in a poor family. A mechanic engaged in manual labour; his wife occupied in the lowest domestic offices; a child sharing the toils of both, first assisting his mother, and then, as his strength increases with his age, helping his father in the labours of his trade;—this is a faithful image of what took place at Nazareth.

Consider attentively—

1. *The dignity of Him who thus labours.* How is the condition of a workman regarded by the world? What pity is inspired by the misfortune of a man who is obliged, by reverse of fortune, to descend to this condition? From this conclude how little suitable such a condition is to Jesus Christ; to the descendant of David; the Messiah who might labour in public with such success in the promulgation of the Gospel; to a God.

2. *The painful and humiliating circumstances of this work.* It is the work of a carpenter, working in wood; using rough tools; his time and toil hired out to any master who will pay him; recommencing each day the same fatigues, scarcely interrupted by hasty

meals and a short sleep; living unknown and despised, like those poor artisans, whose fate is never pitied, who often think themselves fortunate in meeting with persons to hire their services. Such is the position of Jesus Christ;—thus is accomplished what the prophet said of Him: "I am poor and in labours from my youth" (Ps. lxxxvii. 16).

3. *In what manner Jesus Christ works.* Enter into the heart of Jesus Christ. Prayer is constantly united in it to the work of the hands. In the midst of bodily fatigues, Jesus blesses the justice of His Father, that has condemned man to water the earth which gives him bread with the sweat of his brow (Gen. iii. 19). When He receives orders, He adores in creatures the supreme dominion of His Father; when He receives payment, He returns thanks to His providence, which gives subsistence to all men; when He suffers disdain and rebuffs, He accepts them as a reparation to His glory outraged by sin.

4. *The motive of the labour of Jesus Christ.* Among so many different professions, why did Jesus Christ choose one so laborious and so low? It is to teach men that since original sin they have two great disorders to combat,—pride and luxury,—and that the only way to arrive at their final end is by the path of humiliation and suffering.

5. *The merit of the labour of Jesus Christ;* a merit so excellent that it fixes the looks and complaisance of His celestial Father. At the same time that Jesus Christ hides Himself at Nazareth, there are in the world famous politicians, celebrated orators and poets, captains of high renown; but the eyes of the Lord are

turned from all these men, and rest on Nazareth, a city so despised, and of which it was said, "Can any thing good come from Nazareth?" (John i. 46.) They are fixed on the Son of the carpenter; Him alone the celestial Father points out to His angels, saying, "Behold My beloved Son"—how He obeys, how He humbles Himself, how He annihilates Himself, for My glory and My love.

THIRD POINT.

At Nazareth Jesus Christ grew in grace and wisdom before God and before men.

Jesus Christ could not grow interiorly in virtue, since from the first moment of His conception the plenitude of grace dwelt in Him, and therefore the words of the Gospel signify that each day He produced new acts and allowed new marks of holiness to appear.

Represent our Saviour to yourself in spirit as if you contemplated Him with your eyes; follow Him in all the details of this life, so simple and so common; study all the virtues that were developed in Him with age —

1. *Humility,* which makes Him prefer to the labours of an apostolic life obscurity, retreat, a hidden life in the workshop of a mechanic.

2. *Detachment,* which makes Him support with joy the most painful privations in His dwelling, His dress, His food; in a word, all the wants of the poor.

3. *Charity,* which fills His heart with an immense compassion for the miseries of men; above all, with a burning zeal for their salvation.

4. *Modesty,* which regulates admirably His looks, His words, all His movements, all His steps.

5. *Recollection*, which, in the midst of conversation, work, or recreation, always keeps His holy soul elevated and united to the Divinity.

6. *Perfection in the commonest actions;* so that it is written of Him "that He did all things well" (Mark vii. 37). Recall to yourself that holiness of life depends on the sanctity of ordinary actions; consequently, that it is by the perfection or imperfection of the actions of common life that we approach our end or go farther from it. Take, then, Jesus Christ for your model, and learn from the example of His private life to do all things well.

COLLOQUY.

Let us adore Jesus Christ as our master and model; humble ourselves for having followed His example so little; beg of Him, through the intercession of Joseph and Mary, to give us the intelligence to understand and the strength to practise what He teaches us.

Anima Christi. Pater. Ave.

HIDDEN LIFE OF JESUS AT NAZARETH.

CONTEMPLATION.

Preparatory Prayer.

Preludes, same as in the meditation, p. 150.

FIRST POINT.

Contemplate the persons.

(1) In this world, men, thinking only of advancing themselves :—the learned, the rich, the great, — all

)ccupied with thoughts of fortune, elevation, celebrity; the poor, who envy them, who cannot resign themselves to indigence and degradation. (2) At Nazareth, Mary in silence and prayer, attending to the cares of a poor household; Joseph working with his hands in an obscure workshop; Jesus associating Himself with the troubles and labours of His parents; the grace spread over all His sacred person—"Grace is poured abroad in Thy lips" (Ps. xliv. 3); the modesty of His countenance and demeanour; the recollection which keeps His mind and heart constantly united to His Father. (3) Finally, in heaven, the angels, who look on this scene with admiration; and the celestial Father, whose looks dwell with complacency on His beloved Son.

SECOND POINT.
Listen to the words.

They are few. Charity or necessity alone interrupt occasionally the silence of this family, whose conversation is in heaven. They are always regulated by humility, by meekness, by zeal, in a word, by the Spirit of God. They are always holy and perfect. St. Joseph speaks little; Mary still less; the Infant God scarcely ever. In the holy house at Nazareth they converse little with men, but they converse constantly with the heavenly Father. Recollect yourself profoundly, and listen to these holy conversations, which ravish the angels.

THIRD POINT.
Consider the actions.

The painful toil to which the Son of God voluntarily submits;—how He assists Mary in her domestic cares;

how He shares with Joseph the rude and humble trade of a carpenter; with what simplicity and zeal He obeys the least wish of His parents; with what patience He bears the fatigues of His condition; with what humility He resigns Himself to the caprices, the repulses, the disdain of strangers, who command Him as a hireling; His charity in His relations with His neighbour; His fervour in prayer; His divine perfections in the smallest actions, &c.

COLLOQUY WITH THE THREE PERSONS OF THE HOLY
FAMILY.

Adore Jesus Christ in the humble exercise of His hidden virtues, and beg of Him to fill us with His Spirit. Ask, through the intercession of Joseph and Mary, the grace to imitate after them the examples of the Divine Saviour.

Anima Christi. Pater. Ave.

HIDDEN LIFE OF JESUS AT NAZARETH.

APPLICATION OF THE SENSES.

Preparatory Prayer.

Preludes, as in the preceding contemplation.

1. *Sight.* Consider St. Joseph, the holy Virgin, our Lord Jesus Christ, at their work, their repasts, their prayers, their intercourse with their neighbours; the angels, who look with love on this holy house; the heavenly Father, who takes delight in His Son; &c.

2. *Hearing.* Listen to the words of Jesus, of Mary, of Joseph; their silence, their recollection; their

conversations, regulated by meekness, humility, modesty, &c.

3. *Taste.* Taste the peace which fills their souls, their interior joy, their bitterness, &c.

4. *Smell.* Respire the sweetness, and, as it were, the perfume of their virtues,—obedience, charity, fervour, care in little things, love of a hidden life, &c.

5. *Touch.* Kiss inwardly the walls, witnesses of the virtues of Jesus Christ; the rude tools of His trade; the earth sanctified by His steps and His labours.

Colloquy as in the preceding contemplation.

Anima Christi. Pater. Ave.

THE PUBLIC LIFE OF JESUS CHRIST.

Preparatory Prayer.

First prelude. Represent to yourself our Lord Jesus Christ showing Himself to you as the apostles and inhabitants of Judea saw Him, and saying to you, "Look, and make it according to the pattern" (Exod. xxv. 40).

Second prelude. Ask the grace faithfully to imitate your divine Model.

Third prelude. Consider our Lord as the most perfect model man can propose to himself, in regard to God, to himself, and to his neighbour.

FIRST POINT.

Conduct of Jesus Christ in regard to His Father.

To pray to God, to obey the will of God, to labour

for the glory of God, are the principal obligations of man towards his Creator.

Consider how Jesus Christ accomplished these obligations in His public life.

1. *Jesus Christ obeying.* He is not subject to the law, since He is the first author of it, and comes to substitute another of a more perfect kind; yet, as He sees in it an expression of the Divine will, He observes all its rules with religious exactness. Recall what the Gospel tells us of His fidelity in coming to pray in the Temple, in sanctifying the Sabbath-day, in celebrating the Passover. He carries His respect for the law so far as to honour its ministers even in the Scribes and Pharisees: "The Scribes and the Pharisees have sitten on the chair of Moses. All things, therefore, whatsoever they shall say to you observe and do" (Matt. xxiii. 2, 3).

2. *Jesus Christ labouring for the glory of God.* The three years of His public life were devoted to the preaching of the Gospel. Admire with what zeal He seizes all occasions to speak to men of salvation, and the obligation of serving God. Represent to yourself this God-apostle in the midst of His disciples, and surrounded by an innumerable crowd.

With what force and with sweetness combined does He reprove sinners! With what patience He repeats the same truths under different forms to their simple and coarse minds, which can scarcely understand them! With what abnegation of Himself and His own glory, at the price of what toils and perils, does He announce the word of His heavenly Father!

3. *Jesus Christ praying.* Although He has only three years to give to His preaching, He retrenches

whole days of even this short space to devote them exclusively to prayer: "He went up into a mountain
alone to pray" (Matt. xiv. 23); "He went into a
desert place, and there He prayed" (Mark i. 35). After
the fatigues of the day, instead of giving Himself up
to the necessary sleep, He retires to a distance from His
apostles on the mountains, or to some desert place, to
pray in the silence of night. Meditate on all the circumstances of this divine prayer. It is a prayer made in
solitude; a prayer accompanied by outward signs of
the most profound respect,—He prays kneeling, or with
His face bowed to the ground; it is a prayer consist-
ing of the purest and most heroic sentiments of charity,
—He offers Himself as a victim ready to immolate
Himself to repair His Father's glory and to save men.

Look in upon yourself. Do you pray? Do you
fulfil the precepts of your religion? Do you labour for
the glory of God?

Learn from the example of Jesus Christ to fulfil
your duties towards God in a Christian manner.

SECOND POINT.

Conduct of Jesus Christ in regard to Himself.

Consider our Lord—

1. *In the use of His creatures.* Admire His *humility,*
—how He hides His knowledge and His virtues; how
He forbids those He has cured to publish His miracles;
how He steals away from the enthusiasm of the people
who wish to proclaim Him king. His *poverty;*—His
want is so great that often He has not even a little bread
to support His strength, and only a stone whereon to rest

His head, and—oh, most admirable!—He who lavishes miracles when required for the necessities of His neighbour, refuses them for Himself. His *continual mortifications;*—He renounces, He crucifies Himself in all things; His life is a course of fatigues, of fasts, of watchings: "The whole life of Christ was but one cross and one continual martyrdom" (*Imit. of Christ*, i. 2-12).

2. *With regard to the exterior.* Contemplate the simplicity of His garments; the gravity of His deportment; the modesty which regulates His bearing; the reserve of His words and looks; the serenity and sweetness of His looks, which draw all men to Him;—in a word, recognise in Him what the prophets had announced: "Behold My servant, My elect; My soul delighteth in Him. I have given My spirit upon Him. He shall not cry, neither shall His voice be heard in the streets. He shall not be sad nor troublesome" (Is. xlii. 1, 2, 4).

3. *With regard to the interior.* Penetrate into the sacred soul of Jesus Christ: study His admirable virtues; His purity of intention, which refers all to His Father; His charity, which leaves but two affections in His heart,—zeal for the glory of God, and zeal for the salvation of men; His detachment in success, when the people, in raptures at hearing Him, cried out, "Never did man speak like this man" (John vii. 46); His resignation and profound peace when His enemies wished to stone Him; His interior calm when He turned the sellers out of the Temple, or when He confounded the Pharisees.

Practical reflections and affections.

M

THIRD POINT.

Conduct of Jesus Christ towards His neighbour.

Consider—

1. *The reserve of Jesus Christ in His intercourse with His neighbour.* His conversations were few and short; He feared, as it were, to be in the midst of men. And yet what had He to dread from communication with them? and, on the contrary, what graces might not men draw from Him who had the words of eternal life? Yet Jesus Christ avoids mingling with them as much as His ministry permits, and prefers silence, prayer, and solitude.

2. *The charity of Jesus Christ towards His neighbour.* He bears with divine meekness the hatred and persecutions of the Pharisees, the rudeness of His disciples, the unworthy treatment of His neighbours, who wish to bind Him as a fool and a madman. He receives with kindness, even with a sort of predilection, the ignorant and the common people: "His communication is with the simple" (Prov. iii. 32); with the poor: "The poor have the Gospel preached to them" (Matt. xi. 5); with little children : "Suffer the little children, and forbid them not to come to Me; for of such is the kingdom of heaven" (Matt. xix. 14); with sinners: witness Zacheus, the Samaritan, the adulteress, Magdalen. He could not refuse miracles when they brought to Him one possessed, a paralytic, &c.; thus it is written of Him that He " went about doing good" (Acts x. 38).

3. *The end Jesus Christ proposed to Himself in His intercourse with His neighbour.* His sole end was

to instruct, to convert, to save men : thus He was never
known to speak of vain or curious things; He only
spoke of the kingdom of God—"Speaking of the kingdom of God" (Acts i. 3) ; of the value of the soul—
"What will it profit a man if he gain the whole world
and lose his own soul" (Matt. xvi. 28) ; of the obligation of loving God—"Thou shalt love the Lord thy
God" (Matt. xxii. 37) ; of the necessity of renouncing
and conquering ourselves—"If any man will come after
Me, let him deny himself" (Matt. xvi. 24) ; of the happiness of sufferings and poverty—"Blessed are the
poor in spirit" (Matt. v. 3).

Practical reflections and affections.

Colloquy with our Lord, to beg of Him the grace of
a faithful imitation of His virtues.

Anima Christi. Pater. Ave.

"Paint to yourself in your heart the conduct and the
whole life of Jesus Christ. What humility He displayed
among men; what benignity towards His disciples;
what commiseration towards the poor, to whom He
made Himself like in all things, and who appeared to
be the most cherished portion of His family. How He
contemned not nor spurned one; how He flattered not
the rich ; how free He was from the solicitudes of this
life, and the fears that men entertain for temporal necessities. What patience He showed under insult; what
mildness in His answers. How He sought not to vin-
dicate Himself by bitter or sharp words, but to triumph
over malice by gentle and humble replies ; how willing
to suffer labour and poverty, and how compassionate
towards the afflicted ; how He condescended to the

imperfections of the weak; how He avoided all scandal; how He disdained not sinners, but received the penitent with infinite clemency; how calm in all His words, in all His gestures; how solicitous for the salvation of souls, for love of whom He deigned to become incarnate and to die; how fervent in prayer; how prompt in the service of others, as He says Himself: 'I am in the midst of you as he that serveth' (Luke xxii. 27).

"In all your actions, then, in all your words,—whether you walk or eat, whether you speak or keep silence, whether alone or in company,—lift your eyes to Him as your model. By this you will inflame your love; you will increase your confidence in Him, you will enter into a holy familiarity with Him, and you will become perfect in every kind of virtue. Let this be your wisdom, your study, your prayer, always to have something about Him in your mind, in order that you may be stirred up to a greater love and imitation of Him. For the more we conform ourselves to Him in the imitation of His virtues, the nearer we shall approach and be like to Him in His celestial beauty and glory." (St. Bonav.)

Note.

It is more especially from this time that the person in retreat must occupy himself seriously with the choice of a state of life, or a reformation to be made in his state of life, if already fixed.

INTRODUCTION TO THE MEDITATION ON THE TWO STANDARDS;

OR, PRELUDE TO THE CONSIDERATIONS TO BE MADE ON THE PARTICULAR STATE OF LIFE TO WHICH WE MAY BE CALLED.

Our Lord, subject to His parents at Nazareth, presents to us the model of that first state of life which consists in observing the commandments, and which is called *common life.*

But from the time that Jesus Christ, at the age of twelve years, leaves His foster-father and her who, according to nature, was His mother, and goes to the Temple to attend to His Heavenly Father's service, as He was to do during the three years of His public life, He appears to give us the idea and the example of a second state, which is that of *evangelical perfection.*

It is therefore proper here, while we are contemplating the life of Christ, to examine and earnestly beg the grace to know the kind and state of life in which it would most please His Divine Majesty that we should serve Him and promote His glory. We shall be guided in this search by the following exercise, which places in parallel and contrast the thoughts and views of Jesus Christ and those of His mortal enemy. We shall thus learn what ought to be our dispositions, in order that we may arrive at perfection in that state, whatever it may be, which the Divine goodness may counsel us to choose.

THE TWO STANDARDS.

Note. This exercise is a sort of *parable*, in which St. Ignatius represents our Lord and Lucifer as two captains armed one against the other, and calling all men to their standards. The object of it is to place before our eyes the right of Jesus Christ to our service, and to engage us to serve under His banner for ever.

Preparatory Prayer.

First prelude. Consider, on one side our Saviour, on the other Lucifer, who both invite men to follow their standard.

Second prelude. Construction of place. Represent to yourself two vast plains; in one, near to Babylon, Lucifer assembles round him all sinners; in the other, near to Jerusalem, our Lord is surrounded by all the just.

Third prelude. Ask the grace to discover and avoid the snares of Lucifer, and to know and imitate the virtues of Jesus Christ.

FIRST POINT.

The standard of Lucifer.

1. Represent to yourself the prince of the reprobate in the vast plains of Babylon, on a throne of fire surrounded by thick smoke, spreading terror around him by the hideous deformity of his features and by his terrible looks. Meditate on the hidden meaning of these figures. These vast plains designate the broad path where sinners walk. Babylon, the city of confusion, signifies the disorder of a guilty conscience. The throne of fire is the symbol of the pride and the passions which

devour the soul like a fire. The thick smoke is the
image of the blindness of the sinner and of the vanity
of his pleasures. The hideous features and terrible
look of Lucifer express the deformity of sin and the
operations of the evil spirit in the soul; that is to say,
its trouble, its agitation, its depression, its sorrows.

2. Consider the innumerable crowd of followers and
ministers around Lucifer. Here are found united the
sinners of all ages;—the spirits who first, even in heaven, raised the standard of revolt against God, degraded
beings, with whom evil is become as a nature; all the
men who have made themselves the slaves of their passions and sins,—the proud, the impure, robbers, homi-
cides, all the wicked men who at different times have
startled the world by their crimes, and of whom there
is not a single one who is not, in some way, an object
of aversion and disgust. But why does Lucifer convoke these under his standard? For the most perfidious
and cruel design that can be imagined; he wishes to
seduce the whole human race, and after having seduced
it, to drag it down to eternal misery.

3. Listen, in spirit, to Lucifer addressing his ministers, and ordering them to lay snares on all sides for
men, in order to their perdition: "Come with us, let
us lie in wait for blood, let us hide snares for the innocent without cause. Let us swallow him up alive like
hell. We shall find all precious substances; we shall
fill our houses with spoils" (Prov. i. 11-13). Remark
his artifices, and the three ordinary degrees of temptation;—how, first, he catches souls by the love of riches;
next, how he throws them into the paths of ambition;
then, from ambition to pride—a bottomless abyss, from

whence all vices rise as from their fountain. See with what patience and active zeal the ministers of Lucifer execute the task imposed on them by their master, how they make every thing conduce to the one end,—the ruin of souls; defects of the understanding, inclinations of the heart, the character, the habits, the passions, the faults, the virtues even, and graces of God. Finally, contemplate the success of hell in its enterprise;—how many fools are taken in these snares every day; how many blindly throw themselves in; how many who, not content to allow themselves to be seduced, seek also to seduce their brethren. Look on yourself. Be astonished at having given way so often and so easily to the temptations of the enemy; weep over your folly and your past weakness, and resolve to be wiser and more courageous for the future.

SECOND POINT.
The standard of Jesus Christ.

1. Represent to yourself a beautiful plain near Jerusalem, and there, not on a throne, but mingling with His subjects, our Lord, attracting all hearts by the beauty and irresistible charm of His looks. Meditate on the hidden meaning of these figures. This plain signifies the way of the just, rough in appearance, but in reality pleasant and happy. Jerusalem, the city of saints, the vision of peace, is the symbol of a pure conscience. Our Lord is represented without a throne and mixing among His subjects, to express the lowness and self-humiliation of His mortal life. He shows Himself as the most beautiful of the children of men—" Thou art beautiful above the sons of men" (Psalm xliv. 3);

and with all the marks described by the prophets:
"He shall not be sad, nor troublesome" (Isaias xlii. 4);
"His conversation hath no bitterness, nor His company
any tediousness, but joy and gladness" (Wis. viii. 16);
"The bruised reed He shall not break, and the smoking
flax He shall not quench" (Isaias xlii. 3). It is the
image of beauty, of virtue, and the operations of the
good Spirit in souls, that is, of joy, of calm, of consolation, &c.

2. Consider, around our Saviour, His disciples and
apostles. Where shall we find a more august assembly? There are united the just and the saints of all
ages,—patriarchs, prophets, apostles, martyrs, penitents,
virgins, doctors, holy pontiffs; none of the vices or
weaknesses that dishonour humanity; on the contrary,
all virtues, and these carried even to heroism. But
for what purpose does Jesus Christ convoke His disciples under His standard? For the most just, the most
noble, the most generous purpose that can be,—to recall
men to virtue, and through virtue to happiness in time
and eternity.

3. Listen, in spirit, to our Saviour addressing His
disciples, and commanding them to go into the world
to save men: "For the Son of Man is come to seek
and to save that which was lost" (Luke xix. 10); "I
am come that they may have life, and may have it
more abundantly" (John x. 10); "I am come to cast
fire on the earth, and what will I but that it be kin-
dled?" (Luke xii. 49); "Go ye into the whole world,
and preach the Gospel to every creature" (Mark xvi.
15); "Teaching them to observe all things whatsoever
I have commanded you" (Matt. xxviii. 20). Observe

by what degrees, exactly opposed to the temptations of
Lucifer, Jesus Christ leads souls to perfection. He
wishes His apostles first to inspire them with indifference to riches, and then the desire of abjection, from
whence arises humility as from its source, and with it
every other virtue. See with what ardour, what constancy, the apostles accomplish the mission intrusted
to them by the Son of God. Represent to yourself all
the labours and sacrifices that their ministry entails:
" In all things let us exhibit ourselves as the ministers
of God, in much patience, in tribulation, in necessities,
in distresses. In stripes, in prison, in seditions, in labours, in watchings, in fastings. In chastity, in knowledge, in long-suffering, in sweetness, in the Holy
Ghost, in charity unfeigned. In the word of truth, in
the power of God, by the armour of justice on the right
hand and on the left" (2 Cor. vi. 4-7). Finally, contemplate the success of the enterprise;—how many sinners snatched from hell; how many disciples won to
evangelical poverty and humility; how many apostles
trained and prepared for the saving of souls and the
glory of God. Examine yourself, and make practical
reflections.

THIRD POINT.
Election between the two standards.

Consider that we are all placed between Jesus Christ
and Lucifer, and that it is equally impossible either to
serve both at once—" No one can serve two masters"
(Matt. vi. 24)—or to remain neutral without serving
one or other, for Jesus Christ says, " He who is not
with Me is against Me" (Luke xi. 23). It is, then, ne-

cessary to *make a choice.* And to do so wisely, let a examine attentively—

1. *The qualities of the two leaders.* In Jesus Christ, all that can captivate the heart; in Lucifer, all that can merit aversion and hatred.

·2. *What they have done for you.* Jesus Christ has been the most generous of benefactors; Lucifer the most cruel of enemies.

3. *Their design.* That of Jesus Christ is to make you a sharer in His labours, and then in His glory; that of Lucifer is to make you first the accomplice of his crimes, and then the companion of his punishment.

4. *Their promises.* Jesus Christ promises you possessions honourable, unfailing, infinite, eternal. Ask the elect; all render homage to the truth of His promises; all confess that they have only been surprised in being rendered happier even beyond their hopes. Lucifer promises you things unworthy of you, uncertain, which will leave a void in your heart, which will only add to your disgusts and agitations, which will soon pass away, and will end in everlasting punishments.

5. *Their rights.* Jesus Christ has the most sacred and incontestable rights over your heart. Recall what, as a man and as a Christian, you owe Him, what you have promised Him so often, so freely, and so solemnly. Lucifer has no right but to your contempt. You renounced him before heaven and earth at the baptismal font, at the holy table; you cannot give yourself to him without perjury.

COLLOQUIES.

1. With the Blessed Virgin. Ask her to obtain for

you from her Son the grace to be received and to march under His standard; first, in the love, or even, if He should deign to call you to it, in the practice of poverty; then, in the love of abjection and humility. *Ave Maria.*

2. With our Saviour.   Ask Him the same grace. *Anima Christi.*

3. With the Eternal Father.   The same.   *Pater.*

EXERCISE ON THE THREE CLASSES.

Preparatory Prayer.

First prelude. Represent to yourself three men attacked by serious illness, who all desire health. One will not take any remedy; the second only certain remedies of his own choice; the third will take whatever remedy may be necessary for his cure.

Second prelude. Figure to yourself that you are in the presence of God and His saints, and offer to the Lord a sincere and ardent desire to please Him.

Third prelude. Ask the grace of a good election; that is, the grace to choose what is the most agreeable to the Divine Majesty, and the most useful for your salvation.

PRELIMINARY OBSERVATIONS.

In the meditation of the two standards, we have resolved to attach ourselves to that of Jesus Christ. It is requisite, then, to examine whether this resolution is a serious and solid one. There are three ways of giving ourselves to Jesus Christ; and thus those who call themselves His disciples may be divided into three classes, who correspond to the three sick men presented to us in the first prelude. All, in appearance, wish to follow Jesus Christ; but the first only give Him desires; the next certain works; the third give themselves entirely to Him, and without reserve. To which of these three classes do we aspire to belong?

FIRST POINT.

The first class consists of those who only *give desires to Jesus Christ.* To this class belong all those Christians who are convinced of the truth of religion, of the rights and dominion of God over men, of the malice of sin, of the misery of a soul surprised by death in a state of mortal sin, of the necessity of salvation. They wish, they say, to save themselves, to be converted, to be sanctified.

But they stop there, and put aside all the means necessary for holiness, for conversion, for salvation. These Christians may be compared to the sick man who wishes to be cured, but will not submit to any remedy. Evidently this sick man does not wish to be cured with a serious will, and all his desires of health are only illusions.

Examine before God whether this disposition is not yours. You wish to be converted, to be saved, to be sanctified; but conversion, salvation, sanctity, require *efforts;*—for example, prayer, regular frequenting of the sacraments, avoidance of occasions of sin, the reform of the passions and bad habits: do you seriously will all this?

If this disposition is yours, consider how criminal it is; for it supposes the abuse of the graces and inspirations of the Holy Ghost. In this state men know the obligation of belonging to God; they feel at the bottom of their heart the desire to belong to Him; they have around them all the means of conversion and sanctification and yet they stop at a barren and inefficacious will, that is, they resemble the rebellious Jews at the voice of our Saviour, of whom He said, " If I had not come, and spoken to them, they would not have had sin; but now they have no excuse for their sin" (John xv. 22). Or that cursed land of which St. Paul speaks: " For the earth that drinketh in the rain which cometh often upon it, and bringeth forth thorns and briers, is reprobate, and very near unto a curse, whose end is to be burnt" (Heb. vi. 7, 8).

SECOND POINT.

The second class is of those who will only give Jesus Christ certain works. To this class belong those Christians who wish to be saved, to be converted, to be sanctified; but who will not adopt the most certain means, nor all the means of salvation, conversion, or sanctification. They are like the sick man who wished to be cured, but would only take certain remedies, and rejected the others which were the only efficacious ones.

Look into yourself. Are there not certain sacrifices that God asks of you because they are, you know well, the necessary condition of your sanctification or your salvation, and which you dispute with Him ? Is there not in your heart some predominant passion, the source of all the others, the occasion of all your falls, and which you yet wish to spare. Are there not certain exercises of piety, certain rules of Christian mortification, which are necessary for your return to, or your advancement in, the ways of virtue, and which you have not dared to embrace? Consider well that to remain in this disposition is—

1. *To lose the principal fruit of this retreat;* for it is to renounce the degree of virtue to which God calls you, and consequently all the graces that were to follow it, and the degree of glory which would have crowned it in heaven.

2. *It is to expose your eternal salvation to serious peril;* for God punishes those who resist His voice by withdrawing from them those superabundant graces by which He rewards the sacrifices of those generous souls who give themselves to Him unreservedly.

3. *It is to increase the difficulty in trying to avoid it;* for God generally pours such bitterness into the passions we try to spare, that it costs us more to spare them than it would have done to sacrifice them.

THIRD POINT.

The third class consists of those who give themselves to God entirely and without reserve. To this class belong exclusively those who desire conversion, salvation, holiness, whatever they may cost, and by the most effectual means. These souls are like the sick man who desires health at any price, and gives himself up without restriction into the hands and to the treatment of the physician. Meditate on the motives which urge you to place yourself in this last class.

1. *The example of worldlings.* They sacrifice them-

ꞅelves without reserve for the world, and for what a ꞷorld! Will you not do for God what they do for men? "And they, indeed, that they may receive a corruptible crown; but we an incorruptible one" (1 Cor. ix. 25).

2. *The example of the devil.* Is there any one means that he neglects, any one difficulty before which he recoils, when there is the question of destroying a single soul? Shall we have less courage for our salvation than he has for our ruin?

3. *The example of our Lord.* Did He give Himself to us by half, or with reserve? Ask the manger, the cross, the tabernacle. Shall we be niggardly of ourselves with so generous a God?

4. *The blessings attached to this disposition of heart.* These are: a superabundance of graces, peace of heart, and the unction of the Holy Ghost, which will soften all sacrifices; the moral assurance of salvation; great merits in time, and an immense weight of glory for eternity.

Let us, then, resolve to follow Jesus Christ in this third class; and let us say with the apostle, "I most gladly will spend and be spent myself" (2 Cor. xii. 15). "I fear none of these things, neither do I count my life more precious than myself, so that I may consummate my course" (Acts xx. 24).

COLLOQUIES.

1. With the Blessed Virgin. 2. With our Lord. 3. With the Eternal Father, as in the exercise of the Two Standards.

Observe here that when we feel a reluctance for perfect poverty, which consists not only in being detached in spirit, but in being really deprived of riches; when, on the contrary, we feel ourselves inclined towards the possession of the goods of this world, it is very useful, in order to destroy the effect of this inclination, to ask of God, notwithstanding the repugnance of nature, that He will deign to call us to this complete and effective detachment; and this we must not only ask, but strive to desire and earnestly beg, solely for the interest of the service and glory of God.

EXERCISE ON THE THREE DEGREES OF HUMILITY.

Preparatory Prayer.

First prelude. Represent to yourself our Lord Jesus Christ pointing to His sacred Heart, and saying to us, " Learn of Me, because I am meek and humble of heart" (Matt. xi. 29).

Second prelude. Ask the grace of a perfect renouncement of yourself, after the example of Jesus Christ.

PRELIMINARY OBSERVATIONS.

1. The exercise of the "Two Standards" points out the motives for following Jesus Christ. The exercise of the "Three Classes" points out the motives for following Him by giving ourselves to Him entirely and without reserve. In the exercise of the "Three Degrees of Humility," we are about to consider in what this perfect gift of ourselves to Jesus Christ consists.

2. This exercise is called, in the first place, the

N

"Three Degrees," because it contains the three degrees of Christian perfection, which consist (1) in the firm resolution to avoid mortal sin, even at the risk of life; (2) in the firm resolution to avoid deliberate venial sin at any price; and (3) in the voluntary choice of whatever is most perfect for the service of God: in the second place, it is so called because these three degrees suppose the abasement and, as it were, the annihilation of the old man within us.

FIRST POINT.

Text. *The first degree of humility consists in perfect submission to the law of God, so that we should be ready to refuse the empire of the whole world, or even to sacrifice our lives, rather than willingly transgress any precept which obliges us under pain of mortal sin.*

This first degree is absolutely necessary for eternal salvation, and is as it were the fruit of the exercises of the first week. To establish ourselves firmly in it, we may recall what faith teaches us: (1) of the infinite malice of mortal sin, and the terrible vengeance with which the justice of God pursues it in time and in eternity; (2) of the supreme dominion of God, and His right to the obedience of every creature; (3) of the certainty and nearness of death, which will leave the sinner without resource in the hands of the living God; (4) the rewards which await in eternity the faithful observers of God's law; (5) the sacrifices of the saints and martyrs, who renounced every thing—fortune, pleasures, liberty, life itself—in order to escape mortal sin: "They were stoned, they were cut asunder, they were tempted, they were put to death by the sword" (Heb. xi. 37).

End by turning back upon yourself. Examine if you are ready to sacrifice all rather than consent to mortal sin; if there is not some obstacle to this necessary disposition of heart, and what that obstacle is; and what means you are willing to take for the future, in order to arrive at this first degree, and to strengthen yourself in it.

SECOND POINT.

Text. *The second degree is more perfect; it consists in the indifference of the soul towards riches or poverty, honour or shame, health or sickness, provided the glory of God and salvation are equally secured on both sides; further, that no consideration of interest or temporal disgrace, not even the consideration of immediate death, should be capable of drawing us into deliberate venial sin.*

This second degree is the consequence of the exercise on "The end of creatures." In that exercise we saw that, according to the order of creation, creatures are only the means given to man to lead him to his true end. Reason tells us that, in the choice of means, man should only consider what brings him nearer or takes him farther from this end. Hence it follows that man should be indifferent to poverty or riches, honour or shame; and that to commit venial sin in order to escape shame or poverty, is to sin against this indifference, is to reverse the order, and convert the means into the end itself.

To arrive at this second degree, we may meditate —(1) on the malice of venial sin, the greatest of evils after mortal sin; (2) the hatred with which God pursues it, and the torments with which He punishes it in the other life; (3) its effects with regard to the soul, in which it weakens charity and disposes to mortal sin; (4) the examples of the saints, of whom several have preferred to die rather than consent to one slight fault (5) above all, the example of Jesus Christ.

Examine what is your disposition towards venial sin, &c., as in the first point.

THIRD POINT.

Text. *The third degree is the highest degree of Christian perfection. It consists in preferring, for the sole love of Jesus Christ, and from the wish to resemble Him more, poverty to riches, shame to honour, &c., even if on both sides your salvation and the glory of God were equally to be found.*

To arrive at this third degree of humility, we may consider—

1. *Its excellence.* It contains all that is most heroic in virtue, and the perfect imitation of Jesus Christ, who for love of us willingly embraced the ignominy of the cross: "Having joy set before Him, endured the cross, despising the shame" (Heb. xii. 2).

2. *Its happiness.* To this degree is attached (1) peace of heart, since nothing can trouble him who professes to love all that nature fears and abhors; (2) intimate union with Jesus Christ, who communicates Himself fully to those souls who give themselves to Him without reserve; (3) the choice graces and blessings of God on all that we undertake for His glory: "The foolish things of the world hath God chosen, that He may confound the wise" (1 Cor. i. 27).

3. *Its utility.* This degree is the *most certain* way of salvation, because it snatches us away from all the dangers inseparable from fortune and honour; the *shortest*, because it delivers us at once from sin, and raises us to every virtue; finally, the *most meritorious*, because it is one uninterrupted course of sacrifices, and consequently of merits, for eternity.

COLLOQUIES.

1. With Mary; 2. with Jesus Christ; 3. with the Eternal Father,—to obtain the grace of arriving at the third degree of humility.

Anima Christi. Pater Ave

THIRD WEEK.

THE purpose of the third week is to confirm the soul in
the resolution of a new life, and in the determination
to serve God better.   It is for this purpose that it is
devoted to meditations on the touching and admirable
examples that are offered to us by the Passion of our
Lord Jesus Christ.

The remarks peculiar to this week are—

1. The order and method of the preceding meditations must be followed.   The preparatory prayer and
the three preludes as usual.   In the second prelude, or
construction of place, however, the person must imagine himself present at a mystery accomplished for *him*,
—according to the words of the Apostle, " He loved me,
and delivered Himself for me" (Gal. ii. 20); and must
dwell upon the consideration that *his* sins are the cause
of the sufferings of Christ.

2. In the meditation we shall continue to consider
(1st) the persons, (2d) the words, (3d) the actions.
But three other points must be added: (4th) what our
Saviour suffers and desires to suffer in His humanity;
(5th) how His divinity hides itself as it were, allowing
His enemies to work their will; (6th) what we must do
and suffer for a God whom our sins have reduced to
such a state.

On each of these points we must excite ourselves to
sorrow, sadness, and **tears**.

Although these three last points are in a degree comprised in the three first, St. Ignatius has chosen to present them separately, that the soul may attach itself in a particular manner to the sentiments they express, and which are to lead it to the third degree of humility.

In the fourth point, it will be useful to compare the sufferings of Jesus Christ to the kinds of pain which have been spoken of in the meditation on the end of man,—to weakness, to the sufferings He endured in body and soul, to poverty, to constant separation from all dear to Him, to contempt, to insults, to a short life, to the death He suffered on the cross.

The fifth point relates to these words of Isaias (liii. 3) : "He was offered because it was His own will." Jesus Christ could have destroyed His enemies, as His miracles prove, and yet He spared them and freely gave Himself up to their hate. This thought ought to inspire us with the desire to prefer with Jesus Christ poverty to riches, contempt to reputation and the esteem of men, provided always that both shall be equally conducive to the glory of God.

The sixth point is a sort of abridgment of the colloquy of the first meditation on sin, except that in one we consider what we ought to do for Jesus Christ, and in the other what we ought to suffer for love of Him.

Finally, St. Ignatius wishes that, in these three last points, we should excite ourselves to sorrow, sadness, and tears ; but these affections must not stop at an interior sentiment, they must above all tend to the imitation of Jesus Christ suffering.

3. The colloquies must be made according to the disposition of the soul; for example, according as it feels trouble or consolation, as it desires such or such a virtue, or wishes to make such or such a resolution. We may make one single colloquy, addressed to Jesus Christ; or we may make three,—one to the Blessed Virgin, another to her Divine Son, the third to the Eternal Father.

4. The observance of the ten additions must undergo the following modifications:

(1.) As soon as you awake, you must recall the summary of the prayer; then, in dressing, excite yourself to sadness and sorrow, in union with Jesus Christ suffering.

(2.) Dismiss, as so many distractions, agreeable and consoling thoughts, however holy they may be in themselves, and encourage feelings of sadness by the remembrance of all that Jesus Christ suffered from His birth to His death.

(3.) It is useful to read some passages from Scripture relating to the Passion of our Saviour,—for example, the Psalms or Isaias, St. Paul or the Gospels,—in order to recall the greatness of our Lord's sufferings, or His mercy, or the admirable effects of His death for the redemption of mankind.

(4.) You may also occupy yourself usefully in reciting the "Stabat Mater," according to the second method of prayer.

Note. Although the sentiment of compassion is good, though it ought to be asked for earnestly, desired with humility, and received with gratitude, yet there are other sentiments which we must endeavour to excite in ourselves, because they are more useful for our spiritual progress. Such are—(1) *Hatred of sin :* this hatred must be excited in the soul by the consideration of the insult that sin offers to God,—an insult that can only be fully repaired by the sufferings and death of a God-man. (2) *Admiration of the infinite goodness* and wisdom of God, who has found so efficacious a means of touching and drawing to Him the hearts of men : " But God commendeth His charity towards us, because when as yet we were sinners Christ died for us" (Rom. v. 8). (3) *Confidence:* " For," says St. Augustine, "can He who gave us the most precious thing in the world, the blood of His only Son, refuse us eternal glory, which is certainly of less price?" (4) *Love ;* by way of gratitude for this wonderful love of God, who gives Himself to us and gives Himself in this manner. (5) *Imitation of Jesus Christ :* it is for you that He suffered, says St. Peter, leaving you an example that you may follow in His footsteps. (6) *The salvation of souls,* which God has so much esteemed, has so much loved, that He has redeemed with so much pain, and at so high a price.

FIRST EXERCISE ON THE MYSTERY OF THE
EUCHARIST.

MEDITATION.

Preparatory Prayer.

First prelude. Represent to yourself the Last Supper, and our Saviour seated at the same table as His

Apostles, and by His all-powerful word changing the bread into His own body, and the wine into His own blood.

Second prelude. Ask a lively faith in the mystery of the Eucharist, and a tender love for Jesus present in the tabernacle.

FIRST POINT.

The presence of Jesus Christ in the Eucharist.

Contemplate in spirit our Saviour present on our altars, and, after having adored Him with profound respect, ask Him why for eighteen hundred years He has remained shut up and, as it were, a captive in our tabernacles. Is it to redeem the world? But the redemption was accomplished on Calvary. Is it solely to confer grace upon us? But from the height of heaven Jesus Christ could sanctify us without there being any need of His presence on earth. Why, then, remain in the midst of us? Because He loves us, and all His delight is to be with the children of men: " My delights were to be with the children of men" (Prov. viii. 31). And how does He dwell among us? He dwells under the veils of the Sacrament, for fear that the splendour of His glory should keep us away from His person, either through fear or respect. He wishes to dwell not merely in a single city or a single sanctuary, but in all the temples of the Catholic Church, so that there shall not be any Christian who may not enjoy converse with Him. Finally, He wishes to inhabit our temples, not on certain days or certain solemnities only, but all days, all hours, all moments, so that there shall not be any person in his family who cannot come at all times before Him, to ask and to receive light, strength, and consolation.

What happiness for you to live thus in the society of Jesus Christ! You have, then, nothing to envy the Apostles, the disciples, the inhabitants of Judea,—all those who possessed our Saviour during the days of His mortal life. Between them and you there is only one difference, and that appears to be to your advantage. They possessed Jesus Christ, but in the state of His infirmity; you possess Him in the state of His glory. They only possessed Him at intervals, for Jesus Christ frequently retired from the company of men into solitude; you possess Him constantly, you can enjoy His presence at any hour, as often, as long as you wish. Your happiness is so great that it may be compared to that of the elect in heaven; for this Jesus, whose possession forms the beatitude of the saints, is the same you possess on earth; and He does not reside more really in heaven than He resides in our sanctuaries.

SECOND POINT.

The life of Jesus Christ in the Eucharist.

Consider that our Lord reproduces in His eucharistic life all the states and all the virtues of His mortal life.

1. His mysterious birth on the altar at the voice of the priest represents His birth at Bethlehem. In the solitude of our churches you find the deserted stable where Mary gave to the world its Saviour; in the sacramental species, the swaddling clothes which enveloped the Divine Child; in the indifference of men for the Sacrament of Divine Love, the conduct of the inhabitants of Bethlehem towards the Messiah

2. The tabernacle represents the humble house at Nazareth. What was the life of Jesus at Nazareth? A life of retreat, of prayer, of obedience. What is His life in the tabernacle? Contemplate it. He dwells in the midst of the world, and is at an infinite distance from its societies and its feasts. He prays, but with a continual prayer that has not been interrupted a single instant for eighteen hundred years. He is in a state of absolute dependence, always submissive to His ministers, equally ready, according to their will, either to remain hidden in the tabernacle, or to present Himself to the adoration of the faithful, or to transport Himself to the houses or to the hospitals, to visit His suffering members.

3. Recall to yourself what the Gospel relates of the public life of the Son of God. You will still meet with all this in the Eucharist. In His public life Jesus taught, and He supported His teaching by miracles. In His eucharistic life what does He do? He teaches still, no longer by His words, but by His example,—by His poverty, by His humility, by His flight from the world. He says always, "Blessed are the poor in spirit. Woe to the world" (Matthew v. 3, xviii. 7). He still works miracles; He still restores sight to the blind, life to the dead,—that is, the light of faith to those who walk in the darkness of the world, the life of grace to those who are buried in the grave of sin.

4. The suffering life of our Saviour on Calvary is perpetuated in the Sacrament of the Altar. On the altar, as on the cross, the same trials: the same sadness of the heart of Jesus Christ at the sight of men's crimes; the same abandonment of Jesus Christ by those souls who ought to be most faithfully attached to Him ; the same

insults on Calvary by the Jews, and on the altar by heretics and impious men; the same torment of His sacred body, equally crucified by His executioners on Calvary and on the altar by the profane; in fine, on Calvary and at the altar the same examples of patience, of detachment, of charity, in a word, of the most heroic sacrifices.

Meditate with lively faith on the mystery of the eucharistic life of Jesus Christ, and excite yourself to the imitation of His virtues.

THIRD POINT.

The union of Jesus Christ with us in the Eucharist.

Consider that the Eucharist, according to the idea of the Fathers, is an extension of the mystery of the Incarnation. In the Incarnation, the Word, it is true, unites Himself to us in an ineffable manner; but much more wonderful is the union He contracts with us in the Eucharist. In the Incarnation He takes a nature like ours; He enters into our family, He makes Himself one of us,—in a word, our brother. In the Eucharist He goes farther; it is no longer to a nature like ours He unites Himself, He unites Himself to each one in particular; it is no longer to our family He allies Himself, it is to our person.

Enter into this mystery of the charity of Jesus Christ, and meditate on all the circumstances.

1. How does He unite Himself to us in the Eucharist? By the nearest and most intimate union. The Fathers compare it to the union of two waxes melted into and mixed together (St. Cyril of Alex.).

Our Lord compares it to that which exists between His Father and Himself: "As the living Father hath sent Me, and I live by the Father: so he that eateth Me, the same also shall live by Me" (John vi. 58). As, in the Holy Trinity, the Father, without losing any thing of His infinite being, communicates it entirely to His Son, who is His Word; so, in the Eucharist, the Word incarnate retains His humanity and His divinity, yet always communicates both to the person receiving Him.

2. With what sentiments does He unite Himself to us? With sentiments of the most ardent love; and this love He reveals by His desires, His promises, His threats: "If any man eat of this bread, he shall live for ever; and the bread that I will give is My flesh for the life of the world. Except you eat the flesh of the Son of man, you shall not have life in you" (John vi. 52, 54).

3. What does He do to unite Himself to us? He multiplies miracles and reverses all the laws of nature. He does more, He exposes Himself to all insults; for example, to the insults of indifferent Christians, who leave Him alone, and do not come to adore Him in His tabernacle; to the insults of profaners, who in their souls unite themselves with sin and the devil; to the insults of heretics and the impious, who have so often trampled Him under foot and cast Him in the mire.

4. What does He give us in uniting Himself to us? He gives us all He has and all He is,—His body, His soul, His divinity, and with this every grace. He is generous even to exhaustion; and what is most admirable is, that He gives Himself thus entirely, not once only, but every day, if we wish it. Every fresh com-

munion is a new gift which Jesus Christ makes of Himself to us.

Practical reflections and affections. Colloquy with our Lord.

Anima Christi. Pater. Ave.

SECOND EXERCISE ON THE MYSTERY OF THE EUCHARIST.

APPLICATION OF THE SENSES.

Preparatory Prayer.

First prelude. Represent to yourself heaven opening at the voice of the priest, and our Lord descending upon the altar amidst choirs of angels.

Second prelude. Beg a lively faith in the mystery of the Eucharist, and a tender love for Jesus Christ present in the tabernacle.

Application of sight. By faith pierce through the veils of the Sacrament. Contemplate our Saviour present in the tabernacle and impatient to give Himself to you. Represent to yourself the glory of His adorable humanity; the majesty, and at the same time the sweetness, of His countenance; the dazzling light which flashes from His wounds; the flames which escape from His heart. Then penetrate in spirit to His divinity, to the Word consubstantial with the Father and the Holy Ghost, and with them One only God. Consider with what goodness this Divine Saviour casts on you those eyes, one look from which converted sinners in the days of His mortal life; and after having adored Him with a lively faith, profound respect, and fervent love, say to Him with the prophet : "Lord, cast Thine eyes upon

me, and have pity on my miseries. Look Thou upon
me, and have mercy on me" (Ps. cxviii. 132). Make the
light of Thy countenance to shine on Thy servant, and
save me because of Thy mercy: "Make Thy face to
shine upon Thy servant: save me in Thy mercy" (Ps.
xxx. 17).

Practical reflections and affections.

Application of hearing. Listen to our Saviour, the
incarnate Wisdom, who speaks to you. And what does
He say to you? Words of *consolation:* "Blessed are
the poor in spirit. Blessed are they that mourn. Blessed
are they that suffer persecution" (Matt. v. 3, 5, 10).
Perhaps words of *reproach,* but of sweet and tender reproach: "I know thy works, and thy labour, but I
have somewhat against thee, because thou hast left thy
first charity" (Apoc. ii. 2, 4). Words of *counsel* and
invitation: "Take up My yoke upon you, and learn
of Me, because I am meek and humble of heart, and ye
shall find rest to your souls; for My yoke is sweet and
My burden light" (Matt. xii. 29, 30). Words of
encouragement: "I know thy tribulation and thy
poverty, but thou art rich. . . . . Be thou faithful unto
death, and I will give thee the crown of life" (Apoc. ii.
9, 10). Words of *desire* and *love:* "Behold I stand
at the gate and knock" (Apoc. iii. 20). "My son,
give me thy heart" (Prov. xxiii. 26).

Gather together with holy attention the words of
our Saviour, and say to Him: "Speak, Lord, for Thy
servant heareth" (1 Kings iii. 9). "Thou hast the
words of eternal life" (John vi. 69). "Say to my soul,
I am thy salvation" (Ps. xxxiv. 3).

Practical reflections and affections.

Application of smell and taste. Respire the celestial perfume of the divinity and the humanity of Jesus Christ. Taste in spirit, sometimes the bitterness which His sacred Heart suffers from the indifference, the contempt, the insults, the profanations of men; at other times the sweetness of the virtues He practises in His Eucharistic life,—His patience, His charity, His obedience, His poverty, His humility, His solitude, His prayer, &c. Unite yourself to Him as a model, to imitate His example; as a victim, to sympathise with His sorrows, and to make reparation for the outrages He suffers.

Practical reflections and affections.

Application of the touch. Recall to yourself the woman in the Gospel who touched the hem of the garments of Jesus Christ, and obtained health as the price of her faith; Magdalen, who embraced His sacred feet and watered them with her tears; St. Thomas, who placed his finger in His wounds; St. John, who reposed on His breast, &c. Enter into their sentiments, and put yourself in their places, according to the different states of your soul. Thus, present yourself before Jesus Christ, sometimes as a sick man, and in spirit touch His garments to obtain your cure; sometimes as a penitent, embracing His sacred feet and asking pardon for your faults; sometimes as a disciple, whose confidence requires animating and strengthening, then place your finger in His wounds to convince yourself of His love; sometimes as a friend admitted to intimate familiarity, and then figure to yourself that our Lord presses you to His heart, &c.

Practical reflections, &c. Colloquy with our Lord. *Anima Christi. Pater. Ave.*

o

EXERCISE ON THE DISCOURSE OF OUR LORD AFTER THE LAST SUPPER. (St. John xiii.-xvii.)

Preparatory Prayer.

First prelude. Represent to yourself the disciple whom Jesus loved reposing on His bosom, and drawing from His heart the understanding of His sublime teachings.

Second prelude. Ask the grace to partake with him this place of honour during your meditation.

FIRST POINT.

Jesus answers the questions of His Apostles.

1. Peter asks Him, " Lord, whither goest Thou?" Jesus answers, " Whither I go thou canst not follow Me now, but thou shalt follow hereafter." Peter replies, " Why cannot I follow Thee now? I will lay down my life for Thee." Jesus answers, " Wilt thou lay down thy life for Me? Amen, amen, I say to thee, the cock shall not crow till thou deny Me thrice."

2. Thomas says to Him, " We know not whither Thou goest; and how can we know the way?" Jesus answers him, " I am the way, the truth, and the life. No man cometh to the Father but by Me. If you had known Me, you would without doubt have known My Father also, and from henceforth you shall know Him, and you have seen Him."

3. Philip saith to Him, " Lord, show us the Father, and it is enough for us." Jesus saith to him, " So long a time have I been with you, and have you not known Me? Philip, he that seeth Me, seeth the Father also. How sayest thou, show us the Father? Do you not

believe that I am the Father, and the Father is Me? The words that I speak to you, I speak not of Myself. But My Father who abideth in Me, He doth the works. Believe you not that I am in the Father, and the Father in Me? Otherwise believe for the very works' sake. Amen, amen, I say to you, he that believeth in Me, the works that I do, he also shall do, and greater than these shall he do: because I go to the Father. And whatsoever you shall ask the Father in My name, that will I do: that the Father may be glorified in the Son. If you shall ask Me any thing in My name, that I will do. If you love Me, keep My commandments. And I will ask the Father, and He shall give you another Paraclete, that He may abide with you for ever. The Spirit of truth, whom the world cannot receive, because it seeth Him not, nor knoweth Him: but you shall know Him, because He shall abide with you, and shall be in you. I will not leave you orphans. I will come to you. Yet a little while, and the world seeth Me no more. But you see Me, because I live, and you shall live. In that day you shall know that I am in My Father, and you in Me, and I in you. He that hath My commandments and keepeth them, he it is that loveth Me. And he that loveth Me shall be loved by My Father: and I will love him, and will manifest Myself to him."

4. Judas saith to Him, not Iscariot, " Lord, how is it that Thou wilt manifest Thyself to us and not to the world?" Jesus answered him, " If any man love Me, he will keep My word, and My Father will love him, and We will come to him, and will make Our abode with him. He that loveth Me not keepeth not My words,

and the word which you have heard is not Mine, but the Father's who sent Me. These things have I spoken to you, abiding with you; but the Paraclete, the Holy Ghost, whom the Father will send in My name, He will teach you all things, and bring all things to your mind, whatsoever I shall have said to you."

5. The Apostles asked each other what the words signified that Jesus had just said: "A little while, and you shall not see Me; and again a little while, and you shall see Me." Jesus, knowing they wished to ask Him, said to them, "Of this do you inquire among yourselves, `ecause I said: A little while, and you shall not see Me; and again a little while, and you shall see me? Amen, amen, I say to you, that you shall lament and weep, but the world shall rejoice, and you shall be made sorrowful, but your sorrow shall be turned into joy. A woman, when she is in labour, hath sorrow because her hour is come; but when she hath brought forth the child, she remembereth no more the anguish for joy that a man is born into the world. So also you now indeed have sorrow; but I will see you again, and your heart shall rejoice, and your joy no man shall take from you. And in that day you shall not ask Me any thing. Amen, amen, I say to you, if you ask the Father any thing in My name, He will give it you. Hitherto you have not asked any thing in My name. Ask, and you shall receive, that your joy may be full."

SECOND POINT.

Jesus announces His passion; recommends charity, peace, intimate union with Him and with our brethren, constancy in persecutions: He promises the Holy Ghost.

1. *He announces His passion.* " Now is the Son of man glorified, and God is glorified in Him. If God be glorified in Him, God also will glorify Him in Himself, and immediately will He glorify Him. Little children, yet a little while I am with you" (John xiii. 31-33).

2. *He recommends charity.* "A new commandment I give unto you, that you love one another; as I have loved you, that you also love one another. By this shall all men know that you are My disciples, if you have love one for another" (xiii. 34, 35).

3. *Peace.* " Let not your heart be troubled. You believe in God, believe also in Me. In My Father's house are many mansions. If not, I would have told you that I go to prepare a place for you. And if I shall go and prepare a place for you, I will come again, and will take you to Myself, that where I am you also may be" (xiv. 1-3).

4. *Union with Him and with our brethren.* " I am the true Vine, and My Father is the husbandman. Every branch in Me that beareth not fruit He will take away; and every one that beareth fruit, He will purge it, that it may bring forth more fruit. Now you are clean by reason of the word which I have spoken to you. Abide in Me, and I in you. As the branch cannot bear fruit of itself unless it abide in the vine, so neither can you unless you abide in Me. I am the Vine; you the branches. He that abideth in Me and I in him, the same beareth much fruit : for without Me you can do nothing. If any one abide not in Me, he shall be cast forth as a branch, and shall wither, and they shall gather him up and cast him into the fire, and he burneth. If you abide in Me, and My words abide in you, you shall ask what-

ever you will, and it shall be done unto you. In this is
My Father glorified, that you bring forth very much
fruit, and become My disciples. As the Father hath
loved Me, I also have loved you. Abide in My love. If
you keep My commandments, you shall abide in My
love, as I also have kept My Father's commandments,
and do abide in His love. These things I have spoken
to you, that My joy may be in you, and your joy may
be filled. This is My commandment, that you love
one another, as I have loved you. Greater love than
this no man hath, that a man lay down his life for his
friends. You are My friends, if you do the things that
I command you. I will not now call you servants: for
the servant knoweth not what his lord doth. But I
have called you friends: because all things whatsoever
I have heard of My Father I have made known to you.
You have not chosen Me, but I have chosen you; and
have appointed you that you should go and should
bring forth fruit, and your fruit should remain; that
whatsoever you shall ask of the Father in My name, He
may give it you. These things I command you, that
you love one another" (xv. 1-17).

5. *Constancy in persecutions.* "If the world hate
you, know ye that it hath hated Me before you. If you
had been of the world, the world would love its own;
but because you are not of the world, but I have chosen
you out of the world, therefore the world hateth you.
Remember My word that I said to you: The servant
is not greater than his master. If they have persecuted
Me, they will also persecute you: if they have kept My
word, they will keep yours also. But all these things
they will do to you for My name's sake, because they

know not Him that sent Me. If I had not come and spoken to them, they would not have sin; but now they have no excuse for their sin. He that hateth Me hateth my Father also. If I had not done among them the works that no other man hath done, they would not have sin; but now they have both seen and hated both Me and My Father. But that the word may be fulfilled which is written in their law: They have hated Me without cause. But when the Paraclete cometh, whom I will send you from the Father, the Spirit of truth, who proceedeth from the Father, He shall give testimony of Me: and you shall give testimony, because you are with Me from the beginning. These things have I spoken to you, that you may not be scandalised. They will put you out of the synagogues; yea, the hour cometh that whosoever killeth you will think that he doth a service to God. And these things will they do to you, because they have not known the Father, nor Me. But these things I have told you, that when the hour of them shall come, you may remember that I told you" (xv. 18 to end, xvi. 1-4).

6. *He promises the Holy Ghost.* " But I tell you the truth: it is expedient to you that I go; for if I go not, the Paraclete will not come to you: but if I go, I will send Him to you. And when He is come, He will convince the world of sin and of justice and of judgment. Of sin: because they believed not in Me. And of justice: because I go to the Father, and you shall see Me no longer. And of judgment: because the prince of this world is already judged. I have yet many things to say to you; but you cannot bear them now. But when He, the Spirit of truth, is come, He

will teach you all truth. For He shall not speak of Himself; but what things soever He shall hear, He shall speak, and the things that are to come He shall show you. He shall glorify Me; because He shall receive of Mine, and shall show it to you. All things whatsoever the Father hath are Mine. Therefore I said, that He shall receive of Mine and show it to you" (xvi. 7-15).

THIRD POINT.
The prayer of Jesus.

1. *Jesus prays for Himself.* Lifting up His eyes to heaven, Jesus said : "Father, the hour is come ; glorify Thy Son, that Thy Son may glorify Thee. As Thou hast given Him power over all flesh, that He may give eternal life to all whom Thou hast given Him. Now this is eternal life : That they may know Thee, the only true God, and Jesus Christ whom Thou hast sent. I have glorified Thee on earth. I have finished the work which Thou gavest Me to do. And now glorify Thou Me, O Father, with Thyself, with the glory which I had, before the world was, with Thee" (John xvii. 1-5).

2. *Jesus prays for His disciples.* " I have manifested Thy name to the men whom Thou hast given Me out of the world. Thine they were, and to Me Thou gavest them : and they have kept Thy word. Now they have known that all things which Thou hast given Me are from Thee: because the words which Thou gavest Me I have given to them, and they have received them, and have known in very deed that I came out from Thee, and they have believed that Thou didst

send Me. I pray for them : I pray not for the world, but for them whom Thou hast given Me; because they are Thine. And all My things are Thine, and Thine are Mine : and I am glorified in them. And now I am not in the world, and these are in the world, and I come to Thee. Holy Father, keep them in Thy name whom Thou hast given Me; that they may be one, as We are also. While I was with them, I kept them in Thy name. Those whom Thou gavest Me have I kept : and none of them is lost, but the son of perdition, that the Scripture may be fulfilled. And now I come to Thee : and these things I speak in the world, that they may have My joy filled in themselves. I have given them Thy word, and the world hath hated them, because they are not of the world, as I also am not of the world. I pray not that Thou shouldst take them out of the world, but that Thou shouldst keep them from evil. They are not of the world, as I also am not of the world. Sanctify them in truth. Thy word is truth. As Thou hast sent Me into the world, I also have sent them into the world. And for them do I sanctify Myself: that they also may be sanctified in truth. And not for them only do I pray, but for them also who through their word shall believe in Me. That they all may be one, as Thou, Father, in Me, and I in Thee : that they also may be one in Us : that the world may believe that Thou hast sent Me. And the glory which Thou hast given Me I have given to them : that they may be one, as We also are one. I in them, and Thou in Me; that they may be made perfect in one ; and the world may know that Thou hast sent Me, and hast loved them as Thou hast also loved Me.

Father, I will that where I am, they also whom Thou
hast given Me may be with Me : that they may see
My glory which Thou hast given Me, because Thou
hast loved Me before the foundation of the world. Just
Father, the world hath not known Thee; but I have
known Thee ; and these have known that Thou hast
sent Me.   And I have made known Thy name to them,
and will make it known : that the love, wherewith Thou
hast loved Me, may be in them, and I in them" (xvii.
6 to end).

Affections at the foot of the crucifix.
Anima Christi.

FIRST EXERCISE ON THE PASSION OF OUR LORD.

Jesus Christ in the Garden of Olives.

Preparatory Prayer.

First prelude.   Jesus entering into the garden of
Gethsemani, took with Him Peter and James and John;
and He began to fear and be sorrowful ; and He said to
them : My soul is sorrowful even unto death, wait here
and watch with Me.   And going a little way off, He
prayed, saying, Father, if it be possible, remove this
chalice from Me; but yet not My will, but Thine be
done.   And being in an agony, He prayed the longer.
And His sweat became as drops of blood, trickling
down upon the ground (Mark xiv. 32; Luke xxii. 40).

Second prelude.   Represent to yourself the garden
of Gethsemani, and our Saviour prostrate on the ground
praying for the salvation of mankind.

Third prelude. Ask God to grant you tears of sorrow in union with Jesus Christ suffering for love of us. In each of the scenes of the passion of our Lord we may consider what He suffers, and how He suffers; that is, a God as a victim, and a God as a model. As the one, we owe Him love; as the other, we owe Him imitation.

FIRST POINT.

Jesus Christ as victim.

Recall to yourself that our Lord is the most holy of the children of men; that He is the beloved Son of the living God; that He is Himself the God of all consolation, the sight of whom forms the beatitude of the angels and the elect. He ought not, then, to have known pain or suffering; and yet what does He not suffer! He endures the most violent interior trials of the soul, —fear, " He began to fear" (Mark xiv. 33); weariness, " and to be heavy" (ibid.); sorrow, "My soul is sorrowful even unto death" (ibid. 34); finally, a sort of agony, " Being in an agony" (Luke xxii. 43).

In order fully to understand the excess of the suffering of Jesus Christ, meditate on all the circumstances told by the evangelists. Jesus Christ complains; He who had never uttered a single complaint until then. And to whom does He complain? To common and almost unconcerned men, who do not know how to console Him, nor even to pray with Him. In what terms does He complain? In the most energetic—He tells them His soul is sorrowful even unto death. And this Jesus who complains in this way, is He who said a short time before, speaking of His approaching passion, " I have

& baptism, wherewith I am to be baptised, and how am
I straitened until it be accomplished!" (Luke xi. 50.)
In fine, His desolation is such, that His heart appears
to break; He suffers convulsions like a dying person
struggling violently against death; it reduces Him to
sweat blood from all His members: "His sweat became
as drops of blood trickling down upon the ground"
(Luke xxii. 44).

And what are the causes of this desolation of the
Saviour? The eternal misery that sin is preparing for
us; this is cause of His fear. The infinite injury that
sin does to the majesty of His Father; this is the
cause of His sorrow. The uselessness of His sufferings
for so many miserable creatures who persist in the way
of perdition; this is the cause of His weariness.

The sight of God basely insulted, and of so many
souls miserably damned, is the cause of His agony.
Return to yourself. You see what Jesus Christ suffered
on your account and for you: what will you do for
Him?

SECOND POINT.

Jesus Christ our model.

Recall these words of St. Peter,—Jesus Christ suffered for us, that we might walk in His footsteps:
"Christ also suffered for us, leaving you an example, that
you should follow His steps" (1 Peter ii. 21). Consider, then, all the examples of this Divine Saviour, and
endeavour to imitate Him in your life.

1. Jesus Christ knew beforehand the trials which
awaited Him in the Garden of Olives; but it does not
make Him less faithful to the holy custom of retiring

into solitude to pray. With what intrepidity and what peace He goes to the first theatre of His bloody passion ! From this example of the Saviour, learn fidelity to good resolutions in spite of obstacles and trials.

2. Jesus Christ leaves His disciples at the entrance of the garden ; He only takes with Him three of His apostles, Peter, James, and John; and yet, if He admits them to the confidence of His prayers and sorrows, it is rather for their instruction than His own consolation. From this example of the Saviour, learn detachment from human consolation in afflictions.

3. Jesus Christ, given up to all the agitation and bitterness of His heart, has recourse to prayer. And in this prayer what lessons for a Christian ! A lesson of recollection and solitude : " Withdrawn away from them a stone's cast" (Luke xxii. 41). A lesson of humility : " Kneeling down He prayed" (ib.). A lesson of confidence in God : " Abba, Father, all things are possible to Thee ; remove this chalice from Me" (Mark xiv. 36). A lesson of resignation : " Not what I will, but what Thou wilt" (ib.). A lesson of fervour : " And leaving them He went again, and He prayed for the third time" (Matt. xxvi. 44). Finally, a lesson of heroic constancy : " Being in an agony, He prayed the longer" (Luke xxii. 43).

Practical reflections and affections. Colloquies with our Lord suffering in the Garden of Olives · then with God the Father.

Anima Christi. Pater. Ave.

SECOND EXERCISE ON THE PASSION OF OUR LORD.

On the sufferings of Jesus Christ from His agony in the Garden of Olives to His death on the Cross.

Preparatory Prayer.

First prelude. Recall the account of the evangelist. Jesus Christ is betrayed by the traitor Judas, abandoned by His disciples, bound with cords by the soldiers, dragged to the tribunal of Caiphas; then to that of Pilate, and of Herod; again sent back before the Roman governor, and cruelly scourged by his orders, crowned with thorns in the judgment-hall; finally, loaded with His cross and led to Calvary, there to undergo the last suffering. (Matt. xxvi., xxvii.; Mark xiv., xv.; Luke xxii., xxiii.; John xviii., xix.)

Second prelude. Represent to yourself the different scenes of our Saviour's passion: the Garden of Olives, the tribunal of Caiphas, that of Pilate, the palace of Herod, the judgment-hall, the way of Calvary.

Third prelude. Beg a lively contrition for your sins, and a tender love for Jesus Christ suffering for us. In the Garden of Olives you have contemplated Jesus Christ making the sacrifice of His *interior* consolations. Contemplate Him in Jerusalem, making also the sacrifice of all *exterior* things, which consist in these five things,—His liberty, His friends, His reputation, His happiness, His own body. In each of these sacrifices consider the Saviour as a victim and as a model; meditate on what He suffers and how He suffers.

FIRST POINT.
Jesus Christ as victim.

Consider—

1. *What our Lord suffers in His liberty.* He is deprived of it in the most unjust, the most violent, the most ignominious manner possible. He is seized in the midst of His disciples by the Pharisees and their followers. He is bound like a vile malefactor. He is dragged from tribunal to tribunal in the same city, and amidst the same people that have so often witnessed His preachings and His miracles. He is delivered up to the brutality of the soldiers and of the vilest populace. Finally, His bonds are loosed, only that He may be nailed to the cross where He is to expire.

2. *What He suffers from His friends.* He suffers all that is most cruel from friendships disowned and betrayed. All His apostles forsake Him; one of them denies Him three times, and at the voice of a servant; another sells Him to His enemies for thirty pieces of money. And when is it that His friends put His heart to these sore trials? At a time the most painful, and when He had the greatest need of consolation; at the moment when His most implacable enemies are the masters of His person; at the moment of His sufferings and death. And who are these friends who treat Him in this way? Men whom He has admitted to intimate familiarity; the depositories of His secrets; men to whom He had just given the institution of the Eucharist, the most splendid testimony of His love: "My friends and my neighbours, and they that were near me, stood afar off" (Ps. xxxvii. 12, 13). "My heart hath ex-

pected reproach and misery, and I looked for one that would grieve with me, but there was none; and for one that would comfort me, and I found none" (Ps. lxviii. 21).

3. *What He suffers in His reputation.* What reputation more universal or more glorious than that of Jesus Christ! In all Judea men only spoke of His wisdom, His power, His holiness. Now they only see in Him an ignorant stupid person, who does not know how to answer accusations the coarsest and the most easy to refute : " Answerest Thou nothing? Jesus held His peace" (Matt. xxvi. 62, 63). An impostor, who has deceived the people by illusions, and who with all His power cannot withdraw Himself from the hands of His enemies : " He saved others, let Him save Himself" (Luke xxiii. 35). A seditious impious man, deserving the greatest punishment: " All condemned Him to be guilty of death" (Mark xiv. 64).

4. *What He suffers in His honour.* Not any kind of insult is spared Him. At the tribunal of Caiphas, He is struck in the face, as guilty of irreverence towards the high-priest. In the house of this pontiff the soldiers, covering His eyes, struck Him by turns, and cried: " Prophesy, O Christ! and say who it is that struck Thee" (Luke xxii. 64). At the court of Herod He was shamefully clothed in a white robe as a madman. At the tribunal of Pilate, He is placed on a level with Barabbas, whom the people unanimously prefer before Him. In the hall of judgment they cover Him with purple rags, crown Him with thorns, put a reed in His hand, and bending before Him in derision, say : " Hail, King of the Jews !"

5. *What He suffers in His body.* Represent to

yourself the cruel scenes of the scourging, the crowning with thorns, the crucifixion. Contemplate the sacred body of our Lord torn by the scourgers, and presenting to the eye one bleeding wound : " There is no beauty in Him, nor comeliness; and we have seen Him, and there was no sightliness, that we should be desirous of Him — a Man of sorrows, and acquainted with infirmity and we have thought Him as it were a leper, and as one struck by God and afflicted" (Isaias liii. 2-4). His head pierced by sharp thorns, which the soldiers make more painful every moment by striking Him; His shoulders bruised by the overpowering weight of the cross, which He carries to Calvary; and lastly, His feet and hands nailed to the cross, with horrible torture to the nerves, and all His body suspended and, as it were, sustained by His wounds. Then ask yourself why were all these sufferings of your God, and say with lively contrition : " He was wounded for our iniquities, He was bruised for our sins; the chastisement of our peace was upon Him, and by His bruises we are healed" (Is. liii. 5).

SECOND POINT.
Jesus Christ as model.

Meditate on the examples of virtue our Saviour gives us in the different circumstances of His passion.

1. *In the loss of His liberty,* He gives you an example of perfect resignation to the will of His Father, which He adores in the criminal will of His enemies. He knew their designs beforehand, since He had foretold them to His Apostles, and yet He will neither withdraw Himself by a miracle nor by flight

He anticipates the Pharisees and the soldiers by going to meet them; He voluntarily delivers Himself into their hands; He allows Himself to be bound, then led from tribunal to tribunal, and finally nailed to the cross, and that without offering the least resistance, without making one complaint. Learn from so great a model the characters of perfect obedience to the will of God— that is, docility, promptitude, and constancy.

2. *In the desertion of His friends,* He gives you an example of the most generous charity. To the indifference of His disciples He opposes a lively and tender friendship; He watches over their perils, forgetting His own; and while He delivers Himself without defence into the hands of His most cruel enemies, He obliges them to respect the liberty of His Apostles. " I have told you that I am He. If therefore you seek Me, let these go their way. That the word might be fulfilled which He said: Of them whom Thou hast given Me, I have not lost any one" (John xviii. 8, 9). To Peter, who had denied Him, He does not even utter a reproach, and only replies to his perjury by a look full of sweetness, and which converted the unfaithful Apostle : " The Lord turning looked at Peter, and he going out wept bitterly" (Luke xxii. 61, 62). With regard to Judas, He does not repulse his perfidious embrace; He contents Himself with saying, less to confound him than to convert him, " Friend, whereto are thou come ?" (Matt. xxvi. 50.) " Judas, dost thou betray the Son of man with a kiss ?" (Luke xxii. 48.)

3. *In the loss of His reputation,* He gives you an example of perfect detachment. It was easy for Him to confound His enemies, and to reëstablish with more

splendour than ever His renown for wisdom, sanctity, and power. For this a miracle or even a few words would have sufficed. What does Jesus Christ do? He refuses for Himself the miracles He lavishes on others, and if He speaks, it is only in the interest of truth. Are you the Son of God? You have said it. Yes, I am. Learn, then, from your Divine Master to despise the opinion and the esteem of men. What matters the contempt of the world, if you have the approbation of the Lord? "Those who praise me while Thou blamest me, can they save me when Thou shalt condemn me?" (St. Aug.)

4. *In the ignominies and insults which Jesus Christ endured,* He gives you an example of profound humility. To calumny He only opposes silence : " He held His peace and said nothing" (Mark xiv. 61). Yet it appears that the interest of His doctrine, of His mission, of His Church, that the glory even of His Father, required from Him at least a few words for His justification. But Jesus is silent : " I as a deaf man heard not ; and as a dumb man not opening his mouth, and that hath no reproofs in his mouth" (Ps. xxxvii. 14, 15). To derision and insult He only opposes meekness ; and He fulfils to the letter what was written of Him : "I have given My body to the strikers, and My cheeks to them that plucked them ; I have not turned away My face from them that rebuked Me and spit upon Me" (Is. l. 6) ; " He shall be led as a sheep to the slaughter, and shall be dumb as a lamb before his shearer, and He shall not open His mouth" (Is. liii. 7).

5. *In the different torments of His sacred body,* He gives you the example of an heroic penance. Medi-

tate well on the following circumstances : 1. Wno is He that suffers? A God holy by essence. 2. What does He suffer? Every thing that it is possible for man to suffer. 3. From whom does He suffer it? From those whom He has loaded with benefits. 4. Why does He suffer? For your sins. 5. How does He suffer? With infinite love. These, in a few words, are the motives and practice of penance.

COLLOQUIES.

1. With the Blessed Virgin. Recite some verses of the *Stabat Mater*, for example.

2. With our Lord. *Anima Christi.*

Pater. Ave.

THIRD EXERCISE ON THE PASSION OF OUR LORD

CONTEMPLATION ON THE DEATH OF JESUS CHRIST CRUCIFIED.

Preparatory Prayer.

First prelude. They fasten Jesus to the cross, and crucify Him between two thieves, one on His right and the other on His left. Thus were accomplished the words of Scripture, "With the wicked He was reputed" (Mark xv. 28).

Second prelude. Represent to yourself Calvary, and there our Lord Jesus Christ fastened to the cross.

Third prelude. Let us beg a lively contrition for our sins, and a tender love of Jesus Christ dying for us.

FIRST POINT.
Contemplate the persons.

1. The crowd of strangers and inhabitants of Jerusalem assembled round our Saviour. What motive brings them to Calvary? With some it is compassion; but with a great number it is curiosity; with a still greater number it is hatred. 2. The Roman soldiers, the Pharisees, the princes of the priests, who insult the Son of God, and who feel a malignant joy at His sufferings and death. 3. The two malefactors crucified beside Jesus Christ. 4. The Blessed Virgin, Mary the wife of Cleophas, Magdalen, and the beloved disciple, gathered together at the foot of the cross. 5. Our Lord on the cross; His head crowned with thorns, His eyes blinded by the blood trickling from His forehead, His arms violently stretched out, His hands and feet pierced by sharp nails, His body torn so that the bones may be counted through the still bleeding wounds of His scourging.

Practical reflections and affections.

SECOND POINT.
Listen to the words.

1. *The words of the people.* Those who pass by loading Him with maledictions, shaking their heads, and saying, "Thou that destroyest the temple of God, and in three days dost rebuild it, save Thy own self; if Thou be the Son of God, come down from the cross" (Matt. xxvii. 40).

2. *The words of the chief priests and scribes.* They said, " He saved others; Himself He cannot save. If

He be the King of Israel, let Him now come down
from the cross, and we will believe in Him. He trusted
in God; let Him now deliver Him if He will have
Him, for He said: I am the Son of God" (Matt. xxvii.
42, 43).

3. *The words of the soldiers,* who come to Him and
offer Him vinegar, saying, "If Thou be the King of
the Jews, save Thyself" (Luke xxiii. 37).

4. *The words of the two malefactors.* One of them
blasphemed against Him, saying, "If Thou be Christ,
save Thyself and us" (ib. 39). The other rebuked
him, saying, "Neither dost thou fear God, seeing
thou art under the same condemnation. And we indeed justly, for we receive the due reward of our deeds;
but this Man hath done no evil. And he said to Jesus,
Lord, remember me when Thou shalt come into Thy
kingdom" (ib. 40-42).

5. *The interior words of Mary,* of the holy women,
of St. John, and their communion with the Sacred
Heart of Jesus.

6. *The seven words of Jesus Christ on the cross.*
1. To His Heavenly Father: "Father, forgive them,
for they know not what they do" (Luke xxiii. 34).
2. To the good thief: "To-day thou shalt be with Me
in Paradise" (ib. 43). 3. To Mary and John: "Woman,
behold thy son; son, behold thy mother" (John xix. 26).
4. "My God, My God, why hast Thou forsaken Me?"
(Matt. xxvii. 46.) 5. "I thirst" (John xix. 28). 6. "It
is consummated" (ib. 30). 7. "Father, into Thy hands
I commend My spirit" (Luke xxiii. 46).

Practical reflections and affections.

THIRD POINT.
Consider the actions.

1. In the Jews, indifference, or rather hate. 2. In the priests and Pharisees, a barbarous joy at the sight of their enemy dying. 3. In the soldiers, a fierce cruelty: they divide the garments of Jesus at the foot of the cross, and give Him vinegar to quench the thirst of which He complains. 4. In one of the thieves, an impenitence and hardness which resists every grace. In the other, faith, humility, contrition, confidence in God. 5. In the holy women and St. John, the heroism of fidelity and devotion. 6. In Mary, the union of her heart with the sufferings, the patience, the humility, the charity of Jesus Christ. 7. In Jesus Christ, the perfection of all virtues: the perfection of humility,—He dies under the ignominy of the most disgraceful of sufferings: the perfection of poverty,—He dies in a state of the most complete privation: the perfection of abnegation,—He sacrifices all His liberty, His honour, His affections; His body, in which every sense suffers torture; His soul, of which every faculty has its pain.

Practical reflections and affections.

End by the three following considerations:

1. What our Saviour suffers in His humanity.

2. How His divinity hides itself, and allows His enemies to act, instead of striking them and annihilating them.

3. What we ought to do and suffer for a God whom our sins have reduced to this state.

COLLOQUY WITH OUR SAVIOUR CRUCIFIED.

Excite in yourself the sentiments pointed out in the

advice on the third week: 1. hatred of sin; 2. admiration of the goodness and wisdom of God; 3. trust; 4. love; 5. imitation of the Saviour; 6. zeal for the salvation of souls.

Anima Christi. Pater. Ave.

FOURTH EXERCISE ON THE PASSION OF OUR LORD

APPLICATION OF THE SENSES ON JESUS CHRIST CRUCIFIED.

Preparatory Prayer.

Preludes the same as last.

1. *Application of the sight.* Contemplate the bloody scene of Calvary; the crowd of strangers and of the inhabitants of Jerusalem assembled through compassion, curiosity, or hatred; the soldiers and Pharisees, who insult the agony of the Son of God; the two malefactors crucified beside Him; the Blessed Virgin, the holy women, and the beloved disciple at the foot of the cross; and on the cross Jesus Christ, just giving the last sigh, His feet and hands violently stretched, His head crowned with thorns, His eyes dim, His whole body torn, and allowing the bones to be seen through the wounds which furrow it.

Practical reflections and affections.

2. *Application of the hearing.* Listen to the discourse of the people; the blasphemies of the soldiers; the words of the bad thief who insults Jesus Christ, and those of the good thief who acknowledges Him as God; the interior words of Mary, of the holy women, of St. John; the seven words of Jesus Christ.

Practical reflections and affections.

3. *Application of the taste.* Taste the bitterness of the heart of Mary at the sight of her Son nailed to the cross, and dying in the most cruel and ignominious tortures. Taste, above all, the bitterness of the heart of Jesus, suffering at once from His own sorrows and those of His Mother, and from the rigour of His Father, who seems to have forsaken Him.

Practical reflections and affections.

4. *Application of the smell.* Respire the perfume of the virtues of Jesus Christ dying; of His poverty, His humility, His patience, His charity.

Practical reflections and affections

5. *Application of the touch.* Kiss inwardly the cross and the bleeding wounds of Jesus Christ.

Practical reflections and affections.

COLLOQUY WITH OUR LORD.

Recite slowly the *Anima Christi,* stopping at each clause.

Pater. Ave.

FOURTH WEEK.

In the fourth week, the soul occupies itself entirely with the love of God, and the desire of a blessed eternity, of which a pledge is given in the resurrection of Jesus Christ.

The following are the directions proper to this week:

1. In the first, second, and third points of the meditation, you must contemplate the persons, the words, and the actions, as in the preceding week.

In the fourth point, you must consider how the divinity of Jesus Christ, which was as it were hidden during the time of His passion, is manifested in His resurrection, and afterwards declares itself by all kinds of miracles.

In the fifth point, you must remark with what promptitude, what tenderness, and what effusion of heart Jesus Christ deigns to console His faithful followers.

To meditate with fruit on each of these points, you must recall to yourself that we shall participate in the victory and happiness of the Son of God in proportion as we have partaken of His sufferings, as has already been said in the contemplation on the reign of Jesus Christ. It is for this purpose that St. Ignatius proposes to us—

(1) Jesus Christ as glorious and triumphant after His

resurrection, in proportion as He had been cast down and humiliated in His death; (2) the Apostles and disciples as consoled by our Saviour, in proportion to their past trials and sufferings.

2. During this week some change must be made in the "additions" observed during the preceding weeks. Thus: (1) As soon as you awake you must, in recalling the subject of the meditation, endeavour to unite yourself to the joy of our Saviour after His resurrection with His disciples. (2) You must occupy yourself with all the thoughts that can excite you to spiritual joy, such as celestial glory. (3) No longer deprive yourself of light or of the sight of heaven, but profit by whatever the season offers of agreeable, that we may rejoice with our Creator and Saviour: in spring, with the appearance of verdure, the flowers, and the fresh rich fields; in winter, with the warmth of the sun or the fire; in a word, with the innocent pleasures of nature. Abstain also from corporal mortifications, and be satisfied with temperance in your repasts, unless there should be some fast or abstinence prescribed by the Church, of which the precepts must always be observed, unless some legitimate reason should dispense with them.

FIRST EXERCISE ON THE RESURRECTION OF JESUS CHRIST.

MEDITATION.

Preparatory Prayer.

First prelude. When our Lord had breathed His last sigh, His body, taken down from the cross, was placed in the sepulchre: His soul descended into Limbus to deliver the souls of the just; then returned to the sepulchre the third day, and withdrew from it His body, which was then united to it never more to be separated. The risen Saviour appeared, first, to His blessed Mother, then to the holy women, and at different times to the disciples and Apostles.

Second prelude. Represent to yourself the sepulchre from which Jesus Christ arose, and some of the places that witnessed His apparitions,—for example, the road to Emaus, &c.

Third prelude. Beg the grace to participate in the joy of Jesus Christ and of His blessed Mother.

FIRST POINT.

The glory of Jesus Christ in His resurrection.

Consider the glory of the Saviour in His resurrection, and how faithfully His Father rewards all the sacrifices of His suffering life.

1. In His passion Jesus Christ had made the sacrifice of His body. We have seen this sacred body scourged and on the cross, only offering to the eye one bleeding wound, and scarce allowing the features of the Son of man to be recognised: "From the sole of the foot unto the top of the head there is no soundness therein" (Is. i. 6); "There is no beauty in Him, nor comeliness; and we have seen Him, and there was no sightliness" (Is. liii. 2). In the resurrection the body of Jesus Christ takes a new life—an immortal life. He is raised in a manner to the nature of spirits; like them He is endowed with agility and impassibility. In the

place of that beauty destroyed by His executioners, He
is clothed with a splendour surpassing that of the sun.
This glory of the body of Jesus Christ is promised to
our body also, but on the condition that, after the example of Jesus Christ, we offer up ourselves by penance:
"Yet so if we suffer with Him, that we may be also
glorified with Him" (Rom. viii. 17). Let us courageously
embrace Christian mortification, of which the following
are the three principal degrees : (1) to suffer patiently
all the trials that are independent of our will, — for
example, sickness, infirmities, the inclemencies of the
seasons, &c. ; (2) not to allow our senses any criminal
enjoyment ; (3) to resist our senses, whether by impos-
ing voluntary afflictions on them or by refusing them
allowable enjoyments.

2. In His passion Jesus Christ had made the sacrifice of His honour and glory.   Before the tribunals and
on Calvary we have seen Him, according to the oracle
of the prophets, treated as the lowest of men, with the
reproach of mankind : "The most abject of men" (Is.
liii. 3) ; "The reproach of men" (Ps. xxi. 7). Classed
with the wicked : "And was reputed with the wicked"
(Is. liii. 12). Loaded with ignominy ; trodden under
foot like a worm of the earth : "A worm and no man"
(Ps. xxi. 7).   Now, in the resurrection, all is repaired :
Jerusalem is filled with the news of His triumph ; the
judges who condemned Him are confounded ; the soldiers,
who insulted Him as a seducer and a madman, are the
first witnesses of His glory ; His disciples and Apostles,
who had abandoned Him every where, proclaim His
resurrection ; the angels and the holy souls He has
delivered from Limbus bless Him as the Conqueror of

death and hell: "Thou wast slain, and hast redeemed us to God in Thy blood, and hast made us to our God a kingdom and priests. The Lamb that was slain is worthy to receive power and divinity" (Apoc. v. 9-12). Conceive a holy contempt for the opinion and esteem of men; place your honour in the hands of God, and know how to make the sacrifice of it to Him when He requires it, being assured that He will faithfully return it to you a hundredfold: "I also suffer; but I am not ashamed. For I know whom I have believed, and I am certain that He is able to keep that which I have committed unto Him against that day" (2 Tim. i. 12).

3. In His passion Jesus Christ had made the sacrifice of His interior consolations. His soul was steeped in bitterness: in the Garden of Olives we have heard Him cry out, "My soul is sorrowful even unto death" (Matt. xxvi. 38); and on the cross, "My God, My God, why hast Thou forsaken Me?" (Mark xv. 34.) Now the time of desolation is passed never to return; His soul enters into possession of a happiness without end; it is inundated with the delights of Paradise, with all the joys of the divinity which is united to Him. Animate your hope by your faith. Recall to yourself that you are called to share this felicity of the Son of God one day in heaven. And when sacrifices alarm you or trials depress you, say to yourself with the Apostle, "For that which is at present momentary and light of our tribulation worketh for us above measure an eternal weight of glory" (2 Cor. iv. 17).

SECOND POINT.

The apparitions of Jesus Christ after His resurrection.

Consider to whom Jesus Christ appeared, how He appeared, and why He appeared.

1. *To whom Jesus Christ appeared.* He appeared (1), according to the general opinion, to His blessed Mother; not only on account of the incomparable dignity of Mary, but above all, because no one had participated so much in His sorrows and in the opprobrium of His passion. So Jesus Christ teaches you that you will only participate in His consolations in proportion to your constancy in suffering after His example and for His love.

(2) He appeared next, not to the Apostles, but to Magdalen and the holy women. And why to these holy women? To reward their simplicity and fervour, and to teach you that it is to simple and fervent souls that He is pleased to communicate Himself: "His communication is with the simple" (Prov. iii. 32).

(3) Lastly, He appears to the Apostles; but it is after Peter and John have been to the sepulchre and have merited the grace of seeing our Saviour by the zeal of their search. Learn from this that to find Jesus Christ we must seek Him long by prayer and desire. Happy they who know how to draw Jesus Christ to them! Happy they who know how to retain Jesus Christ with them! "It is a great art to know how to converse with Jesus, and to know how to retain Jesus is a great prudence" (*Imit. of C.* book ii. ch. 8).

2. *How Jesus appeared.* All the apparitions of the Saviour brought joy and consolation to their souls.

He appeared to Mary ; and who can express with what a torrent of spiritual delight He inundated her heart? He appeared to Magdalen, saying to her, " Mary;" and this word alone, making Him known, transports and ravishes the soul of Magdalen.   He appeared to the Apostles, saying to them, " Peace be with you; and He said to them again, Peace be with you" (John xx. 19, 21).   And the sight of Him and these words filled all their hearts with joy: "The disciples therefore were glad when they saw the Lord" (John xx. 20).

Let us learn to recognise by these signs the presence of Jesus Christ, and the characteristics which distinguish the action of His spirit in our souls from the action of the evil spirit.   The one announces himself by obscurity, trouble, depression, and agitation ; the other, on the contrary, announces Himself by light, peace, interior consolation.   Above all, let us know how to profit by the visits of Jesus Christ; and let us not forget that to lose His sensible grace and the consolation of His presence, it suffices only to bestow too much of our thoughts on exterior things : " You may easily banish Jesus and lose His grace if you give yourself too much to exterior things" (*Imit. of C.* book ii. ch. 8).

3. *Why Jesus Christ appeared.* For three reasons, which the Gospel indicates to us ;—to strengthen the still hesitating faith of the Apostles ; to prepare them for an approaching and long separation; to animate them to the sacrifices He is going to ask of them.   The interior visits with which Jesus Christ favours souls are for the following purposes.   If He honours us with lights and consolations, it is always to impress a greater liveliness on our faith,—to prepare us for interior deso-

lation and trials,—to animate us for the sacrifices He will soon ask of us in the practice of virtue.

COLLOQUIES.

1st. With the holy Virgin. Congratulate her on her happiness, and join in her joy.

Regina cæli.

2d. With our Lord Jesus Christ. Adore Him in the glory of His resurrection, and consecrate yourself anew to Him as to your Saviour and your King.

Prayer—Suscipe, p. 236.

SECOND EXERCISE ON THE RESURRECTION OF JESUS CHRIST.

CONTEMPLATION.

Preparatory Prayer.

Preludes. The same as last.

FIRST POINT.

Contemplate the persons.

Represent to yourself Jesus Christ rising gloriously from the tomb; the angel seated on the stone of the sepulchre, of whom it is said in the Gospel, "His countenance was as lightning, and his raiment as snow" (Matt. xxviii. 3); the guard terrified and taking to flight; the holy women, then the Apostles Peter and John, coming to the sepulchre; Jesus Christ appearing to the holy women; the disciples refusing to believe; Jesus Christ appearing to them several times.

Q

SECOND POINT.

Listen to the words.

Listen to the angel saying to the holy women : "You seek Jesus of Nazareth; He is not here; He is risen, as He foretold," &c. To Jesus Christ, appearing to His disciples and addressing words of consolation to them : "Peace be to you. It is I; fear not," &c.; then explaining to them the mysteries of His passion and of the redemption of men: "Thus it behoved Christ to suffer and to rise again. . . . Blessed are ney who have not seen and yet have believed. . . . Receive ye the Holy Ghost. . . . All power has been given Me in heaven and on earth. . . . Whatsoever you shall loose upon earth shall be loosed also in heaven. . . . Go, teach all nations, baptising them in the name of the Father. the Son, and the Holy Ghost" (Matt. xxviii.; Luke xxiv.).

THIRD POINT.

Consider the actions.

Jesus Christ, after having delivered the souls of the just from Limbus, rises from the tomb through the massive stone which closes up the entrance. The earth trembles. An angel dazzling with light descends from heaven, and seats himself on the stone of the sepulchre after having overturned it; the terrified guards run to tell the priests, who bribe them to say that the disciples have carried off the body of their Master. The holy women arrive at the sepulchre, and are seized with terror at the sight of the angel; the celestial spirit reassures them. The Saviour appears to them as well as to Peter; soon He shows Himself to His Apostles to console them, instruct them, strengthen them: He bestows upon them His peace.

FOURTH POINT.

Consider how the divinity of Jesus Christ, which was, so to say, hidden during the time of His passion, manifests itself in His resurrection, and is declared by all kinds of miracles.

FIFTH POINT.

Consider with what loving tenderness, what effusion of heart, Jesus Christ deigns to console His Apostles, —like a friend who, knowing the affliction of a friend tenderly loved, hastens to console him. Finish by practical reflections, and say to yourself: If I am now raised to grace, I must, like Jesus Christ, make my resurrection shine for the glory of God and the edification of my brethren. Jesus Christ risen dies no more; I must, then, die no more to grace by sin. Jesus Christ risen made only short apparitions of Himself; I must, then, only appear in the world through necessity, through charity, through courtesy, &c.

COLLOQUIES.

1. With the holy Virgin. Congratulate her on her happiness, and participate in her joy.
Regina cæli.
2. With our Lord Jesus Christ. Adore Him in the glory of His resurrection, and renew your consecration to Him as your Saviour and your King.
Prayer—Suscipe, p. 296. *Pater. Ave.*

EXERCISE ON THE BLESSED LIFE OF JESUS CHRIST IN HEAVEN.

Preparatory Prayer.

First prelude. Represent to yourself our Lord seated on His throne at the right hand of His Father; beside Him the Blessed Virgin; around the throne the angels and the elect.

Second prelude. Beg for an ardent desire of heaven, and the courage to suffer on earth with Jesus Christ, that you may one day reign with Him in eternity.

FIRST POINT.

Jesus Christ in heaven suffers no more.

Consider that our Lord in heaven is free from all the trials and pains which He experienced in His mortal life. His body, since His resurrection, is withdrawn from the empire of weakness and death. His soul, inundated with the delights of the divinity united to Him, is henceforward a stranger to sadness and desolation.

In heaven the Christian, like his Divine Head, will be for ever freed from all bodily pains and from all afflictions of the soul.

1. *In heaven there are no more infirmities.* The body, clothed with the glory of Jesus Christ, will be raised, like that of the Saviour, to a state of impassibility: " Who will reform the body of our lowness, made like to the body of His glory" (Philipp. iii. 21). In this abode of perfect beatitude the blessed no longer

know what it is to suffer and die: "And death shall be no more" (Apoc. xxi. 4).

2. *In heaven there is no more grief or sorrow.* "Nor mourning, nor crying, nor sorrow shall be any more" (Apoc. xxi. 4). Here below, what is life but one long unceasing affliction? In heaven all tears are dried: "God shall wipe away all tears from their eyes" (Apoc. vii. 17). They remember past sorrows, but this memory is for the elect a part of their beatitude. Each one of them, like the prophet, applauds his past trials. Each one of them says, Happy tribulations, which are now repaid by an immense weight of glory: "We have rejoiced for the days in which Thou hast humbled us; for the years in which we have seen evils" (Psalm lxxxix. 15).

3. *In heaven there are no more separations.* Here below, to poison the sweets of friendship, this thought alone suffices: "How long will the society of these friends, of these relatives so tenderly loved, continue?" But once in the bosom of God, the elect meet to part no more. What joy for a Christian family to meet again, after the long and sad separation of the grave! What joy to be able to say with confidence, "We are again united, and it is for eternity!"

4. *In heaven there are no more temptations.* Here on earth is for the Christian a struggle of every day and every moment; and in this struggle a continual danger of losing the grace of God, his soul, and eternity. Hence the groans of the saints, who never cease crying out with the prophet, "Woe is me, that my sojourning is prolonged" (Psalm cxix. 5); or with the Apostle, "Unhappy man that I am, who shall deliver me from

the body of this death?" (Rom. vii. 24.) The lament of the exile is never heard in this country. There is no longer any thing to fear from the world, which has no more illusions; nor from hell, which is conquered; nor from our own hearts, which only live for Divine love. There every thing says, as did formerly holy King David, "He hath delivered my soul from death, my eyes from tears, my feet from falling. I will please the Lord in the land of the living" (Psalm cxiv. 89).

5. *In heaven, above all, there is no more sin.* Recall what you have meditated on the malice of sin. It is the supreme evil, the one only evil of time and eternity; the sole evil of the creature, the great evil done against God. Banished into hell, sin cannot penetrate into the kingdom of charity. Oh, the happiness of that day, when, entering into heaven, the elect shall say, My God is now mine, and I am His! "My beloved to me and I to Him" (Cant. ii. 16). I am united to Him for ever, and sin can never separate me from Him: "I held Him, and will not let Him go" (Cant. iii. 4).

SECOND POINT.

Jesus Christ in heaven has no longer any thing to desire.

What our Lord asked of His Father is accomplished: "And now glorify Thou Me, O Father, with Thyself, with the glory which I had, before the world was, with Thee" (John xvii. 5). The holy humanity of our Saviour is glorified, and His glory is this blessed possession of God, in which His soul loses itself in the plenitude of all good.

To possess God, and in God to possess all good—such is also the bliss which awaits us in heaven; a sovereign and universal beatitude, which will be the full satisfaction of the entire man.

1. *Beatitude of the senses.* The body raised up at the last day and united to the soul, whose servant it was, will partake of its felicity. The ear will not weary of hearing the sacred songs of the elect; the eye will never tire in contemplating the light of Paradise, the splendour of the glorified saints, the sweet majesty of Mary on her throne, the lustre of the adorable humanity of Jesus Christ;—all the senses will be inebriated with these pure and spiritual pleasures, which appear to belong only to the celestial intelligences: "They shall be inebriated with the plenty of Thy house; and Thou shalt make them drink of the torrent of Thy pleasure" (Psalm xxxv. 9).

2. *Beatitude of memory.* With what joy will the saints recall the graces they have received from God, the virtues they practised on earth! How will a martyr congratulate himself on his sufferings, an apostle on his labours, a confessor on his sacrifices! How each one of the elect will return thanks to God for His mercies! With what an effusion of gratitude and happiness will they say to themselves, On such a day God inspired me to serve Him alone; and it is this inspiration that has led me to heaven: on such a day God preserved me from this temptation, withdrew me from this occasion or habit of sin! What care His providence took for my salvation! and what had I done to merit that He should save me in preference to so many who are lost for ever?

3. *Beatitude of the intellect.* Closely united to God, the intelligence of the elect sees all truth in Him

as in a mirror. Suppose the rudest man in the world, the most ignorant of science, enters heaven; that moment his soul is inundated with lights so vivid that before them the lights of the greatest geniuses are but darkness: it sees God without veil and face to face; and in God sees all things,—the wonderful laws that govern the world; the mysteries of providence; the secrets of the redemption of men and of the predestination of the elect; the attributes of the Divine nature,—wisdom, power, goodness, immensity, eternity; the Three Persons of the Trinity, with their relations and ineffable operation. The soul sees God, and this sight, in a manner, transforms it into God Himself, according to the words of St. John: "We know that when He shall appear, we shall be like to Him; because we shall see Him as He is" (1 John iii. 2).

4. *Beatitude of the will.* This beatitude will be to love and possess God. To love God is the true object of our heart. But here below how weak is this love, how it is mingled with lowness and imperfections, how subject it is to change and inconstancy! In heaven, scarcely does God show Himself to the soul before He subjugates it and ravishes it for ever;—sovereign love which rules all the affections; love so pure that the blessed forget themselves to be lost in God; love so ardent and so strong that it absorbs and exhausts all the power of loving; love so ecstatic that the soul goes out of itself and passes entirely into God to be consummated in unity with Him. It is the expression of our Lord: "The glory which Thou hast given Me, I have given to them, that they may be one, as We also are one" (John xvii. 22).

" O God! when shall it be given to me to see the glory of Thy kingdom? When will the day arrive that Thou shalt be all in all to me? When shall I be with Thee in the mansions which Thou hast eternally prepared for Thy beloved?" (*Imit. of Christ*, book iii. ch. 43.)

THIRD POINT.
Jesus Christ in heaven has no change to dread.

The reign of Jesus Christ in heaven is safe from all vicissitudes: it will have no end. He will reign eternally at the right hand of His Father, always triumphant, always sovereign, always the object of love to the saints and angels, as of the sweetest approbation of His Father: *Cujus regni non erit finis*, " Of whose kingdom there shall be no end."

The beatitude of the saints is immutable, like that of the Son of God. It is the inseparable condition of worldly goods to be accompanied by fear or distaste, sometimes by both at once: fear, because each moment they may escape; distaste, because we cannot long enjoy them without recognising and feeling their vanity. It is not so with the goods of eternity. These are unchangeable, and therefore have no end or diminution. Add ages to ages; multiply them equal to the sand of the ocean or the stars of heaven; exhaust all the numbers, if you can, beyond what the human intelligence can conceive, and for the elect there will be still the same eternity of happiness. They are immutable, and this immutability excludes weariness and disgust. The life of an elect soul is one succession, without end, of desires ever arising and ever satisfied, but desires without trouble, satiety, or lassitude. The elect will always see God, love God, possess God, anr always will wish to see Him, love Him, and possess Him still more.

This beatitude is the end destined for all; God has given us time only in order to merit it, being and life only to possess it. Reflect seriously on this great truth, and ask yourself these three questions at the foot of the crucifix:

What have I done hitherto for heaven? What ought I to do for heaven? What shall I do henceforward for heaven?

Colloquies with the Blessed Virgin and our Lord glorified in heaven.

Anima Christi. Pater. Ave.

EXERCISE ON THE LOVE OF GOD.

First remark. True love consists in fruits and effects, not in words: " My little children," says the beloved disciple, "let us not love in word, nor in tongue; but in deed and in truth" (1 John iii. 18).

Second remark. The effect of true love is the reciprocal communication of all good things between the persons who love each other; whence it follows that charity cannot exist without sacrifice. Do not, then, content yourself with tender and affectionate sentiments; " For," says St. Gregory, " the proof of love is in the works: where love exists, it works great things, but when it ceases to act, it ceases to exist."

CONTEMPLATION.

Preparatory Prayer.

First prelude. Place yourself in spirit in the presence of God, and figure to yourself that you are before His throne in the midst of saints and angels, who intercede for you with the Lord.

Second prelude. Ask of God the grace to comprehend the greatness of His benefits and to consecrate yourself without reserve to His love and service.

FIRST POINT.

Recall to yourself the benefits of God. These benefits are of three principal orders : *benefits of creation, benefits of redemption, particular benefits.* In the first order are comprised all the natural gifts ;—the soul with its powers, the body with its senses, life with the good things which accompany it. In the second are comprised all the supernatural graces, the sufferings and death of Jesus Christ, the Sacraments, &c. In the third are all the graces that we receive every day and every hour from Divine Providence.

Consider attentively these three orders of the Divine benefits, and in each one meditate on these three circumstances in which St. Ignatius shows us the characters of true charity. In each you will find :

1. A love which acts and manifests itself by works. What more active than the charity of God in the creation, preservation, and redemption of man ?

2. A love that gives, that lavishes its goods. Has God any thing of which He has not given part to man? Has He not given Himself on the cross for an example,

and in the Eucharist, His body, His blood, His divinity, His life, and all His being?

3. A love never satisfied with what it has given, and that would always give more. Is not this the love of God towards us? Is it not true that His greatest gifts have not been able to exhaust the prodigality of His heart? Is it not true that there is in Him a desire to do us good which will never be satisfied until He has given Himself to us entirely and for ever in heaven?

After having meditated on these characters of Divine charity, return to yourself and ask yourself what gratitude and justice require in return for such marvellous generosity. You have nothing of yourself: you hold all from God; what else, then, can you do but offer Him all that you have and all that you are? Say to Him, then, with all the affection of your heart:

Suscipe, Domine, &c. : "Take, O Lord, and receive my entire liberty, my memory, my understanding, and my whole will. All that I am, all that I have, Thou hast given me, and I give it back again to Thee, to be disposed of according to Thy good pleasure. Give me only Thy love and Thy grace; with these I am rich enough."*

SECOND POINT.

Consider that God, your Benefactor, is present in all creatures and in yourself. If you look at every

---

* Or, as the prayer may be paraphrased : " Take, O Lord, for it is Thine,—receive as an offering, for I would give it were it not Thine,—all that I value ; all my liberty, all my memory, will, and understanding. All that I am, all that I have, is Thy free gift to me; this I give back to Thee, that Thou mayest

step of the visible creation, in all you will meet God. He is in the elements, He gives them existence; in plants, He gives them life; in animals, He gives them sensation. He is in you; and, collecting all these degrees of being scattered through the rest of His creation, He unites them in you, and adds to them intelligence. And how is this great God in you? In the most noble, the most excellent manner. He is in you as in His temple, as in a sanctuary where He sees His own image, where He finds an intelligence capable of knowing and loving Him. Thus your Benefactor is always with you; He is more intimately united to you than your soul is to your body. You ought, then,—and this is the second degree of love,—you ought as much as possible not to lose sight of Him. You ought to think and act in His presence, to keep yourself before Him like a child before a tenderly-loved father, studying the slightest sign of His will and wish. Finish this second point by a renewed offering of yourself, and one, if possible, still more affectionate and unreserved.

THIRD POINT.

Consider not only that God your benefactor is present, but also that He acts continually in all His creatures. And for whom is this continual action, this work of God in nature? For you. Thus, He lights you by the light of day; He nourishes you with the

dispose of all according to Thy good pleasure. And now, O Lord, bestow upon me a gift. Give me Thy love, and Thy grace, without which I cannot persevere in that love. With this I am rich enough, and I desire nothing more."

productions of the earth; in a word, He serves you by each one of the creatures that you use; so that it is true to say that at every moment the bounty, the wisdom, and the power of God are at your service, and are exercised in the world for your wants or pleasures. This conduct of God towards man should be the model of your conduct towards God. You see that the presence of God in His creatures is never idle; it acts incessantly, it preserves, it governs. Beware, then, of stopping at a sterile contemplation of God present in yourself. Add action to contemplation; to the sight of the Divine presence add the faithful accomplishment of the Divine will. Meditate well on the two characters of the action of God in the world, so as to reproduce them as much as possible in your own deeds. What more active than God, and at the same time what more calm and tranquil? He is incessantly occupied with the care of His creatures; and yet He is never distracted from the interior contemplation of His essence and of His attributes. Learn in the exercise of the presence of God, to unite movement and repose, work and recollection. Think always of God, but in such a manner that you do not cease to act; act, but in such a manner that you do not cease to think of God. And to arrive at this high degree of perfection, endeavour to seek only one end even in the diversity of your occupations; that is, the good pleasure and holy will of God. End by offering yourself as in the preceding points.

FOURTH POINT.

Recall what you meditated on the first point; that is, that there is in God an ardent desire, and as it were

a need, to communicate all His perfections to you, as
much as the infinite can be communicated to the finite.
Consider that you find the weak and rude image of
these perfections in created things.   All that there is
good and beautiful in creatures, what is it but an ema-
nation of the Divinity?   The power, wisdom, goodness
of men, from whence do they come if not from God,
as the rays come from the sun and the stream from the
fountain ?

From this consideration arises a double consequence,
which is the fourth and last degree of the love of God :
detachment from creatures, and detachment from ourselves.

1. *Detachment from creatures*; because they have
only very limited perfections, and those lent to them ;
while God possesses all perfection and in an infinite
degree.

2. *Detachment from ourselves*; because all our
being and all our happiness depend, not on us, but on
God, as the light of the ray depends on the sun, the
water of the stream on the fountain.   According to the
words of our Lord, to find ourselves is to lose ourselves,
because in us and of ourselves there is only nothingness : " He that loveth his life shall lose it" (John xii.
25) ; and, on the contrary, to hate ourselves, leave ourselves, lose ourselves, is to find ourselves, because then
we find ourselves in God, who alone is our life, our
happiness, and our being : " He that hateth his life
shall keep it unto life eternal" (ibid.).

From this double detachment springs true liberty
of spirit, which consists in no longer being bound either
to creatures or to ourselves, and in reposing perfectly and

solely on the love of God. In this state the soul is absolutely indifferent to all that is not God. For it there is only one thought—to please God in all its actions; only one desire—soon to quit this earth, in order fully to possess God in heaven.

Finish as in the preceding points.

Sum up, in order to profit better by them, the four degrees of the love of God, as they are proposed to us by St. Ignatius.

1. A God from whom I hold all; I ought, then, to render Him all. Hence entire oblation of myself.

2. A God who is present in every creature and in myself; I ought, then, to live in God by a constant and happy remembrance of His presence.

3. A God who acts in every creature and for my service, but without losing any thing of His infinite repose; I ought, then, to act in God and for His service without ever losing sight of His presence.

4. A God who wishes to communicate all His perfections to me, and who beforehand shows me the image of them in a faint degree in His creatures; I ought, then, to leave both creatures and myself, in order to attach myself only to God, in whom I find, as in their source, and in an infinite degree, all perfections.

Colloquy according to the accustomed method.

Suscipe or *Pater. Ave.*

ADDITIONAL EXERCISES.

ON DEVOTION TO THE BLESSED VIRGIN MARY, MOTHER OF GOD.

FIRST EXERCISE.

Preparatory Prayer.

First prelude. Salute Mary, Mother of God, with the angel Gabriel.

Second prelude. Ask of Jesus Christ a high esteem and great veneration for His Mother.

Consider—

1. What union the Divine maternity established between Jesus and Mary.

2. What virtues this august title presupposes in her.

3. What authority it confers on her.

FIRST POINT.

Mary is not only the privileged daughter of the Father, the beloved spouse of the Holy Ghost, she is also the *mother of the Son of God.*

1. In this quality, she is united to Jesus in the eternal decrees and in the promises of the Saviour made in the beginning of all time. It is by her that the head of the serpent is to be crushed (Gen. iii. 13). She is united to her Divine Son in the oracles of the prophets. Isaias announces this branch of Jesse, and the

R

blessed fruit she is to bear (Isaias xi. 1); the Virgin
Mother and the Emmanuel her Son (Isaias vii. 14);
Jeremias predicts this marvellous woman, Mother of a
perfect Man (Jer. xxxi. 22); David sings of this Queen
seated on the right hand of the heavenly King (Psalm
xliv. 10). The book of Wisdom describes the wonders
of the temple that Wisdom had chosen for its dwelling
(Wisdom ix., &c.).

2. She is united to Jesus in the figures of the an-
cient law. Eve, says St. Augustine, was, in more than
one point of resemblance or opposition, a figure of Mary.
Eve was drawn from Adam's side; Mary draws all her
merits from her Divine Son. Eve, seduced by an angel
of darkness, was the first cause of our ruin; Mary, persuaded by an angel from heaven, began the work of our
redemption. Her intercession and power are figured by
Esther obtaining grace for her people, by Judith victo-
rious over Holophernes; her Immaculate Conception by
the burning bush which the flames surrounded without
touching, by that wonderful fleece which alone in a vast
plain received the dew of heaven.

3. She is united to the Son of God, above all, at the
moment of the incarnation. Then her Creator became
her Child (Ecclus. xxiv. 12). The blood of Mary became
the blood of Jesus; Jesus is flesh of her flesh; He lives
with her life, breathes with her breath; He is in her, to
her, of her entirely. Thus the angel says : " The Lord
is with thee" (Luke i. 28). Elizabeth says, " Behold
the Mother of my Lord" (ib. 44). And the Church, in
the third General Council, declares : " If any one refuse to call Mary Mother of God, let him be anathema"
(*Act of the Council of Ephesus*).

4. But, above all, the holy soul of Mary is united to the adorable soul of Jesus. She conceived Him in her heart before receiving Him in her bosom, says St Bernard. She unites herself to Him by the most lively faith, the most ardent charity, by the consent, the memory of which we revere in the "Angelus" three times a day, and which associates her with her whole destiny. So Mary is found with Jesus at Bethlehem, in Egypt, in Nazareth, in Jerusalem, and, above all, on Calvary, where the sword of sorrow pierced her soul when the lance opened the heart of her Divine Son.

5. Jesus ascends to heaven, and Mary is soon placed on His right hand, that is, associated with His glory and His all-powerful action in the salvation of the world; united to the King of Heaven by an ineffable union. Here on earth the Son and the Mother are united in the praises of the Fathers, in the prayers of the Christian Liturgy, in the definitions of councils, in the solemnities of the Church. We see Christians honouring, always in union, the Incarnation of Jesus, the Conception of Mary; the birth of Jesus, the nativity of Mary; the presentation of Jesus, the presentation of Mary; the baptism of Jesus, the purification of Mary; the sufferings of Jesus, the dolours of Mary; the ascension of Jesus, the assumption of Mary; the sacred heart of Jesus, the holy heart of Mary. The names of Jesus and Mary live always united in the hearts and the songs of the faithful; their temples and their altars are always near together, and nothing is more inseparable in their pious remembrances, their confidence, their invocation, their love, than JESUS AND MARY.

SECOND POINT.

And what creature was more like to Jesus than Mary?

The laws of nature ordain that the son should resemble the mother; the laws of grace ordained beforehand that the Mother should possess all the characters suitable to the Son. Here recall with profound respect—

1. *Her Immaculate Conception;* which renders her a stranger to sin and its consequences, and to all the occasions leading to sin. This privilege alone, which separates Mary from the mass of iniquity out of which ~e have all come, raises her above all the saints as much as the heavens are above the earth.

2. *Her celestial virginity;* which the approach of an angel alarms; that would shrink from the Divine maternity, if the Mother of God could cease to be a virgin; which the Holy Ghost renders fruitful and a mother by an ineffable miracle.

3. *Her profound humility;* which, says a holy Father, made her merit the Divine maternity: "Behold," said she, "the handmaid of the Lord. He hath regarded the humility of His handmaid. He hath exalted the humble. He hath filled the hungry with good things" (Luke i. 38, 48, 52, 53).

4. *Her perfect charity;* which made her so prompt in visiting Elizabeth, so faithful in preserving in her heart the words of life, so attentive at the marriage of Cana, so devoted, so heroic during the labours and sorrows of her Son, so useful to the Apostles, so dear to the infant Church.

THIRD POINT.

What authority does not this Divine maternity give to Mary? Jesus Christ the Son of God, and Himself God, obeyed her thirty years; thirty years He executes her will, consults and forestalls her wishes. What a lesson does the docility of this true Son give to us sons by adoption; to us sons of Adam the docility of the Son of God! (St. Bern.)

Jesus Christ on the cross gave her to us for our Mother. The Mother of God is, then, our Mother, exercising over us the maternal authority in all its meaning and extent.

Jesus Christ in heaven, say the holy Fathers, still obeys the humble prayers of Mary. He has made her intercession all-powerful; He has established her the distributor of graces, the succour of Christians, the defence of the Church against infidelity and heresy. Giving us Jesus through Mary was to give us all through Mary. From the conception of Jesus the way was thus traced: "We receive all from her who gave us Jesus" (St. Bern.).

How great, then, is the authority of the Queen of Heaven, how extensive is the power of the Mother of God! In what peril are those who forget her or insult her! how safe are those she protects!

COLLOQUY.

Say to her, with the angel, "Hail, Mary, full of grace," &c.; or, with St. Cyril, the oracle of the Œcumenical Council, "Glory be to you, holy Mother of God, masterpiece of the universe, brilliant star, glory of virginity, sceptre of faith, indestructible temple, inhabited by Him whom immensity cannot contain. Virgin mother of Him who, blessed for ever, comes to us in the name of the Lord, by you the Trinity is glorified, the holy cross celebrated and adored throughout the universe, the heavens are joyful, the angels tremble with joy, the devils are put to flight, man passes from slavery to heaven. Through you idolatrous creatures have known incarnate truth, the faithful have received baptism, churches have been raised over all the world; by your assistance the Gentiles have been led to repentance. Finally, through you the only Son of God, Source of all light, has shone on the eyes of the blind, who were sitting in the shadow of death. But, O Virgin Mother, who can speak your praises! Let us, however, celebrate them according to our powers, and at the same time adore God thy Son, the chaste Spouse of the Church, to whom are due all honour and glory now and through all eternity. Amen" (St. Cyril's Homily against Nestorius).

SECOND EXERCISE ON DEVOTION TO THE BLESSED VIRGIN MARY OUR MOTHER.

Preparatory Prayer.

First prelude. See Mary at the foot of the cross; hear Jesus saying to you, "Behold thy Mother!"

Second prelude. Ask of Jesus a filial love for Mary your Mother.

Consider—

1. That Mary was given you for your Mother.

2 That she has really shown herself a Mother to you.

3 That you ought to be a confiding and devoted son to her.

FIRST POINT.

Mary has been given you for a Mother. Consider, then, in your heart all the circumstances of this gift.

1. She was given to you by Jesus Christ, God and Master of all creatures, from whom emanates all power, paternal and maternal; by Jesus Christ the God-Saviour, who had already sacrificed for you the body and lavished the blood He derived from Mary. Having nothing more to give you but her, He bestows her on you as a complement of all His gifts.

2. She is given to you in the clearest terms, the strongest, the most precise, to enable you to realise what they signify: "Behold your Mother." Jesus said, in showing the bread, "This is My body;" and the bread became His body. Pointing to His Mother, He says, "Behold thy Mother;" Mary immediately became our Mother.

3. She was given to you under the most serious and solemn circumstances. Jesus, dying, makes His last dispositions and signifies His last will. Alone of all the disciples the beloved John is present to receive in the name of all Christians the last gift which their Divine Master makes to them. Thus all the fathers and doctors of the Church have understood it.

4. She is given you "for your Mother." Feel these words at the bottom of your heart. Recall to yourself that man does not live only by bread; that his soul as

well as his body has a life to receive and support. It is
in this supernatural order that Mary is your mother;
if you live to grace, it is through her. The principle of
this spiritual life is in Jesus; but Mary's is the bosom
that bore you, the milk that nourished you, the maternal heart that always loves its children even when ungrateful.

5. Why was a mother according to grace given to
you? and why was this mother the mother of God?
Interrogate Jesus in profound recollection of heart. He
wished to become your brother both by father and
mother; He wished that all should be in common between you; He wished that if the infinite height of
His divinity terrified you, a creature, His mother and
yours, should serve as your advocate, your refuge, and
your mediatrix with Him; He wished to encourage
the most timid, open the hearts most oppressed by fear,
offer to all the sweetest motive for trust, always well
founded, never too great; for a mother always loves
her child; and Jesus, Son of Mary, will always love
His mother.

SECOND POINT.

Mary has always shown herself your Mother.

1. She received you to her heart when Jesus gave
you to her for her child; so the Scripture calls Jesus
Christ her first-born (Matt. i. 25). You ought to be
born in her and by her, after Him.

2. She has nourished you, not only by the graces
her prayers have obtained for you, but also in a real
manner by the Body and Blood of her Son given to
you in the F ~harist.

3. She has anticipated you, cared for you, loaded you with favours. All the graces you have received from the Lord have been solicited and obtained by her. So, your call to the faith, the grace of a Christian education, of a first communion; the grace of conversion and retreat, the grace that now leads you to give yourself entirely to God,—all come to you from Jesus through Mary (St. Bernard).

4. At need, Mary obtains for the defence and salvation of her children extraordinary graces and wonderful miracles. What prodigies have caused, sustained, spread every where, confidence among Christian people What striking proofs of her protection the Church recalls to our memory by solemn feasts and pious practices, enriched by precious indulgences! What titles Christians give her to testify their gratitude: "Help of Christians, health of the sick, comfort of the afflicted, refuge of sinners, gate of heaven, our life, our sweetness, our hope!" What a concourse of people to the places where she is most honoured, where she obtains the most succours to those who invoke her! What prayers and acts of thanksgiving at the foot of her altars! and in our days what conquests made by Our Lady of Victories! What favours bestowed on all hearts devoted to the heart of Mary!

5. Her protection, "strong as an army" (Cant. vi.), preserves her faithful children from all dangers; she is for them an assured pledge of predestination. So the doctors of the Church believe, who assure us "that a servant of Mary cannot perish."

THIRD POINT.

We then owe to our Mother love, confidence, imitation, zeal to spread devotion to her.

1. *Love* for her who is the beloved of our Lord; gratitude towards her who has loaded us with benefits; filial affection for our Mother.

2. *Confidence.* Her power and her title of Mother were given to her that our trust in her might be unlimited, that we might know that she would always be able and willing to help us.

3. *Imitation.* She expects from us this proof of true love. Does not the child naturally resemble the mother? Let this resemblance in us be the fruit of our efforts, of a careful study and practice of her virtues. Sons of a virgin, let us be pure; sons of the Mother of sorrows, let us be faithful to Jesus, even unto the cross.

4. *Zeal* to spread her devotion. A sincere love will produce this zeal. We must praise and defend all the practices authorised by the Church; her images must be venerated and distributed; we must love to bear her livery, to visit the places where she is honoured; take pleasure in singing her praises, in preceding her feasts by penance, and in sanctifying them by the reception of the holy Eucharist. Let us honour the sacred heart of Mary, and honour it by a particular devotion.

COLLOQUIES.

Let us recite the *Magnificat* in union with Mary, or else address these words of St. Bernard to ourselves:

"O thou who feelest thyself tossed by the tempests in the midst of the shoals of this world, turn not away thine eyes from the star of the sea if thou wouldst avoid shipwreck. If the winds of temptation blow, if tribulations rise up like rocks before thee, a look at the star, a sigh towards Mary. If the waves of pride, ambition, calumny, jealousy, seek to swallow up thy soul, a look towards the star, a prayer to Mary. If anger, avarice, love of pleasure, shiver thy frail bark, seek the eyes of Mary. If horror of thy sins, trouble of conscience, dread of the judgments of God, begin to plunge thee into the gulf of sadness, the abyss of despair, attach thy heart to Mary. In thy dangers, thy anguish, thy doubts, think of Mary, call on Mary. Let Mary be on thy lips, in thy heart, and to the suffrage of her prayers lose not sight of the example of her virtues. Following her, thou canst not wander; whilst thou prayest to her thou canst not be without hope; as long as thou thinkest of her thou wilt be in the path; thou canst not fall when she sustains thee; thou hast nothing to fear while she protects thee; if she favour thy voyage, thou wilt reach the harbour of safety without weariness."

RECOMMENDATIONS FOR THE LAST DAY OF THE EXERCISES.

1. He who goes from a warm place to a cold or damp one is, if he is not careful, readily affected by the change of air. So he who passes from a retreat to ordinary life is in danger of losing in a short time the lights and fervour of the Exercises. For the impressions of grace not yet being strengthened by habit, it is almost certain, unless great precaution be used, that they will soon be weakened, and finally dissipated altogether.

2. In coming out from the Exercises, do not fail to thank our Lord for the graces of the retreat. Recall in His presence all the lights, all the inspirations you have received, and look on them as so many testimonies of the special love of our Lord for you. Renew your resolution to adopt all the necessary means to accomplish what you know of His Divine will towards you. Fear lest so great a grace, if it does not make you better, should make you more guilty, and serve to draw down on you a more severe condemnation at the tribunal of God.

3. Be careful on re-entering the world to be on your guard against sin and the occasions of sin. On the one hand, you must expect that the spirit of darkness will neglect nothing to draw you away; on the other, you must not conceal from yourself that you have every thing to fear from your own weakness: for you have in the depths of your heart inclinations like a tree that has been cut, but whose roots still live; or like a torch just extinguished, but which lights again as

soon as it is brought near the flame. You require, then, both a spirit of fear lest you allow yourself to be deceived by the demon and by your own heart, and at the same time great courage to combat both.

4. If after the retreat you fall even into some serious fault, do not think that the fruit of the Exercises is lost, and so give way to discouragement. It is the ordinary artifice of the evil one to draw the soul again into its old faults, and from these faults into dejection and despair; he thus endeavours to make perseverance appear impossible; and finally, to withdraw the soul for ever from the service of God. After each fault, humble yourself before the Lord, repair as soon as possible to the Sacraments, have full confidence in the Divine mercy, and begin again with new ardour to walk in the path of virtue.

5. The following are the most efficacious means of preserving the fruits of the retreat :

(1.) Devote each day half-an-hour, or if possible an hour, to meditation, and a quarter of an hour to a particular and general examination according to the method traced in the Exercises.

(2.) Approach the Sacraments of penance and communion every week.

(3.) Fix a rule for your daily actions, keep to it carefully, and in each action study as much as possible to sanctify it by purity of intention, which consists in proposing to ourselves no other motive but the glory and good pleasure of God.

(4.) Choose an enlightened confessor, who will be a guide to you in the ways of virtue, and with whom you may speak of all that concerns your soul.

(5.) Often read pious books, frequent the company of good men, and carefully avoid the conversation of the wicked.

(6.) Apply yourself with perseverance to the acquirement of some solid virtue, above all, of humility and charity.

(7.) Place yourself under the protection of Mary, have a tender piety to this good Mother, and never allow a day to pass without offering her some homage.

(8.) Finally, every year devote a week, if possible, to a spiritual retreat; and if this be impossible, at least at Easter make a review or general confession of all the faults of the past year.

SECOND PART.

METHOD OF PARTICULAR EXAMINATION.

THERE are two kinds of examination (or examen),
general and particular. The object of the first is to
discover all the faults we have committed. The second
or particular examination has for its object one single
fault or bad habit which we have resolved to correct.
It is made every day in the following manner:

1. In the morning, on rising, resolve to avoid this
sin or defect.

2. Towards noon ask of God the grace to remember how often you have fallen into it, and to avoid it
for the future. Then examine, thinking over the time
passed since your rising to this time, the number of
faults committed, marking them by so many points
in the first line of a figure like the following :*

* Books of this kind, containing a page for every week in
year, may be had of the publishers.

DAYS OF THE WEEK.

1st day _____

2d day _____

3d day _____

4th day _____

5th day _____

6th day _____

7th day _____

This done, renew your resolutions for the rest of the day.

3. In the evening, after supper, a new examination like the first, marking the faults on the second line.

OBSERVATIONS.

1. At each fault against the resolutions you have taken, put your hand on your heart and repent of your fall. This may be done without being perceived.

2. At night, count the points of the two examina-

tions, and see if from the first to the second you have made any amendment.

3. Compare in the same way the day or the week which is ending with the preceding day or week. The lines diminish in length, because it is reasonable to expect that the number of the faults should likewise diminish.

4. The subject of the particular examination should be ordinarily the predominant passion—that is, the one that is the source of the greater number of faults that you commit, and which consequently is the great obstacle to your sanctification.

5. This examination on the predominant passion should be continued until it is entirely overcome, or at least notably weakened.

ADVICE CONCERNING THE GENERAL EXAMINATION OF CONSCIENCE.

Sins of thought.

It may be admitted as a principle that there arise in man three sorts of thoughts, of which one comes of itself, and the other two from the good and the evil spirit.

A bad thought, which if consented to would become a mortal sin, may be an occasion of merit—1, when the thought, as soon as it presents itself, is resisted or banished; 2, when the thought repelled, once or several times, returns soon afterwards, but is constantly resisted until vanquished: and this second victory is much more meritorious than the first. That person sins ve-

s

nially who dwells a little on the thought, as if he listened to it, or who takes a slight pleasure in what flatters the senses, or is negligent in repelling it.

Mortal sin is committed by thought, first, when the thought is consented to; and secondly, when the thought is acted upon, which is a more grievous sin: 1, because it is entertained longer; 2, because we give ourselves up to it more ardently; 3, because we generally injure others by scandalising them.

Sins of word.

There are many ways of offending God by words; for example, by swearing and blaspheming. We must not swear by the Creator, nor by any creature, except with these three conditions—truth, necessity, respect. By necessity is understood the obligation of confirming with an oath, not all sorts of truths, but only those which tend to procure a considerable good, spiritual or temporal. That person swears with respect, who, in pronouncing the name of God, renders Him the honour which is due to Him.

To swear by the Creator rashly and in vain is a greater sin than to swear by the creature. Yet it is easier to observe the required conditions in swearing by the Creator than swearing by created things: 1. because in swearing by the latter we take less care as to the truth and the necessity; 2. because we think less of the respect due to God in calling His works to witness than in uttering His holy name. All idle words must be avoided, that is, such as are neither useful to the speaker nor to others, and which are not said with any intention of being useful. But we must not con-

sider those words idle which of themselves tend to the
spiritual good of our souls or those of our neighbours,
or to a temporal good or interest, or which refer to it
in the intention of the speaker, although he may be
speaking of things foreign to his state—as if, for instance, a monk should speak of trade or war, &c. To
speak with a good intention is a merit; to speak use-
lessly or to a bad end is a sin.

The most common sins of the tongue are, lying, false
testimony, and detraction. As to this last, it is a mortal sin to make known a serious fault which is not public, if done with a bad intention or with notable prejudice
to our neighbour's reputation. If the fault revealed be
less serious, the sin is only venial.

If the intention be good, we may speak of our neighbour's faults, 1, when they are public; 2, when we
speak to persons who may probably withdraw them
from sin.

Insult, derision, and words with such-like tendency
belong also to sins of the tongue.

Sins of action.

All actions by which we transgress the commandments of God or the Church are mortal or venial sins,
according to the gravity of the matter and the degree
of thought and consent with which they were done.

METHOD OF THE GENERAL EXAMINATION
TO BE MADE EVERY DAY.

The first point is an act of thanksgiving to the Lord
for the benefits we have received.

The second is a prayer to know our faults, and to correct them.

The third is an exact discussion and examination of the sins we have committed during the day. We must demand a rigorous account from our souls of what we have thought, said, and done hour by hour. The same order and method must be followed as has been already given for the particular examen.

The fourth consists in asking pardon of God for the sins into which we have fallen.

OF GENERAL CONFESSION AND COMMUNION.

The following are some of the principal advantages of general confession, which is recommended during the Exercises, even though not of absolute obligation.

1. The remembrance and detailed view of the sins of our past life excite in the soul a more lively contrition.

2. As the Exercises give a clearer and more distinct knowledge of the malice of sin, the confession will be made with more care and more fruit.

3. Experience shows that a great number of Christians often approach the sacrament of penance without sufficient examination, without the necessary sorrow, without any, or at least a very feeble, resolution of amendment of life. Thence arise troubles and disquiet, if not during life, at least at the moment of death. The purpose of the general confession made during the Exercises is to purify the soul from all past faults, and to give it peace and tranquillity for the future. So, al-

though we must avoid in this confession anxiety, scruples, and continual returns to the past, yet we must endeavour to give it all the attention and all the care we are capable of, so that we may always be able to assure ourselves that not any thing has been neglected; without which we can never enjoy peace of heart or repose of conscience. It will be desirable, in preparing for this confession, to make use of some method or directory for examination. There are several very good ones which can easily be procured.

4. The last advantage of general confession is, that it is generally followed by a more fervent communion. And nothing is more efficacious than a good communion, whether in avoiding sin, or in preserving and augmenting the grace which we have had the happiness to receive.

RULES OF PENANCE; OR, TENTH ADDITION.

(See p. 12, the " Ten Additions.")

10. I will add to the practices already recommended some satisfaction or penance.

Penance is interior and exterior.

Interior penance is sorrow for our personal sins, accompanied by the firm resolution to sin no more.

Exterior is as the fruit of the interior sentiments. It is a punishment which a sincere repentance causes us to inflict, and is practised chiefly in three ways.

First, in nourishment; if we retrench something, not of superfluous food (that is the office of temperance, not penance), but of something proper for us; and the more we retrench, the better we do, as long as nature does not become too weak or ill..

In the second place, in sleep and rest; if we give up, not only luxury,—that which would give delight,—but also what might be only convenient; always avoiding, however, what would seriously endanger the health or life. For this reason, we must not retrench necessary sleep, or at least very little, and only in case of being obliged to cure ourselves of a bad habit of sleeping too long.

Finally, in the treatment of the body; if we inflict painful sensations on our body, by the use of hair-shirts, cords, or iron girdles, or by wounding or bruising ourselves. In all this, however, it appears more expedient that the pain should affect the flesh only, without penetrating to the interior organs, where dangerous lesions might take place; therefore we ought rather to choose disciplines made with small cords, because they only give pain to the exterior parts without injuring the health.

Exterior penance serves for three purposes, or produces three principal effects: it serves as an excellent satisfaction for past sins; it exercises man in conquering himself and in submitting the inferior part of himself, his senses, to the superior part, or the reason; finally, it solicits and obtains those gifts of Divine grace which we desire—for example, lively contrition for our sins, abundant tears for them, or over the cross of Jesus Christ, the solution of a doubt that has troubled us, &c.

When the desired feelings of consolation or sorrow are not derived from the Exercises, it is useful to modify the regimen a little by mortifying ourselves differently from what we have done before, in our eating, sleeping, or the treatment of our body. So that when a penance has been practised three days, for example, it may be interrupted two days or longer, according as the state of the soul requires more or less penance.

Care in varying and interrupting these exterior mortifications during the Exercises procures the following great advantages. It frequently happens that certain persons neglect all practice of penance, either from excess of sensuality or because they persuade themselves that their constitution cannot bear it without danger: others, on the contrary, relying too much on their strength, pass the bounds of all discretion. But by changing the kind of penance, and trying first one and then another, it happens that we obtain, through this experience, and by the grace of God, who sees the depths of our nature, the knowledge of what will be most useful to us.

RULES FOR THE DISCERNMENT OF SPIRITS.

The soul is moved by diverse spirits, which it is important to discern, in order to follow the good and repel the bad. The following are some rules, of which the first are suited to souls less perfect, and the others to those who are more so.

FIRST RULES.

(More particularly suitable to the first week.)

1. Let us suppose a soul that easily falls into mortal sin, and goes from fall to fall: to plunge it deeper into crime and fill up the measure of iniquity, the infernal enemy ordinarily employs the charms of voluptuousness and all the baits of the senses, which he in-

cessantly places before the eyes. On the contrary, to turn him from sin, the good spirit never ceases to prick his conscience with the sting of remorse and the counsels of reason.

2. But if this soul should set itself to use every effort in order to purify itself from its sins, and to advance every day more and more in the service of God, the evil spirit, to stop and embarrass it, throws in its way every kind of scruple, disquiet, specious pretext, and subject of trouble and agitation. The good spirit, on the other hand, as soon as we begin to amend, encourages, fortifies, consoles, softens even to tears, enlightens the understanding, spreads peace in the heart, smooths all difficulties and obstacles, so that every day more freely, more joyously, and more rapidly, we advance in virtue by the practice of good works.

3. True spiritual consolation may be known by the following signs. A certain interior impulse raises the soul towards the Creator, makes it love Him with an ardent love, and no longer permits it to love any creature but for Him; sometimes gentle tears cause this love, tears which flow from repentance of past faults, or the sight of the sorrows of Jesus Christ, or any other motive that enlightened religion inspires; finally, all that increases faith, hope, charity; all that fills the soul with holy joy, makes it more attached to meditation on heavenly things, and more careful of salvation; all that leads it to find repose and peace in the Lord,—all this is true and spiritual consolation.

4. On the contrary, all that darkens the soul, that troubles it, that inclines it to inferior and terrestrial objects, that disquiets and agitates it, that would lead

it to despair of salvation, that weakens hope and vanishes charity, that renders the soul sad, tepid, languid, distrustful even of the clemency of its Creator and its Redeemer,—this is what may be called spiritual desolation. *Desolation* and *consolation* are two opposite terms; so the thoughts and affections arising from each are diametrically opposite.

5. During times of desolation, the bad spirit makes as feel his influence. By following his inspirations we cannot arrive at any good or useful decision; we must, therefore, beware at such times of reconsidering or making any innovation whatsoever in what relates to our resolutions or choice of a state of life; but we must persevere in what we have decided on in the day or hour of consolation, and consequently under the influence of the good spirit.

6. And yet, without changing any thing that was before laid down and defined, man, when a prey to desolation, would do well to employ means, or to multiply them, in order to dissipate it,—such as prayer offered with more importunity, examination, awakening and arousing the conscience, some penance as a punishment for faults known or unknown.

7. Under the pressure of desolation the following are the thoughts which should sustain us : Divine grace remains to us although it may have ceased to be sensible; although the first ardour of our charity is no longer felt, we still have all that is requisite for doing good and working out our salvation. What, then, does our Lord expect of us? He would see whether, if furnished with the ordinary assistance of nature and grace, we can resist our enemy. Oh, without doubt we can.

8. The unquiet spirit, which agitates and torments us, has a direct antagonist and adversary in the spirit of patience. To preserve patience and calm will, then, be of wonderful assistance to us against it. Finally, we must call hope to our aid; and if we know how to employ the above means against desolation, we may say to ourselves, Consolation will not be long in coming.

9. Desolation most frequently arises from one of these three causes : (1) Perhaps we have deserved from want of diligence and fervour in our spiritual exercises to be deprived of Divine consolations. (2) Perhaps God is trying us, and He wishes to see what we are and how we employ ourselves for His service and glory; even though He does not bestow on us every day the rewards of His Spirit in gifts and sensible graces. (3) Or it is perhaps a lesson He is giving us : He wishes to prove to us by experience that to procure fervour of devotion, ardent love, abundant tears, or to preserve ourselves in these spiritual joys, is beyond our natural strength, and is a gratuitous gift of His Divine bounty. All this cannot be claimed by us as our right, unless we are possessed by a pride and self-love very dangerous to our salvation.

10. When consolation abounds in the heart, we must consider the conduct to be observed in time of trial; and to sustain the shock, we must provide in good time a supply of courage and vigorous resolution.

11. We must also humble ourselves, depreciate ourselves, foresee as much as possible how weak, how cowardly we shall be under the stroke of desolation if Divine grace do not quickly come to our aid ; while the tempted man must, on the contrary, persuade himself that

with the aid of God he is all powerful, and that he will easily overcome all his enemies, provided he establishes his confidence on the Divine strength, and is courageous.

12. Satan, with his weak but obstinate character, may be compared, when he attacks us, to a woman daring to contend with her husband. Let her husband oppose her firmly, she soon lays aside her warlike mood, and quickly leaves the field to him; on the contrary, let her see in him any timidity or inclination to fly or give way, she becomes audacious, insolent, cruel as a fury. So when Satan sees the soldier of Jesus Christ, his heart imperturbable, his head erect, repulsing every attack without flinching, he immediately loses courage; but if he perceives him trembling at the first shock and ready to ask quarter, he immediately attacks him with a rage, a fury, a ferocity which is unexampled among wild-beasts enraged against their prey: obstinate in his infernal malice, he only seeks and breathes our ruin.

13. We may also compare him in some of his artifices to a libertine seeking to lead astray a young girl, the child of good parents, or the wife of an honest man. What he recommends to the object of his passion is, above all things, secrecy,—secrecy as to his propositions, secrecy as to his interviews; if he does not obtain this secrecy, if the daughter does not observe it towards her parents, the wife towards the husband, all is lost for him; his projects are ruined. So the grand artifice of the great calumniator is to induce the soul he wishes to gain to keep secret his suggestions; and when they are discovered to a confessor or an enlightened director, his rage and torment are at their height, because his snare is discovered, and his efforts rendered useless.

14. Finally, in his tactics our enemy imitates a general of an army besieging a citadel, who first studies the ground and the state of the fortifications, so as to concentrate his attack upon the weakest part. To make a like study, our enemy makes as it were the round of our soul: he examines which are the theological or moral virtues that serve as its ramparts, or in which it is wanting, and against the point we have left without guard and defence he turns all his batteries, and says· "It is here I will try the assault."

OTHER RULES FOR THE BETTER DISCERNING OF SPIRITS.

(Applicable more particularly to the second week.)

1. The operation proper to God and His good angels is to shed on the soul on which they act true spiritual joy in banishing the sorrow and trouble that the devil has introduced into it. On the contrary the latter, finding this joy in the soul, labours to destroy it by certain sophistries covered by a false appearance of truth.

2. The Creator alone can penetrate His creature, raise him, change him, enkindle in him the fire of His love. Hence, when nothing has been presented to the senses, the intellect, the will of a nature to cause joy, and yet the soul is consoled all at once without antecedent cause, then it is God that acts upon it.

3. When a natural cause of consolation has preceded, who has sent it? Perhaps our good angel, perhaps the bad. The purpose of the good would be to

assist us to know and to do right; the bad to lead us to evil and to destroy us.

4. The bad spirit knows well how to transform himself into an angel of light. Aware of the pious desires of the soul, he will begin by seconding them, but soon he will begin to lead it to his own ends. Thus at first he will feign to consent to your good and holy thoughts, and even applaud them, but by degrees he will draw you into his hidden snares and entangle you in his dark meshes.

5. We must, therefore, submit our inspirations and thoughts to a strict and attentive examination. Their beginning, progress, and end must all be carefully considered. Are all these good? It is, then, our good angel that inspired them. On the other hand, is there any thing intrinsically bad, any thing that leads us away from good, or that urges us to something below what we had chosen; any thing that fatigues the soul, casts it into anguish and trouble, makes it lose the peace, the repose, the serenity which it enjoyed? If we discover on reflection that such is the case, it is an evident sign that the inspiration comes from the spirit of darkness, and that it conceals some snare he is laying for us.

6. When we have discovered the infernal serpent; when, by the evil result to which his insinuations always tend, we have discovered his diabolical purpose, it is very useful to go over again in spirit the way by which the tempter led us, to take to pieces the plot he had so cleverly laid, to note by what specious pretexts he began to make us listen to him; how he succeeded by degrees in changing that pure taste, that spiritual sweetness, that perfect serenity which we enjoyed before;

how he endeavoured to instil his venom into the soul. This study of his odious manœuvres will render us more capable of escaping them for the future.

7. Both spirits seek to insinuate themselves into the souls of those who advance in the way of salvation; but they make use of very different means: the good angel comes with sweetness, peace, suavity, like a drop of water falling on a sponge; the bad angel rushes in rudely, violently, noisily, like rain in a storm beating on a rock. With those who, day by day, go farther from God, and plunge deeper into evil, the contrary happens. Moreover, a spirit enters the soul gently or harshly, according as the disposition of the soul is suitable to it or opposed to it. If it finds opposition and antipathy, it announces itself by a sudden shock which it is easy to remark; if it finds the soul tending the same way as itself, it enters quietly, as if into a dwelling belonging to it and open to it.

8. We have before stated that it is God who visits the soul when not any natural cause has led to the consolation with which it is suddenly filled. This sentiment, therefore, cannot be subject to illusion; yet we must distinguish with great care this first moment of happiness from those which immediately follow, although the soul still feels its ardour and the heavenly favours it has received; for in this second period it frequently happens, whether from habit, personal manner of judging and seeing, or inspiration of the good or evil spirit, that we conceive certain thoughts or form certain projects which, not coming immediately from God, require to be carefully examined before giving our consent to them or putting them into execution.

OF ELECTION OR CHOICE.

FIRST ARTICLE.

Of the dispositions necessary.

To make a good choice on any matter whatever, we must first meditate with a pure and upright intention on the end of our creation, which is the glory of God and our salvation. Therefore our choice ought never to fall on any thing that does not lead us to this end ; for it is evident that the means ought always to be subordinate to the end, and not the end to the means. Those persons deceive themselves who begin by determining on such or such a state,—for example, on marriage,—and afterwards form the resolution to serve God as well as they can in that state. That is to reverse the order, to take the means for the end, and the end for the means; it is to tend to God obliquely, so to say, and expect to draw the will of God to ours, instead of making ours bow to that of God.

We must do just the contrary : first we must propose for our end what is the true end of man—the service of God ; then, with a view to this end, choose such or such a state, as marriage, or holy orders, &c., and determine our choice by the sole motive of arriving more certainly at our end. In a word, we ought not to decide upon one state in preference to another, but according as one or the other can conduce to the glory of God and our salvation.

SECOND ARTICLE.

Of the matter of choice.

1. All that forms the matter of election ought of necessity to be good, at least neither bad in itself nor contrary to the principles and maxims of the Church.

2. Two kinds of things may be the matter and object of election ; one kind is such, that the choice once made is unchangeable ; for example, the priesthood and marriage. There are other things of which the choice is revocable ; for example, such or such employment, ecclesiastical or secular, that may be accepted at first and afterwards abandoned for just reasons.

3. When the choice has already taken place on an unchangeable matter, there is no longer any election to make. But if imprudence or some unruly affection has dictated a choice that it is not permitted to retract, there is only one decision to take ; it is to repair the fault committed by the regularity of our life and our fidelity to all our duties. There is no question here of change, for that is no longer allowed. Election must have its effect in its full extent, although made imprudently or from suspicious motives it can never pass for a divine vocation ; for there is no divine vocation unless dictated by pure motives and solid reason unmixed with carnal affection or irregular inclinations.

4. With regard to the states that may be changed, if the choice was made with discretion and wisdom, it must not be changed; but we must endeavour to perfect ourselves more and more in this state. If, on the contrary, the election does not appear to have been sufficiently wise and Christian, we must change it, whatever it may

cost, in order to render ourselves more agreeable to
God, and the better to assure our salvation.

THIRD ARTICLE.

Of the three times most favourable for making a good choice

1. When the Divine power gives to the will such an
impulse, that the soul does not and cannot doubt that
it ought to follow it. It happened thus to St. Paul
to St. Matthew, who were called by Jesus Christ, ar
to many others.

2. When the Spirit of God makes us discern His
good pleasure in a manner sufficiently clear and evident
by the application of His grace to our hearts. It is by
submitting the consolations and different movements
we feel to the rules for the discernment of spirits that
we distinguish this Divine action, which always bears
with it the characteristics of God Himself.

3. When, our spirit enjoying a great calm; our soul
free from agitation, and exercising freely its natural
powers; our understanding enlightened, as it always is
in its operations when conducted with rectitude, by the
light of the Divine Word,—we make choice of the most
proper means to lead us surely and easily to our end.
This end is *the glory of God and our salvation.* We
set this truth before us as an established principle;
and, as a consequence or a way to arrive at this term,
we choose, among all the states that the Church au-
thorises, the one that will best of all lead us to it.

If neither the testimony of our senses struck by the
Divine power, nor that of our heart moved by the
Spirit of God, succeed in fixing our choice, we must
appeal to the testimony of our spirit enlightened by

T

eternal truth; and we must have recourse to the two following methods.

FIRST METHOD.

1. Propose to yourself the object of your determination,—for example, such a state, or such an employment. Should it be embraced? Ought it to be renounced? And thus of all that can become matter of election.

2. Keep in view this truth: my end is, in glorifying God, to save myself. Prevent your will from pronouncing prematurely either for or against the object in question; establish yourself rather in a perfect equilibrium, so as to turn entirely and immediately to that side in which you recognise the greatest interest of the glory of God and your own salvation.

3. Beg of the Divine goodness to enlighten your spirit and incline your will towards the calling you should choose; without, however, neglecting to assist yourself by reasonings based on faith, in order to seek and discover the will of God, which is to decide your choice.

4. Weigh exactly the for and against: what advantages, what assistance, such or such an employment or state presents to enable you to arrive at your end; on the contrary, what dangers, what obstacles, await you in it. Examine in the same way the opposite state, —what means it offers you, or what perils; what resources, or what difficulties.

5. After this examination, compare both sides, and without listening to the suggestions of the flesh, decide for that which appears the most according to sound reason.

6. The choice being made, have recourse to prayer; offer your resolution to God, and beg of Him, if it is agreeable to Him, to receive it and confirm you in it.

SECOND METHOD.

1. As the election to be perfect ought to be determined by a celestial movement of Divine love, assure yourself well that whatever inclination you have (whether much or little is of no consequence) for the object you have chosen really comes from the love to God.and regard to His interests alone.

2. If some other person, whose salvation or perfection was of great interest to you, found himself in the same situation you are in, and consulted you in his uncertainty, what would you counsel him for the greater glory of God and the greater perfection of his own soul? The counsel that you would give him is precisely that which you ought to follow yourself.

3. At the moment of death, how would you wish you had conducted yourself in this deliberation? In the same way conduct yourself now.

4. When called before the tribunal of God, what choice would you wish you had made? The same is the choice you must make now; for it is the one that will give you the most confidence at that terrible hour

5. Your resolution once fixed, offer it to God in prayer, and beg of Him to accept and bless it, as in the preceding method.

OF AMENDMENT,

OR REFORM IN A STATE OF LIFE ALREADY EMBRACED.

To persons engaged in the bonds of marriage, or raised to an ecclesiastical dignity impossible or difficult to abandon, we do not propose the rules regarding the choice of a state. Instead of these we subjoin a method of reform, or rules of conduct that will serve for amendment of life in the state already fixed.

The following are the elements of this method:

Do you wish to adopt and follow a plan of life conformable to the end for which God created you?

Perform the Exercises of the second week to be pointed out presently.

Employ the methods of election named above, applying them with much reflection and exactness to the following objects, or others which may serve as matters for your deliberation:

What style of house, what number of servants, is it proper for you to keep?

How does it become you to administer and regulate your affairs?

What instructions and examples ought you to give for the edification of your children and servants?

What part of your revenues ought you to employ for your personal use and that of your house?

What other part ought you to destine to the poor, or consecrate to pious works?

In all this you ought to have nothing in view but the glory of God and your own salvation.

And you ought to be persuaded that the more you

withdraw from yourself, from self-love, and seeking your own ease, the more you will advance in the way of salvation and perfection.

The Exercises to be performed before beginning this work of reform are (besides the meditation on the ordinary mysteries of Jesus Christ), the Contemplation of the Two Standards, the Exercises of the Three Classes, the Prelude of the Elections. These will greatly assist in making the person in retreat conceive the idea and the desire of the perfection of which he is capable, and of which his state is susceptible.

The second article on Election is scarcely applicable here, but rather the third, with its double method. We must proceed in this way:—Each of the points to be examined before God,—for example, the *personnel* of the house, expenses, pious works,—will be considered separately. Whenever deliberation has been made and a resolution taken on a point, pass on to another. The more grave and difficult the question, the more time it requires: sometimes an hour or more must be given to one; sometimes several points successively will have been decided in this space of time.

SOME RULES ON TEMPERANCE.

1. Less care is required about bread than about other food, because it is less pleasing to the palate, and exposes us less to temptation.

2. The use of wine requires more attention. On this point we must examine what is necessary, in order

to keep to it exactly, as well as what is hurtful in order
to retrench it.

3. Abstinence should be observed more particularly
with regard to exquisite and rare meats, because they
stimulate to concupiscence and provoke temptation. We
may succeed in this in two ways—by accustoming ourselves to be contented with the most simple aliments,
and by restraining ourselves in the use of what is more
delicate.

4. The more we retrench in nourishment (always
avoiding privations injurious to health), the more easily
we find the quantity suitable for us, and for this reason—on the one side, abstinence, by meriting for us the
lights and consolations of grace, gives us more facility
in knowing what sustenance our corporal powers require; and on the other, the weakening of the body,
betrayed by the difficulty of fulfilling our spiritual
exercises, teaches us by experience what is necessary to
nature.

5. It is well, during our repasts, to represent to
ourselves our Lord living with His disciples, and eating
at the same table with them, and take Him for our
model in the use of all our senses. The mind being
occupied with these pious objects, it will be easier to be
moderate.

6. We may also occupy ourselves with other
thoughts: for example, the lives of saints, some object of piety, or some spiritual affair, so that this di-
version of mind may weaken the too lively feelings of
nature.

7. We must, above all, in our repasts, be on our
guard against avidity, precipitation, or that effusion of

the soul which is bestowed in a manner on the food It is requisite that we should always rule our appetite and practise temperance both in the quantity of nourishment and the manner of taking it.

8. To extirpate any bad habit of excess in eating or drinking, it would be well to determine before the repast, and before the want of it is yet felt, the quantity that on reflection we judge it well to take. The portion thus determined we ought to content ourselves with, even when nature asks for more, and Satan backs the demand. To conquer both, we might even re·trench something more.

SOME RULES FOR THE DISTRIBUTION OF OUR GOODS IN ALMS

Do you feel inclined to give a part of your goods to your relations or friends from the lively affection you bear them? Submit this disposition to the four rules already given for election, which are a little more developed as follows:

1. All the love I bear my neighbour, to be perfect, ought to be derived from the love of God; I ought to feel that this pure charity is the beginning and the motive of all my affections and attachments. In this circumstance, as in all others, it must appear as the principal motive of my determination.

2. If an unknown person, but one whom I wished to see fulfilling the duties of his state, and acting on a similar occasion with all the perfection possible, came to ask my advice, what should I advise him to do in

the interest of the Divine glory and for his own perfection? I ought to adopt the same course myself.

3. If I were on the point of death, what should I wish that I had done on this occasion? The same I ought to do now.

4. When called before the tribunal of God, what distribution of my goods should I be glad to have made? This certainly is the one I ought to make now.

5. If I feel my heart too much attached to the persons united to me by the bonds of nature, I must first submit this attachment itself to the four preceding rules, without as yet occupying myself with the question of the distribution of goods or alms. Before coming to any arrangement whatever, this inclination must be rectified.

6. What is the portion of the revenues of his church that a perfect ecclesiastic ought to employ in his own expenses? This question gives rise to many scruples, and many are always in fear of going too far. To resolve it, and to determine the just proportion, the above-mentioned rules should be observed.

7. On the subject of the expenses to be determined on for our person, our house, our furniture, or servants, the most perfect and the most sure way is to retrench as much as possible of our convenience and comforts, and to conform ourselves faithfully to the example of Jesus Christ, our great High-priest. It is after this general rule, which is applicable to all states (although we must make due allowance for different persons and even different conditions), that the third Council of Carthage, at which St. Augustine assisted, decided tha˙ all the furniture of a Bishop should be of

!ow price, and should speak of poverty. In the married
state, the best example we can cite is that of St. Joachim
and St. Anne, who every year divided their revenues
into three parts; one for the poor, the second for the
temple and the divine service, and the third for themselves.

REMARKS ON THE SCRUPLES WHICH THE DEVIL RAISES IN THE SOUL.

1. What is generally called scruple is the judgment
by which, with all the liberty of our mind, we call an
action sinful, though it is not. Such would be the
judgment of one who, having walked on two straws
forming a cross, should reproach himself with the oc-
currence as a fault; this, however, is not properly a
scruple, it is rather an erroneous judgment which instruction and good sense must rectify.

2. But you have trampled on this cross, or you
have thought, or said, or done, something equally un-
important; all your intellectual and moral faculties tell
you that you have not sinned, and yet in your conscience the idea arises that you have done wrong. From
this comes perplexity and trouble, which the evil spirit
keeps up; this is a scruple properly speaking.

3. Scruples of the first kind, being moral errors,
ought to be the object of just abhorrence. As to the
second, they serve as purgatives—very active ones sometimes—to a soul which has just arisen from sin. They
are useful to him for some time, and inspire him with fear
and aversion as regards even the shadow of sin. "It
is a good soul," says St. Gregory, "that thinks itself
guilty even when it is not."

4. Our infernal enemy observes with malignant attention what the stamp of our conscience is, whether it is delicate or relaxed. If delicate, he tries to render it more susceptible still; he endeavours to reduce it to the last degree of trouble and anguish, so as to stop its progress in the spiritual life. To this timid Christian, who never consents to any sin either mortal or venial, and who dreads even the appearance of a voluntary fault, as he cannot present the bait of a real sin, he shows an imaginary fault as a frightful phantom. Sin will appear to him in a trifling word, a thought that only crossed the mind, &c. On the contrary, if he finds any where a relaxed conscience, he studies to make it still more so. This soul not being afraid of venial sin, he familiarises it by degrees with mortal sin, and day by day weakens the horror of it in his eyes.

5. That the soul may advance with sure step in spiritual ways, it must walk with constancy in the opposite direction from that in which the enemy of salvation wishes to lead it. If he seek to relax the conscience, let it contract; if he seek to contract it, let it relax. Avoiding the two extremes, it will establish itself in a middle path, that will be for it a state of assurance and peace.

6. When, with regard to a word or an action that presents itself, having nothing contrary to the sentiment of the Church and to Catholic traditions, and which tends to glorify God, a thought strikes you sent by a spirit foreign to your own,—a thought that dissuades you from speaking or acting, under the pretext that it will cause you to be vain-glorious, or excites in you any other chimerical fear, then raise your mind to God; and if it still appears to you that this word or this action

tends to the glory of your Divine Master, or at least that it has nothing contrary to Him, then proceed direct against this thought; and while the enemy murmurs in your ear, reply to him like St. Bernard: " It was not for thee I began ; it shall not be for thee I will desist."

RULES OF THE ORTHODOX FAITH.

1. Always to be ready to obey with mind and heart, setting aside all particular views, the true spouse of Jesus Christ, our holy mother, our infallible and orthodox mistress, the Catholic Church, whose authority is exercised over us by the hierarchy of its pastors.

2. To approve of the confession of sins as it is practised in the Church ; the reception of the Holy Eucharist once a year, and better still every week, or at least every month, with the necessary preparation.

3. To recommend to the faithful frequent and pious assistance at the holy sacrifice of the Mass, the ecclesiastical chant, the divine office, and in general the prayers and devotions practised at stated times, whether in public in the churches or in private.

4. To have a great esteem for the religious state, and to give the preference to celibacy or virginity over the married state.

5. To approve of the religious vows of chastity, poverty, perpetual obedience, as well as the other works of perfection and supererogation.   Let us remark in passing, that we must never engage by vow to take a state (such *e. g.* as marriage) that would be an impediment to one more perfect ; for a vow is essentially an engagement

to *perfection*—the promise of a higher good, as theology says.

6. To approve of the veneration and invocation of saints, respect to images, processions, pilgrimages of devotion, indulgences, jubilees, the custom of lighting candles and burning lamps before altars, and other practices of this kind useful to piety.

7. To observe the abstinences and fasts, not only of precept, as Lent, the Ember-days, vigils, but also such as are of pure devotion, as also of voluntary mortifications and penance, not only interior but exterior.

8. To approve the magnificence of the construction and ornaments of churches, and the holy images which we justly honour because of the things they represent.

9. Far from censuring in any matter the precepts of the Church, to defend them boldly by all the reasons that study can furnish us with against those who attack them.

10. To study to approve the decrees, the statutes, the traditions, the ordinances, the rites and customs of our fathers in the faith or of our superiors. As to their conduct, although there may not be every where the integrity of morals which there ought, yet there is more scandal and disorder than utility in speaking against them in private conversations or public discourses These sort of invectives only embitter the people and raise them against their princes and pastors; we must, then, avoid these reproaches, never incriminating absent masters before their subjects. It would be better to address ourselves in private to those who have in their hands the necessary authority to remedy the evil.

11. To have a great esteem for the teachings of the

Fathers and theologians. The former, like St. Jerome, St. Augustine, St. Gregory, have laboured above all to form the hearts of Christians; the latter, following the course opened by St. Thomas, St. Bonaventure, &c., have had for their aim to cure the errors of the times, and to enlighten the faithful with exact notions and well-defined dogmas. Coming in an age succeeding the Fathers, they have had, like them, the Holy Scriptures and the writings of antiquity to instruct them. They have had besides the ordinances and definitions of councils, the rules and constitutions of the holy Church: and the Spirit of God has powerfully assisted them in profiting by all these resources in order to direct the faithful in the ways of salvation.

12. Avoid all comparison of living men, however great their merit, with the saints; for example, avoid saying: Such a one is more learned than St. Augustine; this is another St. Francis; this one is as zealous, as eloquent as St. Paul, &c.

13. To be with the Church of Jesus Christ but one mind and one spirit, we must carry our confidence in her, and our distrust of ourselves, so far as to pronounce that true which appeared to us false, if she decides that it is so; for we must believe without hesitation that the Spirit of our Lord Jesus Christ is the spirit of His spouse, and that the God who formerly gave the decalogue is the same God who now inspires and directs His Church.

14. Although it is very true that not any one arrives at salvation if not predestined, we must speak with great circumspection on this matter, for fear that, giving too much to grace, we should appear to destroy

ments, humble yourself, accuse yourself; ask for grace
to observe them better for the future; and end by a colloquy addressed to God, suitable to the state and the
dispositions in which you find yourself.

If you wish to take for your subject the capital sins,
the three powers of the soul, the five senses, &c., you
have only to change the matter of the examination; the
rest will be the same as for the commandments.

Let us observe that the Christian who wishes to
imitate our Lord Jesus Christ in the use of His senses
must ask the grace of God the Father to enable him to
do so, and, glancing at each of his senses, examine how
far they approach or depart from his Divine Model.
Before passing from one sense to another, recite a
Pater.

If it is proposed to imitate the Blessed Virgin, we
must ask her to obtain this grace from her divine Son,
and after the examination of each sense recite an *Ave*.

SECOND MANNER.

This consists in reciting some vocal prayer, and rest-
ing successively on the words composing it as long as
we feel taste and devotion.

1. Before beginning, recollect yourself.

2. Address yourself to the person to whom you are
going to pray.

3. Begin the prayer—the *Pater*, for example; dwell
on these words, Our Father; meditate on them as long
as they furnish you with thoughts, affections, &c., and

then pass to the following words, which you will consider in the same manner.

4. When the time comes to conclude, recite the rest of the prayer without stopping, and address yourself in a short prayer to the person to whom you have been praying, to ask the grace or the virtue which you require.

Remark. (1) All vocal prayers, the *Credo*, the *Salve Regina*, the *Anima Christi*, &c., may be recited in this manner. (2) If one single word of the prayer we are reciting in this way suffices to occupy the mind and the heart all the time destined to prayer, we must put off to another day the meditation of the rest. The following day we must commence by reciting, without stopping, what was meditated on the day before, and then continue the consideration of the rest of the words of the prayer.

THIRD MANNER.

This consists in pronouncing a vocal prayer, and, if we choose, several prayers successively, only stopping the interval of a breathing between each, thinking either of the sense of the word, or of the dignity of the person to whom we pray, or of our own unworthiness, or of the distance between the two. Let us take the *Ave Maria* for an example.

1. Think of the action you are going to perform.

2. Beginning with " Hail, Mary," think for a moment what these words signify, or of the dignity of the

Blessed Virgin whom you salute, or of your miseries, which place so great a distance between you and the Mother of God.

3. Then you pronounce the other words, dwelling on each one, as we have said, only the time of a breathing.

ABRIDGMENT OF THE FIRST PART.

ANALYSIS OF THE MEDITATIONS OF THE FIRST WEEK, AND MYSTERIES OF THE LIFE OF OUR LORD FOR CONTEMPLATION DURING THE THREE SUBSEQUENT WEEKS, FOR THE USE OF PERSONS MORE. EXPERIENCED IN MEDITATION.

FUNDAMENTAL MEDITATIONS.

The end of man.

TEXT of St. Ignatius. *Man was created to praise and adore the Lord his God, and in serving Him to save himself. This is his end.*

This meditation comprises three great truths, which are the foundation of the Exercises : *I come from God —I belong to God—I am destined for God;* that is, God is at the same time my first beginning, my sovereign master, my last end.

FIRST TRUTH.

I come from God.

1. Where was I a hundred years ago? I was in nothingness. Oh, how many centuries there were when not any one thought of me! For, can nothing be the

subject of thought? How many ages that an insect, an atom was more than I! for it possessed existence.

Yet I exist to-day; I possess intelligence, a heart, senses, body, soul. Who gave me all this? Was it not God, and God alone?

3. God is, then, my Creator. And what wonderful circumstances in my creation!

God created me; and it was by a pure impulse of His love; for my existence was not necessary either to His happiness or His glory.

God created me; and the decree of my creation is eternal like Himself. During an eternity, then, He was occupied with me; He was thinking of me; He loved me who was as yet nothing.

God created me; and, in creating me, He preferred me to an infinite number of creatures equally possible, and that He will never call into existence.

God created me; and, in creating me, made me the noblest creature of the visible world. All my being bears the stamp of His divine perfections.

Finally, *God created me;* and He continues and renews His work in every moment of my existence. As many moments of life as I count, so many times He makes me a present of life.

SECOND TRUTH.

I belong to God.

1. I come from God, therefore I belong to God. All that I am comes from Him; what I have, then, belongs to Him. To deny this consequence, would it not be to deny reason itself?

2. What do I think of all the rights of a master

over his servant, of a father over his child, of a workman over the work of his hands? Does not God possess over me, in the highest degree and by the most sacred titles, all the rights of men over creatures, since there is nothing in me that is not the fruit of His own resources, and hence His own property?

3. Thus, God has dominion over me. *Essential* dominion: God would cease to be God, if, being my Creator, He ceased to be my Sovereign and my Master. *Supreme* dominion: men have no rights over me except such as the Lord gives them; their rights, then, must be subordinate to the rights of God. *Absolute* dominion: God, then, can dispose of me at His pleasure; and my duty is to receive every thing from His hand with submission. *Eternal* dominion: it will last as long as I shall. *Irresistible* dominion: willing or unwilling, I must glorify Him either by free submission or by inevitable chastisement.

THIRD TRUTH.
I am destined for God.

1. A God infinitely wise must have proposed to Himself some end in creating me. A God infinitely perfect could only create me for His glory; that is, to know Him, love Him, and serve Him.

2. Every thing, both within and without me, agrees in revealing this to me great truth. My *religion*,—all its mysteries, all its precepts, all its promises, only recall my end, which is God. My *reason* shows me that the infinite perfection of God alone can be the object of a mind and a heart ever craving to know and to love. *Creatures* proclaim to me by their nothingness that

they are too insignificant to be the end of my being. My *heart* seeks a happiness without alloy, without li mit; that is, it requires nothing less than God Himself. My *experience* speaks the same language. Away from God, what have I found? trouble, remorse, chastisements for order violated. Faithful to God, what have I found? peace of heart, the fruit and recompense of order faithfully observed.

3. Hence, a God to know, to love, and to serve—behold my final end; and, by the same law, behold my duties, my greatness, my felicity.

SENTIMENTS.

Sentiments of gratitude for a God, my Creator.

Sentiments of submission to a God, my Sovereign and Master.

Sentiments of love for a God, my last end.

Pater. Ave.

———

THE END OF CREATURES.

Text. *All other things which are on the earth are made for man, that is, to aid him in arriving at the end for which he was created.*

FIRST CONSIDERATION.

Creatures belong to God.

Creatures have the same beginning as myself. They were drawn from nothing, like me, and He who drew them from nothing was God. They cannot have the same beginning as I have without having also the same master. Hence, they are from God, and belong to God. It follows from this that I ought to make use of creatures—

1. With a spirit of *dependence;* according to the Divine order and will; not as a master who disposes as he pleases, but as a steward who must give an account.

2. With a spirit of *gratitude;* like a poor man who has of himself no right to the use of the things of this world, and who holds all from the liberality of God, to whom all belongs.

3. With a spirit of *fear;* because, on one side, corrupt nature inclines us incessantly to the abuse of created things; and, on the other, God will rigorously punish this abuse, which overthrows all the economy of creation.

Is it in this spirit that I have hitherto made use of creatures?

SECOND CONSIDERATION.

Creatures are for God by means of man.

Like me, creatures have an end, which is the glory of God; for God could not create any thing but for His glory. Creatures without intelligence cannot connect themselves or be brought into relation with God. They are not, then, made to glorify God in a direct manner; they are made to serve man, who, in exchange for their service, must lend them his intelligence and his heart to praise and love God, and thus refer them to the glory of their common Creator.

This, then, is the order of my connection with God and creatures: I am for God, creatures for me. Hence it follows that I cannot place my end in creatures without rendering myself guilty and miserable. 1. *Guilty.* guilty towards *myself*—it would be to degrade myself; towards *creatures*—it would be to turn them from their end and do violence to their nature; towards *God*— it would be to usurp His dominion. 2. *Miserable*: miserable in *eternity*—I should lose at once God, from whom I should be separated for ever, and creatures, who would become my torment for ever; in *time*—what can creatures do towards my happiness? They have so limited an existence! what a void they would leave in my heart! They are so full of imperfections! what a source of disgust! So frail! what a source of regret! So inconstant! what a source of distrust!

THIRD CONSIDERATION.

How creatures glorify God in leading man to God.

I am made to know, love, serve, possess God; and creatures teach me—

1. *To know God.* Thus the order of the world reveals His wisdom to me, the firmament His power.

2. *To love God.* It is the bounty of God that has given creatures to me; it is His love that serves me in each one of them. What a motive for loving Him!

3. *To serve God.* Consider, O my soul, how all creatures obey the will of their Creator; with what promptitude! Shall I be the only one to refuse to serve God? Shall I be the least faithful of His servants because I am the most indebted?

4. *To merit the possession of God.* For there is not any thing that may not be the occasion of some

virtue, and by the same rule the subject of some merit. There are created things the use of which is necessary: those, for example, that are destined to sustain my existence. What an occasion for practising temperance and detachment !

There are some to the use of which we must submit and that nature shrinks from ; for example, sickness, poverty. What an occasion to practise patience and humility !

There are some which of their nature lead to God, such as assistances of a supernatural order. What an occasion to practise piety and faith!

Finally, there are some that would turn me away from God. What an opportunity for sacrifice !

AFFECTIONS.

Praise God in the name of His creatures. Grieve for having made so bad a use of them hitherto. Resolve to attach ourselves to God only.

Pater. Ave.

ON INDIFFERENCE TOWARDS CREATURES.

Text. *We must use or abstain from created things according as they lead us to, or take us away from, God. This is why we must preserve ourselves in a state of indifference towards all creatures the use of which is left to our free-will; so that, as far as it depends on us, we would not seek health or riches in preference to sickness or poverty, but in every thing seek what will lead us most surely to our end.*

All creatures are given to men to conduct them to their end. How is it, then, that they so often lead us away from God? It is that our nature, degraded by original sin, seeks or rejects them according as they flatter or mortify our corrupt passions. The purpose of this meditation is to reform the disorder of our attachments and our aversions, by establishing in us perfect indifference. This indifference consists in neither seeking nor rejecting of our free and deliberate will any created thing for itself, but solely as it brings us nearer or removes us farther from God.

FIRST CONSIDERATION.
Motives as regards God for this indifference.

1. *The sovereign dominion of God.* Without this indifference, I dispose of my affections according to my own will, not according to the Divine will. Amongst different situations, I choose, not that which God destines for me, but that which pleases myself; I establish myself as my own arbiter and proprietor. Is this not to attack the rights of God?

2. *The sovereign perfection of God.* To love God above every thing, and to love nothing but for Him, is what the infinite perfection of God requires. And without this indifference I shall love creatures for themselves, for the pleasures they procure me; perhaps soon I shall love them above God. Is not this the great disorder of my past life? Is it not this want of indifference that has so often made charity languish, perhaps even die out in my heart?

3. *The providence of God.* God, who created me

for Himself, never ceases to conduct me to my final end by His providence. Shall I fear that this providence, infinitely good, wise, powerful, will not desire or will not be able to procure my greatest good? No, certainly. But without this indifference I derange all its plans. Perhaps God may take from me health, honour, fortune; perhaps He may try me by sickness, poverty, tribulations. Is it not to render myself culpable towards the providence of God, to refuse to accept what He has sent me, and to leave the path He has traced out for my salvation?

SECOND CONSIDERATION.

Motives as regards myself for this indifference.

This indifference is necessary to me in order—

1. *To acquire solid virtue.* What is virtue? It is in fact the spirit of sacrifice—of abnegation: "If any man will come after Me, let him deny himself" (Luke ix. 23). Can there be a spirit of sacrifice where there is not indifference?

2. *To obtain peace of heart.* Without this indifference, what fears, disgust, remorse! On the contrary, with this indifference, what sweet assurance! "The Lord ruleth me, and I shall want nothing" (Ps. xxii. 1). What joy even in the midst of tribulations! "I exceedingly abound with joy in all our tribulations" (2 Cor. vii. 4). What plenitude of peace in the depths of the heart! "Hadst thou hearkened to My commandments, thy peace had been as a river, and thy justice as the waves of the sea" (Is. xlviii. 18).

3. *To ensure my salvation.* What perils threaten the salvation of my soul! Perils from the world; perils

from the devil; perils from within me,—my heart, imagination, memory, senses; perils from without,—friendships, business, pleasures, employment, solitude, society. All these perils are reduced to one, that of making a bad use of creatures. Let me endeavour to arrive at perfect indifference; I shall have nothing more to fear, and my salvation will be assured.

RULES FOR THE PRACTICE OF INDIFFERENCE.

1. In the use of creatures, only to esteem and desire what leads to God.

2. In the use of creatures to be firmly resolved to fly from all that God forbids, that is to say, from sin and the occasions of sin.

3. In the use of indifferent creatures,—that is, such as neither directly lead us nearer to God nor farther from Him,—to be indifferent towards them only according to the rule of the will of God and His good pleasure.

Pater. Ave.

FIRST EXERCISE ON SIN.

MEDITATION OR EXERCISE OF THE THREE POWERS OF THE SOUL ON THREE DIFFERENT SINS: THAT OF THE FALLEN ANGELS, THAT OF OUR FIRST PARENTS, THAT OF A CHILD OF ADAM CONDEMNED FOR A PERSONAL SIN.

Preparatory Prayer.

Ask of God the grace to refer to His glory and service all the powers and operations of your soul.

First prelude. Represent to yourself, during the first point, Lucifer falling from the heights of heaven to the depths of the abyss; in the second, Adam cast out of the terrestrial Paradise into this vale of tears; in the third, a lost soul in the midst of the flames of hell.

Second prelude. Ask of God feelings of shame and repentance at the sight of so many souls expiating by eternal suffering the sin you have committed so frequently.

FIRST POINT.

The sin of the rebel angels.

Consider—

1. *The angels before their sin.* The excellence of their being; the light of their intelligence; the rectitude and innocence of their will; their dwelling, which is heaven, where, without yet seeing the Lord face to face, they have no other life than thinking of Him and loving Him; the happiness of their destiny—that is, a few moments of trial, and then the sight and possession of God for all eternity.

2. *The sin of the angels.* These noble spirits were masters of their liberty, and it proved their ruin; God gave it to them that they might merit, and they abused it to destroy themselves. Lucifer, the highest of all, dared to refuse to God the obedience due to Him; and he drew a third of the angels into his rebellion. Meditate attentively on the circumstances of this sin, and see if you do not find them in great part in your own sins: a sin committed in heaven; a sin committed with great lights; a sin committed after great benefits from Divine grace; a sin of scandal.

3. *The punishment of the rebel angels.* The justice of God falls on them like lightning. They are cast into the depths of hell, and in the midst of flames they

suffer in an eternity of torment the sin of a moment.
Meditate well on this terrible vengeance of God, which
regards neither the multitude of the culprits, nor the
dignity of the victims; neither the rank of the angels,
nor the high place which they occupied in His friendship; neither the service these angels if repentant and
restored to grace might render Him, nor the nature of
their sin; it is their first sin, and the sin of a moment.
"Who shall not fear Thee, O King of nations?" (Jer.
x. 7.)   "How incomprehensible are His judgments,
and how inscrutable His ways!" (Rom. xi. 33.)

SECOND POINT.

The sin of Adam.

Consider—

1. *Adam before his sin.* The excellence of his being;
made in the image of God; the reign of truth in his intellect, of justice in his heart; his empire over his passions and his senses; the profound peace of his soul;
the delights of the terrestrial Paradise where God had
placed him.

2. *Adam's sin.* God had forbidden him to touch
the tree of knowledge of good and evil. Adam did not
obey. Tempted by the serpent, Eve tempts her husband, who by a fatal complaisance becomes a sinner.
Meditate on the characteristics of this sin—imprudence,
sensuality, cowardice, blindness, contempt of God. In
the fall of our first father do you not recognise all
your past falls?

3. *The punishment of Adam after his sin.* The
loss of original justice and grace; disorder in all his
being, in his intellect, in his heart, in his senses; change

in nature,—inclemency of the seasons, barrenness of the earth, the revolt of the animals; tribulations of Adam during his whole life—labour, sickness, desolation at the death of Abel, all the troubles of his mind and heart; and, after 900 years of penitence, death. Finally, consider the anger of God avenging this first sin on all the descendants of the first sinner : pestilence, war, famine, desolation of the earth ; so many disasters, so many violent deaths, so many tears shed, so many crimes committed, so many children for ever deprived of the sight of God, so many souls cast into hell. What consequences and what chastisements for one single sin !

End by recalling your own state, and comparing Adam's sin with your own personal sins.

On Adam's side. One single sin, committed before the Incarnation, before he had experienced the justice of God; above all, a sin which he expiated by nine hundred years of penitence.

On your side. Sins so numerous, committed by a nature sanctified by Jesus Christ, in face of the cross and of hell, and perhaps sins not expiated, and for which you only feel but feeble repentance.

THIRD POINT.
On a particular sin.

Consider that at the moment that you on earth are meditating on the malice of mortal sin, there is, perhaps, in the depths of hell a soul that God has eternally condemned for such or such a mortal sin committed one single time, or at least for sins less numerous and less serious than **yours.**

Represent to yourself this soul for ever deprived o. the sight and the possession of God, plunged into hell amongst demons, delivered up to remorse, to despair, to flames, for a wretched eternity.

Ask yourself what this God is who punishes a single mortal sin in this manner. He is a God infinitely wise, infinitely just, infinitely merciful—a God who has loved this soul so much as to die for it. What an evil, then, is one single mortal sin!

Finally, reflect upon yourself. How long is it since you first committed mortal sin? Why did not God strike you dead after this first sin? Why has God spared you till now, when every thing demanded your condemnation?—the interest of His perfections, which you outraged; of His graces, which you trampled under foot; of the souls whose loss you caused by your scandals. If God had called you before His tribunal on such a day, at such an hour, after such a fault, where would you be at this moment, and in what state? "It is of the mercies of the Lord that we are not consumed" (Jer. iii. 22).

COLLOQUY AT THE FOOT OF THE CRUCIFIX.

Address yourself to Jesus Christ crucified present before you. Ask of your God why He has deigned to become incarnate, to suffer, to die for you. Ask yourself what you have done for Him up to this time that deserves mentioning; what you will do, and what you ought to do, for Him for the future. Fix your eyes upon the cross, and say to Him all that your heart suggests.

Pater. Ave.

SECOND EXERCISE ON SIN.

ON OUR OWN SINS.

Preparatory Prayer.

First prelude. Present yourself before God in the state of a criminal who appears before His tribunal, and is going to hear his sentence.

Second prelude. "I groan in Thy sight as one guilty; shame hath covered my face, because of my sin; spare me, a suppliant, O my God."

FIRST POINT.
Recall all the sins of your life.

Sins of infancy, sins of early youth, sins of more mature age. Examine all your years; what day was there that had not its sin? Question the different places you have inhabited, the societies, the employments, all the scenes of your pleasures; where do you not meet with memories of sin? Ask all the laws of God; is there a single one that you have not transgressed? Ask all your past temptations; are there many before which you have not fallen? Ask all your faculties; which is there that has not been guilty? Ask all your senses; which is there that has not served as an instrument of iniquity?

SECOND POINT.
Consider the malice of all these sins in themselves.

1. *What deformity!* They must be ugliness itself,

x

since they are infinitely opposed to supreme oeauty, which is God.

2. *What ingratitude!* You hold all from God, and yet you dare to say to Him, "Go from me: withdraw Thyself from my senses, which only live by Thy power; retire from my heart, which has received feeling only to love Thee; withdraw from all my being, which I only received to serve Thee."

3. *What audacity!* You have dared to say to God, "I will not serve, I will not obey;" and you have said it to God in face of Himself, on the borders of the grave, on the brink of hell, where He holds you suspended by a slender thread called life.

4. *What folly!* You have left God, God your Father, God your supreme bentitude; and for what? for a perfidious master, for a cruel tyrant, for Satan.

5. *What malice!* You have sinned, and it was with so much eagerness and passion, with so much reflection and liberty, with so much show and scandal. And you have remained at rest in your sin, notwithstanding so many lights, so many solicitations of grace: notwithstanding the voice of conscience and remorse

THIRD POINT.

Consider what you are that have thus offended God.

What are all the angels before God? What are all men compared to the angels? What am I in comparison with the whole human race? What a leaf is in an immense forest, a drop of water in a stream, a grain of sand on the shores of the ocean, an atom in the immensity of the universe! And it is I, vile and worthless dust, that have not feared to declare myself a rebel against God!

FOURTH POINT.

Consider what this God is that you have offended.

Against whom, my God, have I rebelled, when I committed sin? I, weakness itself, rebelled against strength! I, baseness itself, rebelled against sovereign greatness! I, malice itself, rebelled against sovereign goodness! I, who am only corruption and darkness, rebelled against essential wisdom and holiness! I, a nothing, rebelled against the Being of beings!

FIFTH POINT.

Conclude by addressing God and creatures.

Be astonished that, after so many iniquities, creatures have not armed themselves against you, that they continue to serve you when you never ceased to insult their God and yours.

Be astonished that God has not withdrawn His gifts, that He has left you this fortune, this credit, these talents, this mind, this heart, this life, which you abuse to offend Him. Then ask pardon of all the perfections of God that you have offended: "Pardon, O justice of my God, for having so long braved your thunders! Pardon, O holiness of God, for having so long sullied by my crimes your purity! Pardon, O mercy of my God, for having so long forgotten your voice!"

COLLOQUY.

Give thanks to the mercy of God, and protest at

the feet of Jesus Christ that you will never more offend Him.

Pater. Ave.

THIRD EXERCISE ON SIN.

OF THE INFINITE MALICE OF MORTAL SIN.

Preparatory prayer and preludes. As before.

FIRST CONSIDERATION.

God offended by man.

Consider attentively—

1. *The greatness of God who has been offended.* What is God? Who is like to Him in greatness, in power, in holiness, in justice, in wisdom, in goodness? Who is like to God? His age is eternity, His empire every thing that exists, His palace the light, His garments beauty and glory, His subjects and ministers the angels. And this is He whom the sinner dares to offend!

2. *The nothingness of the sinner.* What is man? Flesh full of pollution, dried grass ready to fall under the scythe, a leaf the sport of the winds, a vapour scarce formed and already dispersed in the air, a little dust and ashes. And it is this man who dares to say to God, I will not obey. "Thou hast lifted thyself up against the Lord of heaven, and said, I will not serve" (Dan. v. 23; Jer. iii. 20).

3. *The matter of the sin.* A law of God trans-

gressed; a law infinitely delightful, infinitely wise, the accomplishment of which was so easy, to which were attached such consoling promises and such terrible threats.

4. *The motive of the sin.* To whom have you compared Me? says the Lord: "To whom have you likened Me?" (Isaias xlvi. 5.) To a passion at which you blush; to some low interest, to a pleasure that passes so quickly: "Be astonished at this. They have forsaken Me, the fountain of living water, and have digged to themselves cisterns, broken cisterns" (Jer. ii. 12, 13).

SECOND CONSIDERATION.

A God offended by man, and offended in all His attributes.

What is it you do when you are so unhappy as to commit mortal sin? By a single sin you outrage God in all His titles and in all His perfections. You outrage God the Father. You profane the supernatura being He gave you in holy baptism. You outrage the Word incarnate; you break the bonds that unite you to Him; you renew His passion in your heart; you render His blood and death useless. You outrage the Holy Ghost,—you grieve, you resist Him, you extinguish Him within you.

You outrage God in all His titles. As Creator, in rebelling against His supreme dominion; as Legislator as Redeemer, as your Friend, as your King, as you Father.

You outrage God in all His perfections. In His unity: you adore as many gods as you have passions. In His infinite perfection: you prefer a vile creature before Him. In His wisdom: you overthrow the order He has established, in turning creatures away from their end. In His immensity: you do not blush to sin in His presence, under His eyes. In His justice, which you brave. In His mercy, which only encourages you in your impenitence. In a word, you become guilty of deicide!

THIRD CONSIDERATION.

God offended by man, in spite of so many motives to urge him not to offend.

How many motives there are that ought to engage you to remain obedient to God!

1. *Your respect for your fellow-creatures.* You are so humbly submissive before a sovereign, a protector, a powerful enemy. How is it that you are bold only against God, the first of sovereigns?

2. *What you exact from others.* You are so tenacious of your authority, your honour, your rights, your sentiments, your will. How is it, then, that you have so little respect for the authority, the honour, the rights of God?

3. *The sacrifices you make for the world* When the world speaks, do you not obey at any price,—at the price of your repose, of your pleasures, of your liberty, sometimes even of your life? Why is it that, when the Lord commands, He is not obeyed in this manner? Why is it that then alone sacrifices are painful, and appear impossible?

4. *Your vows to God.* You glory in respecting your pledged word, you would rather die than fail in your sworn faith. But has not God received your

vows a thousand times,—in baptism, at the sacred tribunal, at the holy table? Or is it that the oath that has such strength to bind man to man has none to bind man to God?

5. *The benefits received from God.* You hold all from God;—talents, fortune, life. You can only sin by means of His benefits. What ingratitude, then, not only to forget such a benefactor, but to render Him evil for good! to make use of His gifts to insult Him! to force Him to act against Himself, and to turn against His glory His own goodness and His own power, which preserve you!

COLLOQUY.

Place yourself at the foot of the crucifix, as a rebel subject, as a perjured friend, as a parricide son; and humbly ask of our Lord the pardon of your sins.

Anima Christi. Pater. Ave.

FOURTH EXERCISE ON SIN.

On the effects of mortal sin in the soul of the sinner.

Preparatory Prayer.

First prelude. Present yourself before God as a criminal loaded with chains, taken from a dungeon, and led to the tribunal of his judge.

Second prelude. Beg of our Lord that He will deign to show you the sad state of a soul that has mortally sinned.

FIRST CONSIDERATION.

Mortal sin makes us lose the friendship of God.

When you were in a state of grace God dwelt in your soul; the most august bonds united you to Him; He called you His people, His friend, His child, another self. But what a change since mortal sin has entered into your soul! God has withdrawn Himself from you; the ties which united you to Him have been broken; and with His friendship what have you not lost!

SECOND CONSIDERATION. .

Mortal sin robs us of all the gifts of grace.

1. *It destroys the beauty of the soul.* Before sin this soul was so beautiful a sight that it delighted the heart of God; since its sin, it is as if disfigured by a hideous leprosy, which makes it an object of horror to the Lord and His angels. 2. *It deprives the soul of all its merit:* alms, prayer, sacrifices, good works; one single mortal sin suffices to destroy all. 3. *It deprives the soul even of the power of meriting.* As long as you are in a state of mortal sin, all your good works are useless for heaven. Bestow your goods in alms; embrace the most rigorous austerities; convert the universe, if possible; give your body to the flames;—St. Paul assures you that all this is useless for salvation if there is a single mortal sin in your heart: "If I have not charity, I am nothing" (1 Cor. xiii. 2).

THIRD CONSIDERATION.

Mortal sin enslaves our liberty.

Are you in the grace of God? You are free·

"Where the Spirit of the Lord is, there is liberty" (2 Cor. iii. 17); the sweetest liberty, the most honourable, the only one that human power cannot take away. But have you had the misfortune to sin mortally? you are a slave: "Whosoever committeth sin is the servant of sin" (John viii. 34). All in you is enslaved;—the faculties of your soul, your senses, your talents, your fortune. The devil deals with you as the centurion in the Gospel with his servants: "I say to one, Go, and he goeth; and to another, Come, and he cometh; and to my servant, Do this, and he doeth it" (Luke vii. 8). He cries to you incessantly, "Bring, bring" (Prov. xxx. 15). Again this passion, again this sin; and always he is obeyed. What degrading slavery!

FOURTH CONSIDERATION.

Mortal sin deprives us of peace of heart.

The sinner carries with him every where a trembling heart, and a soul a prey to trouble and grief. Remorse is as a barbed arrow in his heart, as a gnawing worm; his conscience always pursues him; sometimes in the midst of the most serious cares, like David; sometimes in the midst of pleasure, like Baltassar; sometimes in the pains of sickness, like Antiochus; almost always in the silence of solitude, like Cain. Sometimes it reproaches him with a pleasure bought at the price of a long repentance; sometimes it recalls his ingratitude, the malice of his sin; sometimes it represents to him the sword of God's justice suspended over his head. O sinner, how much you are to be pitied, if conscience pursues you in this manner! But how much more if it leaves you at rest! for the peace of a guilty conscience is the sure sign of the great wrath of God.

FIFTH CONSIDERATION.

Mortal sin kills the soul.

The soul is the life of the body, and God is the life of the soul. Sin, then, kills the soul in separating it from God. And what difference is there between a corpse and a soul in mortal sin? The dead no longer see. Every thing ought to strike the eyes of the sinner,—the state of his soul, death which approaches, judgment, hell; and he sees nothing. The dead are insensible. God moves heaven and earth to touch the sinner, and the sinner remains insensible. The dead exhale an infectious odour; in like manner, the sinner spreads death around him by the contagion of his scandals. O fatal death! who will give us tears to weep over thee?

Affections at the foot of the crucifix.

Pater. Ave.

———

EXERCISE ON HELL.

Preparatory Prayer.

First prelude. Represent to yourself in imagination the length, the width, the depth of hell.

Second prelude. Ask of God a lively fear of the pains of hell, so that if ever you have the misfortune to lose the feeling of Divine love, at least the fear of torments may deter you from sin.

CONSIDERATIONS.

1. *The habitation of the damned.* It is hell. But what is hell? The Holy Ghost calls it the place of torment; a region of misery and darkness, where disorder dwells; the lake of the anger of God; a burning furnace; the depths of the abyss; the winepress of the fury of the Almighty, under which God will trample and crush His enemies.

2. *The society of the damned.* In hell, a triple society will form the torment of the damned soul. (1) The society of his body, which will unite to the infectious corruption of a corpse all the sensibility of a living body, and of which all the members have their torment and their pain. (2) The company of devils, whose sole occupation is to torture the damned; who, not being able to revenge themselves on God for their reprobation, revenge themselves on man, His image, and pursue Him in the condemned with all the fury that can enter the heart of a demon. (3) The society of an infinite number of reprobates like himself. Represent to yourself this assembly, so hideous that nothing like it can be found in the dungeons and galleys of human justice; represent to yourself these miserable creatures bound together like a bundle of thorns, or like a heap of tow thrown into the flames, accusing, cursing themselves, tearing one another.

3. *The torment of the damned in the powers of his soul. His imagination,* which represents to him with irresistible clearness the delights of his past life on earth; the horror of his present sufferings in hell; the eternity of his future sufferings; the happiness of the elect,

of which he might have partaken, and which he has lost for ever. *His memory*, which recalls all his sins, all the graces he received in time, all the warnings that were given him during his life. *His understanding*, which incessantly shows him the deformity of sin, the greatness and beauty of God, the justice of the punishments of hell. *His will*, torn at the same time by regret, remorse, jealousy, desire, hatred of God and of himself.

4. *The torment of the damned in all his senses.* Torment of *sight*: the flames, the devils, the damned his companions in torture, the cross of Jesus Christ imprinted on the roof of hell. Torment of *hearing*: blasphemies, imprecations, reproaches, cries of rage calling on death and annihilation. Torment of the *smell*: the infection exhaled from so many bodies, which preserve in hell all the corruption of the tomb. Torment of *taste*: a maddening hunger, the violence of which will force the damned to devour his own flesh; a devouring thirst, and for refreshment wormwood and gall. Torment of the *touch*: this fire, which surrounds the damned like a vestment, and penetrates all his members,—fire lighted by the breath of God Himself; fire which preserves its victim, and at the same time every moment exhausts and renews his sensibility, so as to render his pain eternal; fire armed with all the attributes of God to avenge them on the damned; fire which identifies itself with the damned, which boils in his veins, escapes and enters at every pore, which makes his body but one burning coal in the midst of the furnaces of hell.

5. *The torment of eternity.* "Always," "Never." Al-

ways regrets and despair, always the company of devils, always flames; *never* any end, never any interruption, never any remission of the pains and tortures. " Which of you can dwell with devouring fire? which of you shall dwell with everlasting burnings?" (Is. xxiii. 14.)

COLLOQUY.

Address yourself to Jesus Christ; recall at His feet, that the causes for which these men are damned is either for having refused to believe in His coming or for not having obeyed His precepts. It is the crime of men damned before His coming on earth, of those who lived in His time, and of those who came into the world after Him. Then attach yourself to Him for ever in mind and heart, that He may save you from eternal death. Finish by returning Him the most lively thanks that He has not permitted you to fall into this terrible abyss, but that He pursues you even to this day, not by His vengeance, but by His immense goodness and infinite mercy.

Pater. Ave.

FIRST EXERCISE ON DEATH.

Preparatory Prayer.

First prelude. Transport yourself in thought to the bedside of a dying person, or beside a grave ready to receive a coffin, or into the middle of a cemetery.

Second prelude. Ask of our Lord a salutary fear of death, and the grace to be prepared for it every day.

1. *What is it to die?* It is to bid adieu to every thing in this world,—to fortune, pleasures, friends

family ; a sad adieu, heart-rending, irrevocable. It is to leave my house, to be thrown into a deep narrow pit, without any garment but a shroud, without any society but reptiles and worms. It is to pass to the most humiliating state, the nearest to nothingness, where I shall become the prey of corruption, where I shall fall to pieces, where I shall decompose into an infectious putrefaction. It is for my soul to enter in the twinkling of an eye into an unknown region called eternity, where I shall go to hear from the mouth of God in what place I am to make that great retreat which will last for ever, whether it be in heaven or in the depths of hell.

2. *Must I die?* Most certainly. And what assures me of it? Reason, faith, experience. Yes ; notwithstanding all precautions, all cares, all the efforts of physicians, I shall die. Where are those who preceded me in life? In the grave, in eternity. And from this grave, from this eternity, they cry to me, " Yesterday for me, and to-day for thee" (Ecclus. xxxviii. 23).

3. *Shall I die soon?* Yes. Why? Because ever since my birth I have been only dying. An action continued without interruption is soon accomplished. All other actions have some cessation; business, study, pleasure, sleep,—all these have intervals ; death is the only action never interrupted. How can I be long dying when I have been dying ever since I was born, and every moment of the day and night? Where is now that portion of my life that death has already taken from me? As death has taken the past from me, so it will take the future ; with the same rapidity, with the rapidity of lightning.

4. *When shall I die?* At what age? In old age? In mature age? Will it be after a long illness? will it be from a fall, from a fire, beneath the knife of an assassin? In what place? In my own house, or in a strange house? at table, at play, at the theatre, at church, in my bed, on a scaffold? What day shall I die? Will it be this year? this week? to-morrow? to-day? In what state shall I die? Will it be in a state of grace, or in that of sin? To all these questions, Jesus Christ answers me, "Watch; for ye know not the day nor the hour" (Matt. xxv. 13).

5. *How often shall I die?* Once only; therefore, any error in this great action is irreparable. The misfortune of a bad death is an eternal misfortune. And on what does this bad death depend? On a single instant. It only requires a moment to offend the Lord mortally. It, then, only requires a moment to decide my eternity. If I had died this year, on such a day, such an hour of my life, when I was the enemy of God, where should I be now?

AFFECTIONS.

Fear; desire; resolution.

COLLOQUY.

Represent to yourself our Lord dying on the cross, and recommend the hour of your death to Him.

Pater. Ave.

SECOND EXERCISE ON DEATH.

FIRST CONTEMPLATION.

Your agony.

Preparatory Prayer.

First and second preludes. The same as in the preceding.

APPLICATION OF THE SENSES.

1. *Application of the sight.* Contemplate, 1. Your apartment dimly lighted by the feeble gleam of a lamp; all the objects that surround you and seem to say : "You are leaving us, and for ever." 2. The persons who surround you,—your servants, your family, the minister of Jesus Christ. 3. Yourself laid on a bed of pain, and violently struggling against death. 4. At your side devils and holy angels, who dispute for your soul.

2. *Application of the hearing.* Listen to the noise of your painfully interrupted breathing, to the stifled sobs of the assistants, to the prayers of the Church recited in the midst of tears : "From an evil death from the pains of hell, from the snares of the devil deliver him, O Lord." "Depart, Christian soul, in the name of God the Father Almighty, who created thee, of Jesus Christ, who suffered for thee; of the Holy Ghost, who sanctified thee." The holy words that the priest suggests to you : "Lord Jesus, receive my soul: Mary, mother of grace, mother of mercy, "&c.

3. *Application of the taste.* Represent to yourself all the bitterness of the agony of a dying man. For the present;—what bitterness in this separation from

your possessions, your family, your body; in the weariness, the fears that precede the last sigh! For the past, — what bitterness in the memory of your infidelities, of your resistance to grace! For the future;—what bitterness in the thought of the judgment you are about to undergo!

4. *Application of the touch.* Imagine yourself holding between your hands the crucifix which the priest presents to you. Touch your own body on the point of dissolution; those icy feet, those rigid arms, that chest labouring painfully with interrupted respiration, that heart beating with an almost imperceptible movement. It is in this state that your relations and friends will see you before very long. Make now on yourself the reflections that your agony will soon inspire in those who witness it.

End by a colloquy with our dying Lord: "Into Thy hands, O Lord, I commend my spirit."

SECOND CONTEMPLATION.

Your state after death.

Preparatory Prayer.

Preludes. The same.

1. *Application of the sight.* Consider, (1) Some moments after your death: your corpse wrapped in a shroud; at your side the crucifix, the holy water, relations and friends; a priest praying for you; the public officer writing in a registry of deaths the day, the hour of your decease; the servants occupied with the preparations for your funeral. (2) The day after your death: your inanimate body in the coffin, taken from your

Y

apartment, laid at the foot of the altar; then taken to
its last home, the grave. (3) Some time after your
death: contemplate that stone already blackened by
time, and under this stone the sad state of your body;
the putrefied flesh, the separated limbs, the bones consumed by the corruption of the grave.

2. *Application of the hearing.* Again go over the
different scenes where you yourself are the spectacle:
the dismal sound of the bells asking prayers for you,
the prayers recited at the foot of your death-bed, "De
profundis clamavi;" the discourse of the servants, who
speak freely of you; the friends and relations, who communicate to each other their reflections on your loss;
the attendants called in to arrange your funeral; the
chants of the Church during the funeral ceremony:
"Deliver me, O Lord, from eternal death in that dreadful day, when the heavens and the earth shall tremble;
when Thou shalt come to judgment—a day of wrath,
calamity, and misery,—that great and bitter day;" the
conversation of the persons attending your funeral;
what is said of you in society after your death.

3. *Application of the smell and the touch.* Imagine that you respire the odour that your body exhales
after your soul has abandoned it,—the infection it would
spread if taken from the coffin a few months after your
death. Imagine that you touch the damp earth where
you have been laid, the shroud in rags, the bare skull,
the separated limbs, the mass of corruption enclosed in
a grave, after a few months the sight alone of which is
horrible.

In presence of this sad scene, ask yourself what the
world is, and what is life? "Vanity of vanities, and

all is vanity" (Eccl. i. 2). End by a colloquy with our Lord dying : " Into Thy hands, O Lord, I commend my spirit."

Pater. Ave.

EXERCISE ON THE PARTICULAR JUDGMENT.

Preparatory Prayer.

First prelude. Represent to yourself the tribunal of Jesus Christ, and your soul led to the presence of its Judge to give an account of all its works.

Second prelude. Remember, O most loving Jesu, that for me Thou didst humble Thyself to this mortal life. Let me not be lost, I beseech Thee, on that day.

CONSIDERATIONS.

1. *The time and the place of the judgment.* The time will be the moment you render your last sigh. Represent to yourself your relatives and your friends around your death-bed, examining your lips, your heart, to discover a breath, a throb, which may still betoken life. While they are yet asking whether you belong to time or to eternity, you are already before the tribunal of your Judge. And where is this tribunal? In the very place where you have just expired, beside your death-bed, in presence of those who surround your inanimate remains, and who assist at this terrible scene without desiring it, and probably without thinking of it.

2. *The accused.* It is your soul; but your soul alone with its works; your soul suddenly enlightened on all its obligations; on all the graces it has received, on all the iniquities it has committed; your soul in presence of its God, without power to escape this formid-

able sight. What a situation! A worldly soul in presence of that God it has never loved,—a voluptuous soul in presence of that God thrice holy, who has witnessed its disorders, and who is about to punish them!

3. *The accusers.* Satan, who recalls your baptismal vows so often renewed, so often broken; the holy angels; your guardian-angel, who reproaches you with nis inspirations that you rejected; the angels intrusted with the souls of your brethren, who reproach you with your scandals; the angels who watch over the holy altars, and who reproach you with that indifference which kept you away from the holy table; your conscience, which places before your eyes all your past life, produces all your works, which cry out, " Dost thou recognise us? we are thy works."

4. *The Judge.* It is Jesus Christ who is your judge Jesus Christ once your father, your spouse, your friend, your brother; but who now is your judge only,—a judge infinitely holy, a judge infinitely clear-sighted, a judge infinitely just, a judge without appeal, a judge all-powerful. What have you not to fear from His justice! "What shall I do when God shall rise to judge?" (Job xxxi. 14.)

5. *Your defence at the tribunal of God.* If you present yourself before the tribunal of Jesus Christ in mortal sin, what will you reply to the accusations brought against you? Will you excuse yourself by your ignorance? but you had the lights of conscience and of faith; on your weakness? but you had grace; on your temptations? but you had prayer and the Sacraments; on the scandals that have led you astray? but you had so many holy examples to instruct you. Leav-

ing excuses, will you have recourse to the intercession
of holy Mary and of the saints? they can no longer do
any thing for you; to the mercy of Jesus Christ? He
is henceforward the God of justice, and no longer the
God of clemency: "My eye shall not spare them,
neither will I show mercy" (Ezech. viii. 18).

6. *The sentence.* To the just will be said : " Come,
O ye blessed of My Father, and possess the kingdom
prepared for you from the beginning of the world"
(Matt. xxii. 34). But to the sinner will be said : " Begone, ye cursed, into everlasting fire, prepared for the
devil and his angels" (ibid. 41). Begone! that is, every
tie between us is broken; go far from Me, unnatural
child ; I am no longer thy father ;—go far from Me,
wandering sheep, I am no longer thy pastor; thou art
cursed in thy senses, which shall each have its torment,
—in thy understanding, in thy heart, in all thy being.
Begone into everlasting fire, to that fire where thy only
dwelling shall be a furnace, thy food flames ;—to that
fire which shall last as long as I am God; begone to the
fire prepared for Satan and his angels. I take heaven
and earth to witness that it was not prepared for thee.
I protest that I have done every thing to save thee
from this eternal fire ; but since thou wouldst not profit
by My grace and friendship, begone from Me, and
begone for all eternity.

Affections.

COLLOQUIES.

1. At the feet of Jesus Christ crucified: " O most
just Judge, grant me, I beseech Thee, the gift of pardon before that great day of reckoning. Behold, I

groan in Thy sight as a guilty sinner; shame covereth my face because of my iniquities. Spare me, O God, crying to Thee for mercy."

2. At the feet of an image of Mary: " O Mary, at once the Mother of God and the Mother of the sinner, Mother of the Judge and of the criminal; let not God your Son condemn your son the sinner."

Pater. Ave.

EXERCISE ON THE PRODIGAL SON.

Preparatory Prayer.

First prelude. Represent to yourself the prodigal son returning to his father after long wanderings.

Second prelude. Ask of our Lord the grace to imitate the repentance of the prodigal, and like him to obtain pardon for the past.

PARABLE OF THE PRODIGAL.

" A certain man," &c. (Luke xv. 11-24).

FIRST POINT.

The wandering of the prodigal.

Consider all the circumstances.

1. *He is young.* The passions of youth, that is, love of pleasure, independence, these are the causes of his wandering. Have not yours arisen from the same cause?

2. *He asks of his father his portion of the inheritance.* What ingratitude, what injustice, what temerity

in this conduct of the prodigal! Is not all this to be found in the steps that have led you from your God?

3. *He goes into a distant country.* An image this of your wandering when you gave yourself to the world. Is it not true that you have fled as far from yourself and from God as possible, for fear that grace should find you, and restore you to your heavenly Father in spite of yourself?

4. *Away from his father, the prodigal squanders all his fortune.* And you, away from God, what treasures of grace have you not wasted! Recall all these losses, and weep over them with tears of blood ;—loss of the friendship of God, loss of your past merits, loss of your Christian education, of your inclinations so favourable to piety, of that taste for virtue, of that delicacy of conscience, of that uprightness of heart,—loss of those talents prostituted to your passions,—loss of reason— perhaps of faith. Oh, what a fatal use of the gifts of God!

5. *The prodigal is soon reduced to want in a country desolated by famine.* Obliged to place himself in the service of a hard master ; condemned to take care of filthy animals; to envy, without obtaining, their degrading food.

Behold the fruits of sin :

(1) *Indigence.* The world is this country a prey to a cruel famine. This hunger is the devouring hunger of the passions, which cry incessantly, " Bring, bring" (Prov. xxx. 15). And this want is the deep craving of a soul tormented by the desire of happiness, and finding in creatures only endless regrets, disgust, and sorrow. (2) *Slavery.* Like the prodigal, the sin-

ner is a slave, not of one master alone, but of numberless tyrants,—of the devil, of the world, of his own inclinations and habits. (3) *Degradation.* There is no pleasure, however base, from which a soul separated from God will not seek happiness. It will even envy the most disgraceful sinners their most shameful excesses; sometimes even envy the condition of the brutes, so as to desire to have like them no law but instinct, no other destiny than the satisfaction of his senses: "Man when he was in honour did not understand; he hath been compared to senseless beasts, and made like to them" (Ps. xlviii. 21).

SECOND POINT.
The return of the prodigal.

1. *The prodigal, deserted by the world, returns to himself.* He begins to reflect on his sins and his misfortunes. What subjects of reflection does he not find within himself! O God, what have I gained by forsaking Thee? What repose, what happiness, have I found in the world? Was it necessary to sacrifice Thy friendship, peace of conscience, my eternity, for pleasures so transient, so empty, so degrading?

2. *The prodigal compares his state with that of his father's servants, and envies them their happiness.* Faithless soul, what a difference between your state and that of the servants of God! What peace, what joy in their hearts! in yours what troubles, what bitterness!

3. *The prodigal takes a courageous resolution.* "I will arise," said he, "and I will go to my father." He does not stop at words and desires; he does not defer

his return; he does not draw back, either before the raillery of the world or the sacrifice of his attachments. What an example of solid conversion!

4. The prodigal hopes, by the acknowledgment of his faults, to regain his father's favour. Let this be also the first step in your conversion. Cast yourself at the feet of Jesus Christ, present in the person of the priest, and say to Him, " Father, I have sinned against Heaven and before Thee. I am no longer worthy to be called Thy child; too happy if Thou wilt deign to receive me among Thy servants."

Consider the welcome the prodigal receives from his father.

1. *His father sees him afar off, and is immediately moved with compassion.* Thus, at the first feelings of repentance that arise in the sinner's heart God is moved with pity; He forgets his past ingratitude; He only sees his misfortunes and his sorrow.

2. *The father of the prodigal fell upon his neck and embraced him.* Recognise in these facts the goodness of God when, abandoned by creatures, we return to Him. Did not God owe it to His glory, His holiness, His justice, to reject us? and yet He meets us; He offers us pardon; He embraces us and presses us to His sacred heart.

3. *The father of the prodigal orders him to be immediately reëstablished in all the prerogatives of his rank.* So the Lord treats the sinner that returns to Him. With His friendship He restores to him all he had forfeited by sin;—innocence, peace, merits, right to heaven, all his dignity as a man and as a Christian.

4. Finally, *the father of the prodigal orders a*

splendid feast to celebrate the return of his son, and invites all his household to take part in the joy of this feast. So our Heavenly Father celebrates the return of the sinner by a solemn festival, in which He gives him His own body. He invites the angels to rejoice in his spiritual resurrection. He wills that the day of his conversion should be a day of gladness and feasting for all His family, that is, the Church. After this, why do we delay returning to the arms and the heart of this good Father?

COLLOQUY.

Throw yourself at the feet of Jesus Christ, like the prodigal at his father's feet, and promise never more to forsake Him.

Anima Christi.

MYSTERIES OF THE LIFE OF OUR LORD,

DISTRIBUTED BY ST. IGNATIUS INTO FIFTY-ONE SUBJECTS OF PRAYER,
CORRESPONDING TO THE THREE LAST WEEKS OF THE EXERCISES.

I.

THE INCARNATION OF THE WORD ANNOUNCED TO THE BLESSED VIRGIN.

(Luke i. 26-38.)

Point 1. The angel Gabriel salutes the Blessed Virgin, and announces to her the conception of the Word of God : "The angel entering, said to her, Hail, Mary, full of grace, &c.   Thou shalt conceive in thy womb, and shalt bring forth a son," &c.

2. The angel confirms what he has just announced by the example of the miraculous conception of St. John Baptist: "Thy cousin Elizabeth, she also hath conceived a son in her old age," &c.

3. The Holy Virgin replies to the angel : " Behold the servant of the Lord ; be it done to me according to thy word."

II.

THE VISIT WHICH MARY PAYS TO HER COUSIN ELIZABETH.

(Luke i. 39-56.)

1. Mary goes to visit Elizabeth.   What impression the approach of Mary, and her voice, made on St. John ! " When Elizabeth heard the salutation of Mary, the

infant leaped in her womb. And Elizabeth was filled with the Holy Ghost, and said, Blessed art thou among women, and blessed is the fruit of thy womb."

2. The Holy Virgin, in the transport of her joy, breathes forth the sentiments of her soul in the canticle, " My soul doth magnify the Lord," &c.

3. Mary remains with Elizabeth three months, and returns to her own home.

III.

THE BIRTH OF JESUS CHRIST.

(Luke ii. 1-14.)

1. The Blessed Virgin sets out from Nazareth with St. Joseph, her spouse, to go to Bethlehem: " Joseph went up from Galilee, out of the city of Nazareth, to Bethlehem, ... to be enrolled with Mary, his spouse, who was with child."

2. " Mary brought forth her first-born Son, and wrapped Him up in swaddling clothes, and laid Him in a manger."

3. " Suddenly there was with the angel a multitude of the heavenly army, praising God and saying, Glory to God in the highest," &c.

IV.

THE ADORATION OF THE SHEPHERDS.

(Luke ii. 8-20.)

1. An angel reveals the birth of Jesus Christ to the shepherds: " I bring you good tidings of great joy. . . · This day is born to you a Saviour," &c.

2. The shepherds hasten to Bethlehem: " They

came with haste, and they found Mary and Joseph, and the Infant lying in a manger."

3. The shepherds return, "glorifying and praising God," &c.

V.

THE CIRCUMCISION.
(Luke ii. 21.)

1. The Child is circumcised.

2. "His name is called Jesus, which was so called by the angel before He was conceived in the womb."

3. The Child, after His circumcision, was placed in His Mother's arms, who feels the most tender compassion at seeing the blood of her Son flow.

VI.

THE ADORATION OF THE MAGI.
(Matt. ii. 1-12.)

1. Three kings, wise men, guided by a star, come to adore Jesus Christ: "We have seen His star in the east, and are come to adore Him."

2. "And falling down at the feet of the Child, they adored Him; and opening their treasures, they offered Him gold, frankincense, and myrrh."

3. Having received an answer in sleep that they should not return to Herod, they went back another way into their country.

VII.

PURIFICATION OF THE HOLY VIRGIN AND THE PRE-SENTATION OF THE CHILD JESUS IN THE TEMPLE.
(Luke ii. 22-39.)

1. Mary and Joseph carry the Child to the Temple

of Jerusalem, to present Him to God as their first-born, and make the offerings prescribed by the law—"a pair of turtle doves or two young pigeons."

2. Simeon comes into the Temple, "and took the Child into his arms, and blessed God, and said, Now dost Thou dismiss Thy servant, O Lord, according to Thy word, in peace," &c.

3. "Anna, coming in at the same hour, confessed to the Lord; and spoke of Him to all that looked for the redemption of Israel."

VIII.

THE FLIGHT INTO EGYPT.

(Matt. ii. 13-15.)

1. Herod wishing to kill the new-born Jesus, orders all the children about Bethlehem to be massacred. But before that an angel had warned Joseph to go into Egypt: "Arise, and take the Child and His Mother, and fly into Egypt."

2. Joseph sets out for Egypt: "He arose, and took the Child and His Mother by night, and retired into Egypt."

3. "He was there until the death of Herod."

IX.

THE RETURN FROM EGYPT.

(Matt. ii. 19-23.)

1. An angel warned Joseph to return to the land of Israel: "Arise; take the Child and His Mother, and go into the land of Israel."

2. Joseph immediately "arose, and came into the land of Israel."

3. Archelaus, son of Herod, reigned in Judea at that time, which induced Joseph to retire to Nazareth.

X.

THE LIFE OF OUR LORD FROM HIS TWELFTH TO HIS THIRTIETH YEAR.

'Luke ii. 51, 52 ; Mark vi. 3.)

1. Jesus was subject and obedient to Mary and Joseph.

2. "He advanced in wisdom and age and grace with God and men," &c.

3. It appears that He Himself worked at a trade, since it is said in St. Mark (chapter vi.), that the Jews said of Him, " Is not this the carpenter ?"

XI.

JESUS AMONG THE DOCTORS AT TWELVE YEARS OF AGE.

(Luke ii. 41-51.)

1. Jesus having attained the age of twelve years went from Nazareth to Jerusalem.

2. He remained in Jerusalem, without Mary and Joseph knowing it.

3. Having sought Him for three days, they found Him in the Temple among the doctors. They asked Him why He had remained in Jerusalem ; He replied, " Did you not know that I must be about My Father's business ?"

XII.

THE BAPTISM OF JESUS CHRIST.

(Matt. iii. 13-17 ; Mark i. 9-11 ; Luke iii. 21-28.)

1. Jesus having bid adieu to His Mother set out

from Nazareth, and went to the banks of the river Jordan, where John, His precursor, was baptising.

2. He is baptised by St. John, who at first excuses himself as unworthy to exercise this function towards Him; but Jesus Christ obliges him, saying, "Do it, for it becometh us to fulfil all justice."

3. The Holy Ghost descends upon Jesus Christ, and the voice of the Eternal Father is heard in heaven: "This is My beloved Son, in whom I am well pleased."

XIII.

THE TEMPTATION OF JESUS CHRIST.

(Matt. iv. 1-11; Mark i. 12, 13; Luke iv. 1-13.)

1. Jesus Christ, after His baptism, retired into the desert, and fasted there forty days and forty nights.

2. There He was tempted three times by the enemy of our salvation: "The tempter coming, said to Him, If Thou be the Son of God, command that these stones be made bread. . . . . Cast Thyself down from this pinnacle. . . . . All these will I give Thee, if, falling down, Thou wilt adore me."

3. "Angels came and ministered to Him."

XIV.

THE CALL OF THE APOSTLES.

1. St. Peter and St. Andrew appear to have been called three times; first, to a simple knowledge of Jesus Christ (John i.); then, to follow Jesus Christ only for a time, intending to return to and continue their trade of fishermen (Luke v.); finally, to follow Him constantly, and not to leave Him any more (Matt. iv.; Mark i.).

2. He called the sons of Zebedee, as is related in St. Matthew, chap. iv.; Philip, as St. John relates, chap. i.; and Matthew, as he himself relates, chap. ix.

The other Apostles were called also, although there is no express mention in the Gospels of the order and circumstance of their vocation.

3. On this three reflections may be made : (1) that the Apostles were taken from a low and poor station; (2) that they were raised to a supereminent dignity with admirable sweetness; (3) that they were honoured with supernatural gifts, as numerous as they were extraordinary, and by that placed above all the patriarchs of the Old Testament and all the saints of the New.

XV.

FIRST MIRACLE OF JESUS CHRIST AT THE MARRIAGE AT CANA
(John ii. 1-11.)

1. Jesus Christ is invited, with His disciples, to the marriage taking place at Cana.

2. His Mother tells Him that the guests are in want of wine : " They have no wine." She said to the waiters, " Whatsoever He shall say to you, do ye."

3. The Lord changes the water into wine : " so manifesting His glory; and His disciples believed in Him."

XVI.

THE BUYERS AND SELLERS TURNED OUT OF THE TEMPLE THE FIRST TIME.*
(John ii. 13-22.)

1. He drives out of the Temple all the buyers and

* This occurred after the first Pasch, which followed our

sellers, having armed Himself with a scourge made of little cords.

2. He pours out the money of the changers and overthrows the tables.

3. With more meekness He says to those who sold doves, "Take these things hence, and make not the house of My Father a house of traffic."

XVII.

THE SERMON OF JESUS CHRIST ON THE MOUNT.

(Matt. v. vi. vii.; Luke vi. 17-49.)

1. Jesus Christ proposes to His beloved disciples eight kinds of beatitudes.

2. He exhorts them to make a good use of the gifts and talents they have received from God: "So let your light shine before men, that they may see your good works, and glorify your Father who is in heaven."

3. He shows that He does not come to destroy the Law, but, on the contrary, to perfect it, by developing the precepts against homicide, theft, fornication, and perjury; by ordaining that we love even our enemies: "I say to you, Love your enemies, do good to them that hate you."

XVIII.

THE TEMPEST CALMED ON THE SEA OF GALILEE.

(Matt. viii. 23-27; Mark iv. 35-40; Luke vii. 22-25.)

1. A violent tempest arose on the sea while Jesus slept.

Lord's baptism. The second time our Lord performed this act was before the fourth Pasch, as is recorded by St. Matthew (xxi. 12), St. Mark (xi. 15), and St. Luke (xix. 45).

2. His disciples being afraid, awake Him. He reproaches them with their want of confidence : " Why are you fearful, O ye of little faith ?"

3. He commands the winds and the sea to be still, and immediately there is a profound calm. All those who witnessed it, struck with astonishment, cried out " What manner of man is this, for the winds and the sea obey Him ?"

XIX.

JESUS CHRIST WALKS ON THE WATERS.

(Matt. xiv. 22-33; Mark vi. 45-54; John v. 15-21.)

1. Jesus Christ, being still on the mountain, orders His disciples to return to their boat; "and having dismissed the multitude, He went up into the mountain to pray alone."

2. During the night a tempest arises. The boat of the Apostles is violently tossed by the waves. Jesus goes towards them, and to reach the boat He walks upon the waters. "The Apostles, seeing Him, were afraid, and thought it was a spirit."

3. Jesus says to His Apostles, " It is I; fear not." After He had reassured them by these words, St. Peter asks permission to join Him. Jesus having permitted him, Peter, walking on the waters, goes to meet Him; but feeling afraid, he begins to sink. The Lord reproves him for the weakness of his faith, and entering the boat, the wind ceases.

XX.

JESUS CHRIST SENDS HIS APOSTLES TO PREACH.

(Matt. x. 1-42, xi. 1; Mark vi. 7-18; Luke ix. 1-6.)

1. Jesus having assembled His disciples, gives them

power to cast out devils and to cure all sorts of diseases.

2. He teaches them prudence and patience: "I
send you as sheep amidst the wolves. Be ye, therefore,
wise as serpents and simple as doves."

3. He explains in what manner they must conduct
their apostolic mission: "Freely have you received,
freely give." "Do not possess silver nor gold."
Moreover, He tells them expressly what they are to
teach: "Go and preach that the kingdom of heaven
is at hand."

XXI.

THE CONVERSION OF MAGDALEN.

(Luke vii. 36-50.)

1. Jesus being at table in the house of a Pharisee,
a woman, a sinner of the city, enters the room, carrying
an alabaster vase full of perfumes.

2. Standing behind at the feet of Jesus, she waters
them with her tears, wipes them with her hair, kisses
them, and anoints them with perfumes.

3. Jesus defends Himself against the Pharisee, to
whom He says: "Many sins are forgiven this woman
because she hath loved much." Then He said to her,
"Thy faith hath made thee safe: go in peace."

XXII.

THE MULTITUDE FED.

(Matt. xiv. 13-21; Mark vi. 30-44; Luke ix. 10-17; John vi. 1-14.)

1. The disciples ask Jesus to send away the multitude who had followed Him into the desert.

2. Jesus tells His disciples to give Him the loaves

they had brought. Having blessed them, He breaks them, and gives them to His disciples to distribute to the people, whom He had first ordered to be seated.

3. All the multitude eat, and after they are satisfied there remain twelve baskets of the pieces.

XXIII.

TRANSFIGURATION OF JESUS CHRIST.

(Matt. xvii. 1-9; Mark ix. 1-8; Luke ix. 28-36.)

1. Jesus takes with Him His three dearest disciples, Peter, James, and John. "He was transfigured before them. And His face did shine as the sun; and His garments became white as snow."

2. Jesus speaks of His passion to Moses and Elias.

3. Peter asks permission to erect three tents on the mountain. A voice is heard from heaven: "This is My beloved Son, hear ye Him." The disciples being afraid, fell on their faces. Jesus reassured them, touched them, and raised them, saying to them, "Arise, and fear not. . . . Tell the vision to no man till the Son of Man be risen from the dead."

XXIV.

THE RESURRECTION OF LAZARUS.

(John xi. 1-45.)

1. Jesus having heard that Lazarus was ill, remains two days in the place where He was, so that the miracle He wished to work in his favour might be more striking.

2. Before raising him, He rouses and animates the faith of his two sisters: "I am the resurrection and the life: he that believeth in Me, although he be dead, shall live."

3. Jesus begins by shedding tears; He addresses a fervent prayer to His heavenly Father; then He raises the dead. On which it may be observed, that it was done by the most positive command : " Lazarus, come forth."

XXV.

THE SUPPER AT BETHANIA.

(Matt. xxvi. 6-13; Mark xiv. 3-9; John xii. 1-11.)

1. Jesus eats at the house of Simon the leper, and Lazarus is one of the guests.

2. Mary anoints the head of Jesus with precious perfumes.

3. Judas murmurs at the action of Mary : " What is the use of this profusion?"   Jesus excuses Magdalen: " She hath wrought a good work upon Me."

XXVI.

PALM-SUNDAY.

(Matt. xxi. 1-11; Mark xi. 1-10; Luke xix. 29-44; John xii. 12-19.)

1. The Lord orders His Apostles to go and seek and bring Him an ass with its foal : " Loose them, and bring them to Me.   And if any man shall say any thing to you, say ye, that the Lord hath need of them, and forthwith he will let them go."

2. The Apostles having laid their garments on the ass, the Lord mounted on it.

3. The people assemble in crowds to receive Him. All hasten to cover the way with their garments and the branches of trees, singing: " Hosanna to the Son of David! Blessed is He that cometh in the name of the Lord.   Hosanna in the highest!"

XXVII.

THE PREACHING OF JESUS IN THE TEMPLE.

(Luke xix. 47, 48.)

1. Jesus teaches every day publicly in the Temple.

2. The preaching over, He returns to Bethania, not any one in Jerusalem receiving Him.

XXVIII.

THE LAST SUPPER.

(Matt. xxvi. 17-30; Mark xiv. 12-20; Luke xxii. 7-23; John xiii. 1-30.)

1. Jesus Christ eats the pascal lamb with His disciples, and warns them of His approaching death : "Amen, I say to you, that one of you is about to betray Me."

2. Jesus washes their feet, even those of Judas, and begins with Peter. He, considering the majesty of Jesus Christ and his own lowness, opposes it at first : "Lord, dost Thou wash my feet?" He did not yet know that it was a lesson of humility that their Divine Master was giving them, who told them of it in these words : "I have given you an example, that as I have done to you, so do you also."

3. Then He institutes the most Holy Sacrament of the Eucharist, to be the pledge of His love. These are His words : "Take ye and eat, this is My body," &c. The supper ended, Judas goes out to sell Him to the chief-priests.

XXIX.

MYSTERIES, FROM THE SUPPER TO THE GARDEN OF OLIVES INCLUSIVE.

(Matt. xxvi. 31-46; Mark xiv. 27-42; Luke xxii. 24-46; John xiii. 31-38, xiv.-xvii., xviii. 1, 2.)

1. The supper being ended, and having returned thanks to His Father, Jesus sets out to go to the mountain of Olives with His eleven disciples, who are filled with fear. He leaves eight of them at Gethsemani : "Sit you here, till I go yonder and pray."

2. Taking with Him Peter, James, and John, He repeats three times the same prayer : "My Father, if it be possible, let this chalice pass from Me. Nevertheless not as I will, but as Thou wilt." The greater His sorrow became in this mortal agony, the more earnest He became in prayer.

3. He allows Himself to be reduced to such an excess of fear and terror that He said, "My soul is sorrowful even unto death." He sweated blood abundantly, according to the testimony of St. Luke : "His sweat became as drops of blood, trickling down upon the ground."

XXX.

FROM THE GARDEN TO THE HOUSE OF ANNAS.

(Matt. xxvi. 47-57; Mark xiv. 43-53; Luke xxii. 47-54; John xviii. 3-24.)

1. Our Lord allows Judas to betray Him by a kiss, and the soldiers to seize Him like a malefactor : "Ye are come out as it were to a robber with swords and clubs to apprehend Me. I sat daily with you teaching in the

Temple, and you laid not hands on Me." Then, having interrogated them in these terms, " Whom seek ye?" all His enemies fall backwards to the ground.

2. Peter strikes one of the servants of the high-priest and wounds him. Jesus says to Peter, " Put up thy sword into the scabbard ;" and He cures the servant.

3. Jesus is arrested, abandoned by His disciples, dragged to the house of Annas. Peter follows Him a short time after, and there denies Him the first time.* Jesus receives a blow from another servant of the high-priest, who reproaches Him with being wanting in respect: " Answerest Thou the high-priest so?"

XXXI.

FROM THE HOUSE OF ANNAS TO THAT OF CAIPHAS.

(Matt. xxvi. 57-75 ; Mark xiv. 53-72; Luke xxii. 54-71 ; John xviii. 24-27.)

1. Jesus bound is led from Annas to Caiphas. There Peter denies Him twice. But the Lord casts a look at His apostle ; "and he going out wept bitterly."

2. Jesus remains bound all the night.

3. The guards who surround Him insult and tor-ment Him. They blindfold Him, strike Him, and say in derision, " Christ, prophesy unto us, and say who it is that struck Thee." They insult Him by a thousand blasphemies.

* SS. Matthew, Mark, and Luke do not separate in their narrative the first denial from the other two, as if all three took place in the house of Caiphas. St. John seems to place the first before Annas ; an opinion embraced by St. Augustine, whom St. Ignatius here follows. (See De Ligny's *Life of Christ*, part iii. chap. 1€.)

XXXII.

FROM THE HOUSE OF CAIPHAS TO THAT OF PILATE.

(Matt. xxvii, 1-27; Mark xv. 1-14; Luke xxiii. 1-5;
John xviii. 28-40.)

1. Jesus is led before Pilate, and calumniously accused at his tribunal: "We have found this man perverting our nation, and forbidding to give tribute to Cæsar."

2. Pilate having examined Him several times, answers the Jews, "I find no cause in this man worthy of death."

3. The Jews ask for the release of Barabbas in preference to that of Jesus Christ: "Not this man, but Barabbas."

XXXIII.

FROM THE HOUSE OF PILATE TO THAT OF HEROD.

(Luke xxiii. 6-12.)

1. Pilate sends Jesus to Herod king of Galilee, supposing that He was a Galilean.

2. Herod questions Him to satisfy his curiosity. Jesus answers nothing, though the Jews load Him with accusations.

3. Herod and his court insult Him, and in derision He is clothed in white.

XXXIV.

JESUS SENT BACK FROM HEROD TO PILATE.

(Matt. xxvii. 24-30; Mark xv. 15-19; Luke xxiii. 12-23;
John xix. 1-11.)

1. Herod sends Jesus Christ back to Pilate.   From

this day Herod and Pilate, who had been enemies before, became reconciled.

2. Pilate orders Jesus Christ to be scourged; the soldiers crown Him with thorns, and place an old purple mantle on His shoulders; afterwards they insult Him, saying in derision: "Hail, king of the Jews!" at the same time they strike Him.

3. Jesus comes out of the hall of justice crowned with thorns and clothed in purple. Pilate showing Him to the Jews, says, "Behold the man!" The priests seeing Him, say, "Crucify Him, crucify Him!"

XXXV.

CONDEMNATION AND CRUCIFIXION OF JESUS CHRIST.

(Matt. xxvii. 31-38; Mark xv. 20-28; Luke xxiii. 24-38; John xix. 12-24.)

1. Pilate being seated on his tribunal, judged Jesus, and delivered Him up to the Jews, who renounced Him for their king, saying, "We have no king but Cæsar."

2. Jesus bears His cross until, His strength failing Him, they compel a man named Simon, a Cyrenian, to carry it behind Him.

3. He is crucified between two thieves. At the top of the cross this inscription is placed: "Jesus of Nazareth, king of the Jews."

XXXVI.

JESUS ON THE CROSS.

(Matt. xxvii. 39-56; Mark xv. 29-41; Luke xviii. 39-49; John xix. 25-39.)

1. They blaspheme against Jesus Christ in different

ways: "Thou that destroyest the Temple of God, &c.,
. . . come down from the cross," &c. The soldiers
divide His garments.

2. Jesus pronounces seven words on the cross. He
prays for His murderers. He pardons one of the
thieves crucified with Him. He recommends His
Mother to St. John, and St. John to His Mother. He
cries, "I thirst;" then the soldiers give Him vinegar
and water to drink. He complains to His Father of
the abandonment in which He left Him. He says,
"All is consummated." Finally, before dying, He
pronounces these words: "Father, into Thy hands I
commend My spirit."

3. At His death the sun is darkened, the rocks rent.
the graves opened, the veil of the Temple is torn from
top to bottom. His side being pierced by a spear, blood
and water flow from it.

XXXVII.

THE BURIAL OF JESUS CHRIST.

(Matt. xxvii. 57-66; Mark xv. 42-47; Luke xxiii. 50-56;
John xix. 30-42.)

1. Our Lord being now dead is taken down from
the cross by Joseph and Nicodemus, in presence of His
holy Mother, who is overpowered by the most lively grief.

3. His body, being embalmed, is carried to the
sepulchre, and enclosed in it.

3. Guards are placed at the tomb.

XXXVIII.

THE RESURRECTION OF JESUS CHRIST, AND HIS
FIRST APPARITION.

Jesus Christ appears first to His Blessed Mother

after His resurrection. The Gospel leads us to think
so, by saying that Jesus Christ appeared to several persons; if we do not find in this general expression a
sufficiently sure proof, we deserve that reproach of our
Saviour to His disciples: "Are ye still without understanding?"

XXXIX.

SECOND APPARITION.

(Matt. xxviii. 1-7; Mark xvi. 1-11; Luke xxiv. 1-11;
John xx. 1, 11-18.)

1. Early in the morning Mary Magdalen and the
mother of James and Salome leave Jerusalem to go to
the sepulchre. They say to one another, "Who shall roll
us back the stone from the door of the sepulchre?"

2. They see the stone removed, and in the tomb an
angel, who says to them, "Ye seek Jesus of Nazareth
who was crucified. He is risen; He is not here."

3. Jesus appears to Magdalen, who had remained
alone at the tomb, the other women having gone away

XL.

THIRD APPARITION.

(Matt. xxviii. 8-10.)

1. The pious women of whom we have spoken are
returning to Jerusalem, filled with fear and joy, to tell
the Apostles what they had heard of the resurrection of
their Master.

2. As they walk together, Jesus appears to them,
and says, "All hail!" They kneel at His feet and
adore Him.

3. The Lord speaks to them tenderly: "Fear not.

Go tell My brethren that they go into Galilee; there
they shall see Me."

XLI.

FOURTH APPARITION.

(Luke xxiv. 12-34; John xx. 1-10.)

1. St. Peter, having learned of the holy women
that Jesus was risen, goes in all haste to the sepulchre

2. He enters, and sees only the linen clothes in
which the body of our Saviour had been wrapped.

3. While St. Peter wondered at this event, the Lord
appeared, as it was afterwards said: "The Lord hath
risen indeed, and hath appeared to Simon."

XLII.

FIFTH APPARITION.

(Mark xvi. 12, 13; Luke xxiv. 13-34.)

1. He appears to two disciples, who are talking of
Him on their way to Emmaus.

2. He reproaches them with their incredulity, and
explains to them the mysteries of His passion and resurrection. "O foolish, and slow of heart to believe in
all things which the prophets have spoken! Ought not
Christ to have suffered these things, and so to enter
into His glory?"

3. His disciples beg Him to remain with them.
He remains. Then taking bread and breaking it, He
gives it to them, and disappears. They return to Jerusalem, and relate to the Apostles how they had seen the
Lord, and had recognised Him by the breaking of the
bread.

XLIII.

SIXTH APPARITION.

(Luke xxiv. 36-45; John xx. 19-23.)

1. All the disciples, except Thomas, are shut up in a house, because they feared the Jews.

2. Jesus Christ enters the room where they are all, the doors being closed. " He stood in the midst, and said to them, Peace be to you."

3. He gives them the Holy Spirit, and says to them, " Receive ye the Holy Ghost. Whose sins you shall forgive, are forgiven them."

XLIV.

SEVENTH APPARITION.

(John xx. 24-29.)

1. St. Thomas not having been with the other Apostles when Jesus appeared to them the first time, had protested that he would not believe unless he saw: " If I see not, &c., I will not believe."

2. Eight days after, the Apostles being still together, and Thomas with them, the doors being closed, Jesus appears a second time, and says to St. Thomas, " Put in thy finger hither, &c., ... and be not faithless, but believing."

3. Thomas answers, "My Lord and my God!" Jesus replies, " Blessed are they that have not seen, and have believed."

XLV.

EIGHTH APPARITION.

(John xxi. 1-25.)

1. Jesus appears to seven of His disciples, who were

fishing. They had taken nothing all night; but having cast their net by the order of Jesus Christ, "now they were not able to draw it for the multitude of fishes."

2. John knew Jesus Christ by this miracle, and says to Peter, "It is the Lord." Immediately Peter, casting himself into the sea, hastens to Jesus.

3. Jesus gives them bread and fish to eat. Then, having asked Peter three different times if he loved Him, He gives him the care of His flock, saying to him, "Feed My lambs, feed My sheep."

XLVI.

NINTH APPARITION.

(Matt. xviii. 16-20; Mark xvi. 14-20; Luke xxiv. 46-53.)

1. The disciples, by order of their Master, go to Mount Thabor.

2. There He appears to them again, saying, "All power is given to Me in heaven and on earth."

3. Sending them to preach throughout the whole world, He gives them this command: "Go, teach all nations, baptising them in the name of the Father, of the Son, and of the Holy Ghost."

XLVII.

TENTH APPARITION.

(1 Cor. xv. 6.)

Jesus afterwards shows Himself to more than five hundred disciples assembled together.

XLVIII.

ELEVENTH APPARITION.

(1 Cor. xv. 7.)

He shows Himself to James alone.

XLIX.

TWELFTH APPARITION.

We read in several pious books that He appeared to Joseph of Arimathea alone. This is probable, and we may piously meditate on it.

L.

THIRTEENTH APPARITION.

(1 Cor. xv. 8.)

1. His soul also makes its presence felt by the patriarchs and the just in limbus; and after having delivered them, He showed Himself to them many times.

2. He shows Himself very frequently to His disciples after His resurrection, and converses with them.

3. He appears again, after His ascension, to St. Paul, who declares it himself: "And last of all, He was seen also by me, as by one born out of due time."

LI.

ASCENSION OF JESUS CHRIST.

(Acts i. 1, 11.)

1. Jesus Christ having shown Himself many times to His Apostles during forty days, and having convinced them by many signs that He was really living, "speak-

ing to them of the kingdom of God," He orders them to return to Jerusalem until they shall have received the Holy Ghost.

2. He led them to the Mount of Olives; and "while they looked on, He was raised up, and a cloud received Him out of their sight."

3. While they were looking at Him ascending into heaven, two men dressed in white (whom we believe to have been angels) appeared to them, and said, " Men of Galilee, why stand you looking up to heaven? This Jesus who is taken up from you into heaven, shall so come as you have seen Him going into heaven."

END OF THE EXERCISES.

TABLE L.

mortal sin, 60.—v. Repetition, Abridgment, 317, 320, 308.—
Consid. Rules for discernment of spirits, first seven rules, 263.

DAY 6.

Ex. i. On the particular judgment, points 1, 2, and 3, p. 102.
—ii. Ditto, points 4, 5, and 6, 104.—iii. Effects of mortal sin
on the soul, 67.—iv. v. Repetition, Abridgment, 323, 311.—
Consid. First manner of praying, 287.—General Confession, 260.

DAY 7.

Ex. i. On venial sin, p. 108.—ii. iii. Wandering of the prodigal,
111.—iv. v. Repetition.—*Consid.* Seven last rules for discernment of spirits, 266.—General Examination, 259.

DAY 8.

Ex. i. Return of the prodigal, p. 117.—*Consid.* Object, &c. of the
Second Week, 123.

SECOND WEEK.
DAY 1.   (9.)

Ex. i. Reign of our Saviour, p. 126.—ii. The same repeated, 126.
—Method of Contemplation, 125.—Second manner of praying, applied to the offering of ourselves to Jesus Christ, 288.

DAY 2.   (10.)

Ex. i. ii. iii. Meditation on the Incarnation, p. 133.—iv. v. Contemplation on the same, 138.—*Consid.* Rules for the discernment of spirits for the Second Week, 268.

DAY 3.   (11.)

Ex. i. ii. Meditation on the Nativity, p. 141.—iii. iv. Contem-
plation on the same, 145.—v. Application of the senses, 147.
—*Consid.* Rules for the discernment of spirits for the Second
Week, 268.

DAY 4.   (12.)

Ex. i. ii. Presentation of Jesus in the Temple, and flight into
Egypt, p. 333; or in place of these, on the hidden life of
Jesus at Nazareth, 150; and Contemplation of the same
Mystery, 155.—iii. iv. Repetition.—v. Application of the

senses, 157.—*Consid.* Method of Particular Examination, 255.—Additions or recommendations, 12.

DAY 5. (13.)

Ex. i. Life of our Saviour from the age of twelve years to thirty, p. 335; or the public life of Jesus Christ, point 1, 158. —ii. Jesus among the doctors, 335; or public life of Jesus Christ, points 2, 3, 160.—iii. iv. Repetition.—*Consid.* On election, or choice of a state, art. 1, 271.

DAY 6. (14.)

Ex. i. The two standards, p. 165.—ii. The same, a second time, 170.—iii. iv. Repetition.—v. The three classes, 172.—*Consid.* The choice of state, arts. 2 and 3, 272 ; or of reform, 276.

DAY 7. (15.)

Ex. i. Baptism of our Lord, p. 335.—ii. The three degrees of humility, 177.—iii. iv. Repetition.—v. Choice of state and reform, 271, 276.—Discernment of spirits, 268.

DAY 8. (16.)

Ex. i. Temptation of Jesus Christ ; or vocation of the Apostles, p. 336.—ii. iii. Repetition. — iv. Application of the senses.— *Consid.* Distribution of one's goods and alms-giving, 279.

DAY 9. (17.)

Ex. Sermon on the Mount, p. 338.—*Consid.* Object, &c. of the Third Week, 182.

N.B. If this Second Week were prolonged, we should meditate succes-sively on the following subjects indicated by St. Ignatius : Jesus walking on the water, Jesus teaching in the Temple, the raising of Lazarus, triumphant entry of Jesus into Jerusalem, pp. 339, &c.

THIRD WEEK.

DAY 1. (18.)

Ex. i. Meditation on the Mystery of the Eucharist, points 1 and 2, p. 185.—ii. The same, point 3, 189.—iii. iv. Repetition.— v. Application of the senses, 191.—*Consid.* Rules of temper-ance, 277.—Rules of the orthodox faith, 2, 3, and 8, 283.

Day 2. (19.)

Ex. i. Discourse after the Last Supper, point 1, p. 194.—ii. The same, point 2, 196.—iii. The same, point 3, 200.—iv. v. Repetition.—*Consid.* Rules of the orthodox faith, 11 to 18, 284.

Day 3. (20.)

Ex. i. Jesus in the Garden of Olives, point 1, p. 202.—ii. The same, point 2, 204.—iii. iv. Repetition.—v. Application of the senses.—*Consid.* Tenth Addition, 261.—Remarks on scruples, 281.

Day 4. (21.)

Ex. i. Sufferings of Jesus Christ from the garden to the cross, point 1, p. 206.—ii. The same, point 2, 209.—iii. iv. Repetition.—v. Application of the senses.—*Consid.* The three degrees of humility, 177.

Day 5. (22.)

Ex. i. ii. Contemplation on the death of Jesus Christ on the cross, p. 212.—iii. iv. Repetition.—v. Application of the senses, 216.—*Consid.* Rules of the orthodox faith, 3 and 7, 283.—Rules of temperance, 277.

Day 6. (23.)

Meditation on the whole history of the Passion from the Gospels, making one or more exercises at choice.—*Consid.* The three degrees of humility, p. 177.—Rules of temperance, 277.—On scruples, 281.

Day 7. (24.)

Ex. Burial of Jesus, p. 348.—*Consid.* Object, &c. of the Fourth Week, 218.

FOURTH WEEK.
Day 1. (25.)

Ex. i. Meditation on the Resurrection, point 1, p. 219.—2. Contemplation on the same mystery, 225.—iii. Repetition.—iv. Application of the senses.—*Consid.* On scruples, 281.

Day 2. (26.)

Ex. i. First apparition of Jesus Christ, p. 348; or the apparitions of Jesus risen, point 2 of Meditation on the Resurrection, 223.—ii. Contemplation on the same, 225.—iii. Repetition.—iv. Application of the senses.—*Consid.* Rules for discernment of spirits for Second Week, 268.

Day 3. (27.)

Ex. i. Life of Jesus Christ in Heaven, point 1, p. 228.—ii. The same, point 2, 230.—iii. The same, point 3, 233.—iv. Repetition, or application of the senses.—*Consid.* Rules of the orthodox faith, 283.

Day 4. (28.)

Ex. i. On Devotion to the B. V. M.; Mary, Mother of God, p. 241.—ii. On the same; Mary, our Mother, 246.—iii. iv. Repetition.—*Consid.* Rules of the orthodox faith, 283.

Day 5. (29.)

Ex. i. Contemplation on the love of God, point 1, p. 234.—ii. The same, point 2, 236.—iii. The same, points 3 and 4, 237.—iv. Repetition.—*Consid.* Second and third manner of praying, 288.

Day 6. (30.)

Ex. The prayer "*Suscipe*," according to the second manner of praying, p. 236.—*Consid.* Recommendations for the last day of the Exercises, 252.

TABLE II.

ARRANGEMENT OF SUBJECTS FOR A RETREAT OF FIFTEEN DAYS.

EVE OF THE RETREAT, AS IN TABLE I.

Day 1.

End of man, p. 22.—End of creatures, 31.—Indifference in their regard, 37.—Repetition.—*Consid.* Particular and General Examination, 255, 257.—Method of Meditation, 9.

DAY 2.

On the triple sin, pp. 42, 47, 53.—Our personal sins, 75.—Hell, 79, 87.—*Consid.* The Additions, 1 to 9, 12.—First manner of praying, 287.

DAY 3.

Death, pp. 89, 96.—Infinite malice of mortal sin, 60.—Repetition of the two, 98, 308.—*Consid.* The Tenth Addition, 261.—On General Confession, 261.

DAY 4.

The particular judgment, p. 102.—Effects of mortal sin, 67.—Repetition of the two, 323, 311.—*Consid.* Rules for discernment of spirits for the First Week, 263.

DAY 5.

Venial sin, p. 108.—Wanderings of the prodigal, 111.—His re turn, 117.—Repetition, 326.—*Consid.* Rules for discernment of spirits, 263.

DAY 6.

The reign of Christ, p. 126.—The same subject again, 228.—Object of the Second Week, 123.

DAY 7.

The Incarnation, pp. 133, 138.—The Nativity, 141, 145.—Repetition of these two subjects, 331, 332.—Application of the senses, 147.—*Consid.* Rules for the discernment of spirits for the Second Week, 268.

DAY 8.

Hidden life of Jesus Christ, pp. 150-157.—Public life of Jesus Christ, 158.—Repetition.—Application of the senses.—*Consid.* Of election, or the choice of a state, arts. 1, 2, and 3, 271.

DAY 9.

The two standards, p. 165.—The same repeated.—The three classes, 172.—*Consid.* On election, arts. 3 and 4, 273.

DAY 10.

Baptism of Jesus Christ, p. 335.—The three degrees of humility

TABLE III.

ARRANGEMENT OF SUBJECTS FOR A RETREAT OF EIGHT DAYS.

EVE OF THE RETREAT, AS IN TABLE I.

TABLE IV.

ANOTHER ARRANGEMENT FOR A RETREAT OF EIGHT DAYS.

Day 1.

TABLE V.

SPIRITUAL READING FROM THE NEW TESTAMENT AND FROM THE "IMITATION OF CHRIST."

End of man.	$\begin{cases} N.\ T. \text{ Matt. xvi. 14-28; Luke vi. 20-39.} \\ Imit. \text{ Bk. iii. ch. 9, 22, 26.} \end{cases}$

Mortal sin.	*N. T.* Matt. xxv. 1-31. *Imit.* Bk. i. chap. 21, 22; ii. ch. 5; iv. ch. 7.
Death.	*N. T.* Luke xii. 33-43; Apoc. iii. *Imit.* Bk. i. ch. 23.
Judgment.	*N. T.* Matt. xxv. 31-46. *Imit.* Bk. iii. ch. 14.
Hell.	*N. T.* Luke xvi. 19-31. *Imit.* Bk. i. ch. 25.
Reign of Christ.	*N. T.* John xv.; Col. iii. *Imit.* Bk. i. ch. 1; iii. ch. 13-52.
The Incarnation.	*N. T.* Luke i. 26-56. *Imit.* Bk. ii. ch. 1, 7, 8.
The Nativity.	*N. T.* Luke ii. 1-21. *Imit.* Bk. iii. ch. 1, 2, 18.
The hidden life of Jesus Christ.	*N. T.* Luke ii. 40-52. *Imit.* Bk. i. ch. 20; iii. ch. 44, 53.
Public life of Jesus Christ.	*N. T.* Matt. x. *Imit.* Bk. i. ch. 15, 16; iii. ch. 4.
The two standards, three classes, and three degrees of humility.	*N. T.* Matt. xix. *Imit.* Bk. iii. ch. 23, 27, 31, 56.
Change of a state.	*Imit.* Bk. iii. ch. 54.
The Eucharist.	*N. T.* Matt. xxvi. 17-30. *Imit.* Bk. iv. ch. 1, 2.
The Passion.	*N. T.* Matt. xxvi. 36-75; xxvii. *Imit.* Bk. ii. ch. 11, 12; iv. ch. 8.
The Resurrection and Ascension.	*N. T.* Matt. xxviii.; Mark xvi.; Luke xxiv.; Acts i. *Imit.* Bk. iii. ch. 47, 48.
Love of God.	*N. T.* John xvii.; 1 John iv. *Imit.* Bk. iii. ch. 5, 6, 34.
Holy Communion.	*N. T.* Luke xxii. 14-21; John vi.; 1 Cor. ii. 23-31. *Imit.* Bk. iv. ch. 17.

www.ingramcontent.com/pod-product-compliance
Lightning Source LLC
Chambersburg PA
CBHW030900270326

41929CB00008B/502